SEALS IV

Arizona State University, Program for Southeast Asia Studies, Monograph Series

Also Available

Gamelan Stories: Tantrism, Islam, and Aesthetics in Central Java
Judith Becker

Thai Tellings of Phra Malai: Texts and Rituals Concerning a Popular Buddhist Saint
Bonnie Pacala Brereton

Hill Farms and Padi Fields: Life in Mainland Southeast Asia
Robbins Burling

Prolific Survivors: Population Change in Cambodia, 1975–1993
Jacqueline Desbarats

Patterns of Power and Politics in the Philippines: Implications for Development
James Eder and Robert Youngblood, editors

The Usage of the Traditions of the Prophet in Contemporary Indonesia
Howard Federspiel

Modern Southeast Asian Literature in Translation: A Resource for Teaching
Grant Olson, editor

Purifying the Faith: The Muhammadijah Movement in Indonesian Islam
James Peacock

The Javanese in Suriname: Ethnicity in an Ethnically Plural Society
Parsudi Suparlan

Taking Refuge: Lao Buddhists in North America
Penny Van Esterik

The Jingpo: Kachin of the Yunnan Plateau
Zhusheng Wang

Toward a New Paradigm: Recent Developments in Indonesian Islamic Thought
Mark Woodward, editor

Series

Papers from the First Annual Meeting of the Southeast Asian Linguistics
Society, 1991
Martha Ratliff and Eric Schiller, editors

Papers from the Second Annual Meeting of the Southeast Asian Linguistics
Society, 1992
Karen Adams and Thomas John Hudak, editors

Papers from the Third Annual Meeting of the Southeast Asian Linguistics
Society, 1993
Mark Alves, editor

For further information, check out our web site
http://www.asu.edu/clas/asian/pseas.html

PAPERS
FROM THE
FOURTH ANNUAL MEETING
OF THE
SOUTHEAST ASIAN LINGUISTICS
SOCIETY
1994

EDITED BY
UDOM WAROTAMASIKKHADIT
AND
THANYARAT PANAKUL

Program for Southeast Asian Studies Monograph Series
Arizona State University, Tempe, Arizona 85287-3502

National Resource
Undergraduate Center
Ruth Yabes, Director
Managing Editor
Mark Woodward
Linguistics Series Editor
Karen L. Adams
Associate Editor
Anne Dresskell

This publication was funded in part by the U.S. Department of Education.

♾ The paper used in this publication meets the minimum requirements of the American National Standard for Information Sciences—Permanence of Paper for Printed Library Materials, ANSI Z39.48-1984.

▶ This book is one of a series on Southeast Asia published by the Program for Southeast Asian Studies, Arizona State University, Tempe, Arizona. For a complete list of publications, see our web site ⟨http://www.asu.edu/clas/asian/pseas.html⟩ or contact us via e-mail ⟨pseas@asu.edu⟩.

ISBN 1-881044-16-5

CONTENTS

Semantics

Sociolinguistics and Pragmatics

LANGUAGE/AUTHOR INDEX

Preface

The Southeast Asian Linguistics Society
History and Goals

The Southeast Asian Linguistic Society (SEALS) was conceived by Martha Ratliff and Eric Schiller in 1990 as a needed forum for linguists who have the languages of mainland and Pacific Southeast Asia as their primary research focus. It is our hope that the establishment of this organization will lead to

(1) greater communication within this group of scholars, especially across the gap which has heretofore divided researchers of mainland Southeast Asian languages and the Austronesian languages of the Pacific;

(2) needed publication of descriptive, theoretical and historical accounts of these languages, in the first instance in the form of these proceedings' volumes; and

(3) greater awareness of these languages by non-specialist linguists, many of whom attempt to make universal and typological generalizations about the human language faculty without the important corrective which knowledge of Southeast Asian languages provides.

The Society currently hosts an annual international meeting as the primary means to support these goals. Specific projects, publications, and services beyond those of an annual meeting and the publication of the meeting proceedings will be at the discretion of the members of the Society.

Scope

The Southeast Asian Linguistics Society was founded with the idea of giving language researchers with a 'non-northern' Asian focus a place to share their findings and ideas. In terms of genetic affiliation, investigation into any aspect of Austroasiatic, Austronesian, Hmong-Mien, Tai-Kadai, or Tibeto-Burman languages may be relevant to our members. Although the common thread we recognize in the first instance is geographical, the boundaries of the Southeast Asian area are not clear, and we would not like to be responsible for trying to draw them rigidly. For example, students of languages that have a historical connection to the languages of the area but which are geographically outside and/or typologically unlike those in the Southeast Asian group would be welcome to participate in our meetings and publications, as would students of the typologically similar languages of southern China.

Meetings

The first meeting of the Southeast Asian Linguistics Society was held on the campus of Wayne State University in Detroit, May 9–11, 1991.

SEALS IV was hosted by the Department of English and Linguistics, Ramkhamhaeng University, Bangkok, Thailand. The organizers for the event were Drs. Udom Warotamasikkhadit and Thanyarat Panakul. Future meetings will be hosted by volunteers from the members of the Society. The 1997 meeting, SEALS VII, will be held at the University of Illinois, Urbana. The host of each year's meeting edits the proceedings volume for that year. The volumes are published by the Monograph Series of the Program for Southeast Asian Studies (PSEAS) at Arizona State University. We are grateful to Arizona State University for their commitment to and ongoing support of the Southeast Asian Linguistics Society.

Acknowledgments

As with any conference and proceedings publication, numerous people were involved and deserve our appreciation. The SEALS IV organizers would like to thank their home department and the Faculty of Humanities at Ramkhamhaeng University for the support they provided.

With a note of sadness, the conference organizers would like to acknowledge their friend, Donald A. Leuschel. Dr. Leuschel, who had begun work on editing the papers from SEALS IV, passed away suddenly from a heart attack before he could finish. Dr. Leuschel, whose cremains were scattered in the ocean, began as a professor in Thailand at Songkhla Teachers' College in the 1960s. He then went on to teach at both Chulalongkorn and Ramkhamhaeng Universities. He also taught at various other universities and colleges (such as Sri Patum University), ending his career at Ramkhamhaeng University.

Additional thanks go to Anne Dresskell, editor of the PSEAS Monograph Series, for her aid in the production of this volume. Drs. Karen Adams and Thomas J. Hudak, also from PSEAS at Arizona State University, provided additional help and organized the introductory materials, including the language index.

To Contact SEALS

The host of the May meeting of Southeast Asian Linguistics Society is the head of the Society for that year, and inquiries about the Society should be directed to that person. If the location of the meeting is in doubt, contact Prof. Martha Ratliff for information. She can be reached at the Linguistics Program, Department of English, Wayne State University, Detroit, Michigan 48202 (e–mail address: mratlif@cms.cc.wayne.edu). For further information about SEALS publications, please contact the Program for Southeast Asian Studies, Box 873502, Arizona State University, Tempe, AZ 85287-3502 (e–mail address: pseas@asu.edu).

Udom Warotamasikkhadit
Thanyarat Panakul

The complex acoustic output of a single articulatory gesture:
Pattani Malay word-initial consonant length[1]

Arthur S. Abramson
The University of Connecticut and Haskins Laboratories

INTRODUCTION

1.1. MOTIVATION. A linguistic investigation of Pattani Malay need be justified only as a contribution to Southeast Asian linguistics. My interest in this language, which is spoken by ethnic Malays in southern Thailand, is further motivated by its possibly unique characteristic of having phonemically distinctive word-initial consonant length for all classes of consonants.

The disyllabic pattern C(ː)VCV(C) is the usual structure of the Pattani word. Thus, the initial short or long consonant can appear in three contexts: (1) Utterance-initial, (2) intervocalic, and (3) post-consonantal. The first context requires no comment except, of course, to say that syntactic rules might constrain what classes of words may appear at the beginning of a sentence. The second context is found when a word-final vowel occurs without a following pause before the word in question. Likewise, a word-final consonant without a pause before the word-initial consonant provides the third context.

If the terms 'short' and 'long' are to be taken seriously, the articulatory closure or constriction—henceforth to be called simply CLOSURE—of a long consonant is held significantly longer than that of its short counterpart. For the experimental phonetician this word-initial contrast raises some interesting questions about the limits of human performance in the production and perception of speech: How much information is carried only by the relative durations of the closures? Does the longer articulatory hold have any concomitant perceptually relevant effects on the speech signal? Is the control of relative duration accompanied by a separately controlled mechanism that has its own perceptually relevant acoustic effects?[2]

1

1.2. ARTICULATORY GESTURES AND THE ACOUSTIC SIGNAL.

1.2. ARTICULATORY GESTURES AND THE ACOUSTIC SIGNAL. We can normally recognize an acoustic disturbance, even one embedded in noise or badly distorted, as a speech signal. To do this we need neither understand the linguistic message nor know the language in which it was uttered. Presumably this is so because the acoustic signal sounds like the possible output of a human vocal tract. Indeed, the synthesis of speech or, if you will, speechlike sequences, is feasible only if the parameters of the synthesizer are set well enough to simulate the acoustic effects of states and movements, i.e., GESTURES, of the articulators.[3] Thus, the listener may realize that the 'utterance' has come from a robot or some other sort of machine but still accept it as speech, albeit synthetic speech.[4]

The linguist's concern with phonologically relevant properties of speech, called by some scholars distinctive features, brings us to the question of the links between these fairly abstract properties and phonetic reality. For the work being presented here it is desirable to limit our attention to phonological properties that are defined in terms of actions of articulators or physiological mechanisms (Browman & Goldstein 1986).

The simplest case would be that of a single gesture with a single audible acoustic effect. Perhaps a good example is the movement of the tongue into and out of the position for an apical constriction suitable for the turbulence appropriate to the sound[s].[5]

A more complicated but probably phonologically tolerable case would be that of a single articulatory gesture with multiple acoustic consequences each of which is audible. This is seen in voicing distinctions in initial stop consonants for which the timing of the laryngeal gesture relative to supraglottal gestures causes the valvular action of the glottis to yield a variety of acoustic effects (Lisker & Abramson 1964, Abramson 1977, House & Fairbanks 1953). These include differences along at least three dimensions: the occurrence of glottal pulsing, noise-excitation of formants upon release, i.e., aspiration and fundamental frequency, each of which is detectable by ear. Variation along these acoustic dimensions, even the fundamental frequency of the voice upon release of the stop according to current research (Löfqvist et al.

1989), is apparently a function of the timing of the laryngeal gesture.

Finally, let us consider a phonological distinction involving separately controlled gestures with multiple acoustic consequences. A good example might be the voicing distinction in English word-final consonants. The aforementioned laryngeal gesture can handle the matter of whether or not glottal pulsing persists in the consonant closure. This is audible. At the same time, in some contexts there is a significant correlation between the duration of the preceding vowel and the voicing state of the consonant (Peterson & Lehiste 1960), which is perceptually relevant (Denes 1955, Raphael 1981). The latter property turns out not to be just one more output of the laryngeal gesture but rather part of the separately controlled articulation of the vowel (Raphael 1974). Phonologists of certain schools of thought seem to get around this irregularity by describing it as the application of a 'vowel-lengthening rule' before voiced consonants. The logic may be impeccable, but the phonetic motivation for such an 'explanation' is not at all obvious.

It seems to me that this last situation is phonetically very interesting with important implications for models of speech perception, especially if, as has been argued (e.g., Liberman & Mattingly 1985), the perception of speech directly entails articulatory gestures. It also presents a challenge to those models of phonology that try to be phonetically realistic by incorporating specifications of gestures (e.g., Browman & Goldstein 1986). As suggested earlier (§1.1), the word-initial length distinction in Pattani Malay may offer fertile ground for research into this topic.

1.3. PREVIOUS PHONETIC RESEARCH ON PATTA- NI MALAY. Within a class of unstressed morphemes the Pattani Malay language has developed distinctive consonant length diachronically through reduction and eventual loss of the vowel and assimilation of the final consonant to the initial consonant of the following morpheme (Chaiyanara 1983).[6] Although many words with long initial consonants can still be seen to be sitting astraddle a morpheme boundary, it is also true that such a boundary is no longer obviously present in a good number of other words. I am aware of no statistical treatment of the matter.

4

Of course, the continued presence of a morpheme boundary in much of the lexicon would lead some phonologists to posit gemination rather than distinctive length. Taken seriously as a phonetic statement rather than a phonological abstraction, this would mean a sequence of two instances of the same speech sound, implying rearticulation at the beginning of the second segment. In the absence of a pause during the sustained hold, such a phenomenon seems highly unlikely and is not evident in the available data, so I cling to the concept of distinctive length even while conceding that in this language higher-level grammatical considerations might make it convenient for the phonologist to prefer analyzing phonetic length as a string of two consonants.[7]

Here are some word-pairs with the contrast:

makɛ	'to eat'	mːakɛ	'to be eaten'
labɔ	'to profit'	lːabɔ	'spider'
siku	'elbow'	sːiku	'hand-tool'
dʒalɛ	'way'	dʒːalɛ	'to walk'
butɔ	'blind'	bːutɔ	'kind of tree'

The foregoing words, which are transcribed with symbols of the International Phonetic Association, all have acoustic excitation in the closures of the initial consonants, making it reasonable to suppose that the onsets on the right could be heard as longer than those on the left. In words beginning with voiceless unaspirated stops, however, there is no closure-excitation that might help to hear a difference in length. Here are some examples:

pagi	'morning'	pːagi	'early morning'
paka	'to use'	pːaka	'usable'
tawa	'bland'	tːawa	'to show wares'
katoʔ	'to strike'	kːatoʔ	'frog'
kamɛŋ	'goat'	kːamɛŋ	'goatlike'

In Figure 1 are seen the waveforms of a minimal pair of words differentiated by the relative durations of the voice-excited initial labial closures. The words were not recorded together but were put together for the display. (Curiously enough, if the distinction in question were relevant ONLY for voiced stops, the language could be seen as having an otherwise unattested use of the VOT dimension for a three-way voicing distinction (Lisker & Abramson 1964): long voicing lead, short voicing lead, and short lag, i.e., early prevoicing, late prevoicing, and voiceless unaspirated.)

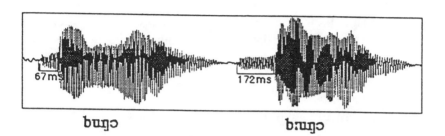

FIGURE 1. Waveforms of /buŋɔ/ 'flower' and /bːuŋɔ/ 'to bloom,' showing the durations of the voiced closures.

In the pair shown in Figure 1, the closure of the long stop, as measured acoustically, is 2.6 times longer than the closure of the short stop. In fact, analysis of a large number of productions (Abramson 1987) showed the closures of long consonants, in both initial and intervocalic positions, to be on average three times longer than those of short consonants. Of course, for voiceless stops and affricates there was no direct acoustic sign of the closure in utterance-initial position, so all durational data for them were obtained in intervocalic position, i.e., utterance medially after words ending in vowels.

The next stage of the work, although my report on it appeared earlier (Abramson 1986), studied the efficacy of closure duration as a perceptual cue. First, to assess the robustness of the distinction, control tests were run with isolated members of 16 short-long pairs that were recorded by two native speakers, randomized, and played through headphones to 21 other native speakers for identification as words. Words with initial nasals, laterals, and fricatives (henceforth to be grouped as CONTINUANTS) were labeled with an accuracy of 90% or better. Labels of voiced and voiceless stops were slightly less accurate at 80% or better. The affricates, especially the voiceless ones, did not fare well, with identifications not much better than chance. These results justified further perceptual experimentation but with the exclusion of the affricates for the time being.

Manipulation of closure duration was the method used (Abramson 1986). Shortening the closures of long utterance-initial /gː/ and long utterance-initial /lː/ in a series of small steps made listeners shift their labels to the short category. For voiceless stops, the tests had to be limited to utterance-medial intervocalic position; shortening the closure of long /pː/ and lengthening the closure of short /p/ caused the listeners' identification functions to shift to the opposite categories.

Although the value of relative duration as a cue had been demonstrated, there remained the question of how subjects could do so well with isolated words beginning with voiceless unaspirated stops, which have no DIRECT acoustic sign of closure duration. Although it is true that in intervocalic position relative duration is a sufficient cue for the voiceless stops, such that any concomitant cues that might be present in the original utterances are overridden by lengthening original short closures and shortening original long ones, it is also true that the crossover points of the identification curves in the two conditions differ significantly from each other. This suggests that even in the presence of the powerful duration cue something else must be contributing to the auditory distinction. Given the fact that words in this language are typically disyllabic, it seemed likely that such an additional differentiating property might reside in intersyllabic relations. Auditory impressions and a quick sampling of acoustic analyses suggested relative amplitude as the most promising feature for investigation.

Root mean square amplitudes of both syllables of a large number of Pattani Malay disyllabic words were obtained for the speech of one man by means of a computer program (Abramson 1987). The difference between his short and long voiceless plosives with respect to amplitude ratio was highly significant. The voiced long plosives also showed a higher ratio than the short ones but with only moderate significance. Although the continuants showed a tendency in the same direction, the effect was not statistically significant. Given the complex effects on speech signals of variation in timing (Lisker 1974), I wondered whether greater duration of consonantal closure entailed a higher buildup of oral air pressure, which, upon release, might yield a higher amplitude peak on the syllable. If so, perhaps this would serve as a cue in the absence of audible closure duration.

The final stage of my previous research was to test the perceptual relevance of the findings on relative amplitude (Abramson 1991). Three pairs of words with short and long initial voiceless stops were recorded at the end of a carrier sentence ending in a vowel. The amplitude peak of the first syllable of words with short initial stops was raised in five 2-dB steps; the peak of the first syllable of words with long initial stops was lowered in five 2-dB steps. These variants were pitted against variants in closure duration. In addition, stimuli with the same amplitude variation, but necessarily without changes in closure duration, were prepared with a pair of isolated words.

The experiments with amplitude pitted against duration revealed that duration is not only sufficient, as before, but also dominant, although relative amplitude turned out to have SOME cue-value in that the perceptual crossover point was earlier for higher amplitude peaks. In the stimuli derived from isolated words, amplitude influenced the identification functions somewhat but was insufficient as a cue to the categories.

NEW WORK

2.1. HYPOTHESIS. Although the ratio of amplitude peaks in disyllabic words physically differentiates short and long voiceless stops, it is by itself a very weak cue for distinguishing the two categories perceptually; nevertheless, the two categories are identified rather well even in isolated words. The hypothesis proposed for testing in the present study holds that some several properties, among them relative amplitude, work together to give greater acoustic salience to the first syllable of words beginning with long stops. In addition, relative salience could also help with the differentiation of short and long voiced stops and perhaps even some of the continuants. In this part of the research, the hypothesis is being tested for validity in speech production. Should it turn out to be tenable, it will be necessary to validate it for perception.

One might ask as to whether a feature of accent or stress is arising in the language in conjunction with the consonant-length distinction. Indeed, in response to my stated plan to look at relative amplitude and perhaps other properties, Christopher Court of Monash University wrote to me on 23 May 1976, 'I have a feeling that what we are dealing with here is something like the Swedish-Norwegian "accentual" system, or the Serbo-Croatian or Japanese one, which is only realized, or at least BEST realized, over the span of two syllables, and that the picture will become clearer when you compare the two syllables.' Looking back at this old letter from a scholar who had done much work with the language, I felt encouraged to return to an idea that I had neglected.

2.2. PROCEDURE. Lists of words forming minimal pairs with respect to consonantal length were recorded in isolation and embedded in carrier sentences by four young adults, all native speakers of Pattani Malay. The utterances of two of them, both women, were given to me by Jimmy G. Harris who, together with Christopher Court, first called my attention to the language. The other two informants, both men, were recorded by me. Since these words were recorded at different times for different purposes, only the lists of the first two speakers are identical. This will be reflected in the statistical treatment of the results. For this stage of the new work, only the isolated words were analyzed.

The choice of acoustic properties for examination was based on the literature on distinctive stress in other languages (e.g., Fry 1955). That is, if one is to test a hypothesis of relative salience or accent accompanying the length distinction, the following aspects of the speech signal are most promising. It was decided to obtain relative values of amplitude, amplitude slope, vowel duration, and fundamental frequency (F_0) across the two syllables of each word. In addition, duration-ratios of the first vowel and the medial closure would be included.

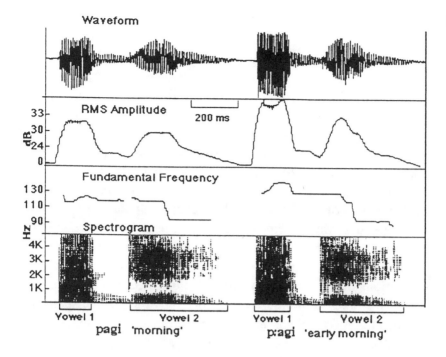

FIGURE 2. Acoustic analysis. The space between Vowel 1 and Vowel 2 in each of the spectrograms is the voiced /g/ closure.

The Signalyze™ program was used on the Macintosh computer for the acoustic analysis. Figure 2 can serve as a guide to the analytic procedures. At the top we see waveforms of a minimal pair of words taken from a randomized set of recordings and put together for this display. This is the starting point for the following analyses. A 200-ms span under the waveforms serves for temporal orientation for all the displays of Figure 2. Just below is a root-mean-square amplitude trace with a decibel scale to the left. For each disyllabic word the ratio of the amplitude peak of the first syllable to that of the second syllable was obtained. In addition, the average rise time of the amplitude slope of the first syllable of each word was obtained by dividing the peak amplitude by the duration of the rise from the baseline to the peak. Next down is an F_0 trace with a scale in Hertz (Hz) to the left. For each disyllabic word the ratio of the F_0 peak of the first syllable to that of the second syllable was obtained. Although the program, with appropriate adjustments, does a good job of extracting F_0, the accuracy of a sampling of the analyses was checked by period-by-period measurements of waveforms on the computer. At the bottom is a sound spectrogram of the two words with a scale in Hz to the left. Spectrograms of the utterances, together with the waveforms, were used for general orientation and, more particularly, for measurements of the vowels and medial closures.

The physical criteria for measuring vowel duration require some comment. Vowel duration was taken to be the span from the moment of release of the first consonant to the moment of achievement of closure for the final consonant. The procedure is illustrated in the spectrograms of Figure 2 where we see the vocalic spans marked. That is, vowels are determined by supraglottal gestures without regard for the excitation source. The durations of the medial closures are unmarked in the figure, but they are taken to be the intervals between the vocalic spans, as seen in the spectrograms and in the waveforms. Acoustic evidence of glottal pulsing at the low end of the spectrum, appropriate to the voiced consonant /g/ is seen in these intervals. For each disyllabic word, then, the duration ratios of the first and second vowel and the first vowel and the medial closure were obtained.

2.3. RESULTS. The amplitude ratios are best shown in numerical tables; however, as a possible aid to the reader, a graphic display of one set of measurements is given in Figure 3. The large dots give the mean amplitude ratios of the first syllable to the second syllable for words beginning with short and long voiceless stop consonants. The vertical bars show one standard deviation about the mean. Note that values below the horizontal line are negative; this indicates a lower amplitude in the first syllable than in the second. (Obviously, some of the values are positive; the amplitude display for /pagi/ with a short initial stop in Figure 2 happens to be such a case.) The values for the mean and the full range of the standard deviation for the long stop are positive, indicating a higher amplitude in the first syllable.

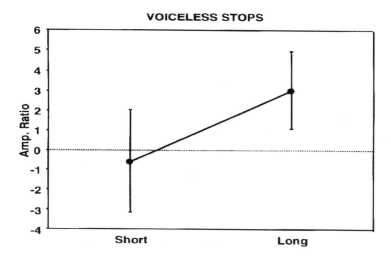

FIGURE 3. Means and standard deviations of the amplitude ratios of the first and second syllables of Pattani Malay words beginning with short and long voiceless stops: Four speakers.

The data underlying the graph for the voiceless stops in Figure 3 are given in Table 1 together with comparable amplitude ratios for the voiced stops and continuants. As stated in the first paragraph of Section 2.2, only two of the speakers, A and B, recorded exactly the same lists of words, so their data are put on one line for each phonetic category here and in the other tables. The data for speakers P and W are necessarily on separate lines. Column 2 shows the numbers of minimal pairs, columns 3 and 4 the means and standard deviations of the amplitude ratios for the short consonants, columns 5 and 6, the means and standard deviations for the long consonants. The three right-hand columns show the results of paired *t*-tests; column 7 gives the degrees of freedom, column 8, the *t*-values, and column 9, the levels of significance.

For the voiceless stops the amplitude ratios in Table 1 are highly significant for all the speakers. For the voiced stops A and B miss significance but not by much, P is highly significant, and W is moderately significant. For the continuants all are significant, although W is only moderately so.

TABLE 1.   Amplitude Ratios

Spkrs	Pairs	Short		Long		Paired *t*-Test		
				Voiceless Stops				
	n	M	SD	M	SD	*df*	*t*	*p*
A+B	24	-.7	3.1	3.6	1.9	23	-7.3	<.001
P	14	-.6	2.2	1.7	1.7	13	-3.6	<.004
W	6	-.1	.8	3.6	1.2	5	-6.0	<.002
				Voiced Stops				
A+B	8	-.6	2.5	.9	1.7	7	-2.2	.07,ns
P	12	-.2	1.2	2.4	3.0	11	-4.0	<.003
W	6	2.0	3.0	4.8	1.5	5	-2.6	<.05
				Continuants				
A+B	20	.6	1.6	2.5	1.4	19	-4.5	<.001
P	10	-1.6	1.7	.9	1.7	9	-3.8	<.005
W	14	1.1	2.7	3.9	2.3	13	-2.7	<.02

TABLE 2.   Average Slope of Amplitude Rise

Spkrs	Pairs	Short		Long		Paired *t*-Test		
				Voiceless Stops				
	n	M	SD	M	SD	*df*	*t*	*p*
A+B	24	-.4	.1	.5	.1	23	-2.4	<.03
P	14	-.5	.3	.9	.6	13	-2.6	<.03
W	6	-.2	.1	.3	.1	5	-1.4	.23,ns
				Voiced Stops				
A+B	8	.1	.04	.3	.1	7	-10.8	<.001
P	12	.2	.1	.6	.3	11	-2.9	<.02
W	6	.2	.1	.4	.1	5	-1.0	.4,ns
				Continuants				
A+B	20	.1	.1	.2	.2	19	-1.8	.1,ns
P	10	.3	.2	.2	.1	9	1.6	.15,ns
W	14	1.1	.04	1.2	.2	13	-2.5	<.03

In Table 2 are shown the average slopes of amplitude rise. The results for three out of the four speakers are moderately significant. W is not significant. For the voiced stops the same three speakers are significant, with the addition that the results for A and B are highly significant, while W is not significant. As for the continuants, only one speaker, W, shows moderate significance. Curiously enough, he is the only one who does not have significant differences in slope for the other two categories.

Table 3 shows the fundamental-frequency ratios. For the voiceless stops all the speakers show highly significant differences between the short and long categories. For the voiced stops W is once again not significant, A and B are moderately significant, and P is highly significant.

TABLE 3. Fundamental-Frequency Ratios

Spkrs	Pairs	Short		Long		Paired t-Test		
	n	M	SD	M	SD	df	t	p
			Voiceless Stops					
A+B	24	.1	.1	1.1	.1	23	-6.1	<.001
P	14	.1	.02	1.1	.6	13	-6.6	<.001
W	6	.1	.1	1.1	.1	5	-4.5	<.007
			Voiced Stops					
A+B	8	1.1	.1	1.2	.1	7	-2.7	<.04
P	12	1.0	.04	1.1	.3	11	-3.6	<.005
W	6	1.0	.1	1.2	.1	5	-1.9	.12,ns
			Continuants					
A+B	20	1.0	.06	1.1	.2	19	-6.9	<.001
P	10	1.0	.04	1.1	.1	9	-3.8	<.005
W	14	1.1	.04	1.2	.2	13	-2.5	<.03

TABLE 4. Vowel-Duration Ratios

Spkrs	Pairs	Short		Long		Paired *t*-Test		
		Voiceless Stops						
	n	M	SD	M	SD	*df*	*t*	*p*
A+B	24	.6	.4	.8	.5	23	-3.8	<.001
P	14	.4	.1	.5	.1	13	-3.7	<.003
W	6	1.0	.5	1.0	.5	5	.8	.47,ns
		Voiced Stops						
A+B	8	.5	.2	.7	.3	7	-3.6	<.009
P	12	.5	.3	.6	.3	11	-2.7	<.02
W	6	.7	.4	.9	.3	5	-1.1	.3,ns
		Continuants						
A+B	20	.6	.2	.8	.3	19	-5.2	<.001
P	10	.5	.2	.6	.2	9	-5.2	<.001
W	14	.7	.3	.8	.3	13	-.7	.5,ns

TABLE 5. Duration Ratios of Vowel 1 and the Medial Closure

Spkrs	Pairs	Short		Long		Paired *t*-Test		
		Voiceless Stops						
	n	M	SD	M	SD	*df*	*t*	*p*
A+B	24	1.9	3.2	1.8	1.7	23	.1	.94,ns
P	14	1.0	.4	1.5	.5	13	-4.1	<.002
W	6	1.1	.1	1.2	.3	5	-1.3	.26,ns
		Voiced Stops						
A+B	8	1.6	.7	2.3	1.1	7	-3.3	<.02
P	12	1.1	.4	1.4	.4	11	-2.0	<.07,ns
W	6	.3	.7	2.3	1.5	5	-2.7	<.05
		Continuants						
A+B	20	1.5	.8	1.8	1.2	19	-2.9	<.001
P	10	.8	.2	1.3	.4	9	-6.0	<.001
W	14	.4	.1	1.4	.5	13	-.7	.52,ns

The duration-ratios of the first vowel to the second are given in Table 4. The findings for W's voiceless stops are not significant. The differences between the ratios for the other three speakers, however, are highly significant. For the voiced stops, we see that W is once again not significant, A and B are highly significant, and P is moderately significant. As for the continuants, W is not significant, but the others are highly significant.

The last dimension, the ratio of the duration of the first vowel and that of the medial consonantal closure, is presented in Table 5. For the voiceless stops only P is significant and highly significant at that. As for the voiced stops, P is the only speaker whose data are not significant although not by much. The others are moderately significant. For the continuants, W is not significant, while the others are highly significant.

CONCLUSION

3.1. SUMMARY OF RESULTS. It seems clear that all the acoustic properties examined in this study tend more or less to help in the differentiation of disyllabic words beginning with short and long initial consonants.

Table 6 is an attempt at summarizing the results in a simple way. Cells are provided under each acoustic property at the intersections between every phonetic category and each speaker or, for A and B, pair of speakers. An entry 'Yes' in a cell means the achievement of a level of significance of at least $p < 0.05$. 'No' means failure to achieve that level; that is, it is not significant.

As for the voiceless stops, the speakers show positive results for amplitude ratio, amplitude slope, and fundamental-frequency ratio. The remaining two properties, vowel-duration ratio and the duration-ratio of the first vowel to the medial closure, are valid for all the speakers except W.

The voiced stops are positive in two out of three cells for every category. All the speakers have 'No' in one phonetic category or another, but speaker W has it more than anyone else.

The best factors for the continuants are the amplitude ratio and the fundamental-frequency ratio. All the rest have 'No' entered once or twice.

TABLE 6. Summary of the Measurements

Amplitude Ratio

Speakers	A+B	P	W
Voiceless Stops	Yes	Yes	Yes
Voiced Stops	No	Yes	Yes
Continuants	Yes	Yes	Yes

Amplitude-Slope Ratio

Speakers	A+B	P	W
Voiceless Stops	Yes	Yes	No
Voiced Stops	Yes	Yes	No
Continuants	No	No	Yes

Fundamental-Frequency Ratio

Speakers	A+B	P	W
Voiceless Stops	Yes	Yes	Yes
Voiced Stops	Yes	Yes	No
Continuants	Yes	Yes	Yes

Vowel-Duration Ratio

Speakers	A+B	P	W
Voiceless Stops	Yes	Yes	No
Voiced Stops	Yes	Yes	No
Continuants	Yes	Yes	No

Duration-Ratio of Vowel 1 and Medial Closure

Speakers	A+B	P	W
Voiceless Stops	No	Yes	No
Voiced Stops	Yes	No	Yes
Continuants	Yes	Yes	No

3.2. DISCUSSION. The speech-production data of this study support the hypothesis (§2.1) that in Pattani Malay several acoustic properties give more salience to the first syllable of disyllabic words beginning with a long voiceless stop consonant than to those beginning with a short voiceless stop. Indeed, this criterion works well for the voiced stops too and, less well, for the continuants. If we count the number of Yes entries, allowing two for each A+B cell, a rank order comes out of Table 6: (1) F_0 ratio, (2) amplitude ratio, (3) vowel-duration ratio, (4) amplitude-slope ratio and duration-ratio of vowel 1 and medial closure. The differences, however, are small.

It is to be recalled, of course, that 'long' consonants do have significantly longer closure durations than their 'short' counterparts, at least for all contexts in which they can be measured acoustically (Abramson 1987). Thus closure duration, the property originally thought to be the sole relevant one, appears to function in combination with a set of prosodic factors in differentiating the two categories in speech production.

What remains to be done is perceptual validation of these findings. My plan, with the earlier perceptual studies as a starting point (Abramson 1986, 1991), is to do perception testing in two contexts, utterance-initial and intervocalic. Stimuli will be prepared with variants along the dimensions measured in this study pitted against each other for presentation to native speakers of Pattani Malay for identification. If the perceptual efficacy of syllable prominence, as provided by combinations of these acoustic cues, is demonstrated, it will be desirable to do studies of motor control to determine whether it is the single factor of closure duration that underlies the several acoustic differences. A possible outcome is that for voiceless initial long stops, and maybe some other consonants, speakers of the language have come over time to enhance the distinction by adding gestures of a prosodic type. If so, it remains to be seen whether this will lead to the emergence of an accentual system.

NOTES

1. This work was supported by Grant HD–01994 from the National Institute of Child Health and Human Development to Haskins Laboratories, New Haven, Connecticut. I am grateful to members of the Department of Islamic Studies of The Prince of Songkhta University, Pattani, for their hospitality and help.

2. Thus, for Turkish voiceless stops, the distinction between 'geminate' and 'non-geminate' consonants includes significant differences between voice onset time (VOT) as well as closure duration; nevertheless, whatever mechanism may be responsible for the VOT difference, experimental

manipulations show that the single overriding cue in perception is closure duration (Lahiri & Hankamer 1988).

3. This description is correct for the traditional terminal-analogue synthesizer. In the newer articulatory synthesizers, the parameter-values are instructions to simulated articulators that determine the configuration of the modeled vocal tract, which when provided with a "voice," emits a speechlike signal.

4. Another possibility is to feed an extraneous source into the vocal tract of a human being who articulates speech with this unnatural carrier. In my childhood in the United States, a soap company, extolling the deodorant properties of its soap, warned against the dangers of body-odor (B.O.) by having a person articulate 'B.O.' with the sound of a foghorn in place of his own voice.

5. It does not pay here to fret that even a single gesture may be physiologically complex and that the turbulence of the fricative has its own spectral and temporal complexity.

6. For a comparison of the consonants of Malay regional dialects and those of Standard Malay see Thavisak (1987: 11–14).

7. In at least one instrumental study (Lehiste, Morton & Tatham 1973) electromyographic data are interpreted as supporting the conclusion that Estonian 'geminate' consonants are rearticulated.

REFERENCES

Abramson, Arthur S. 1977. Laryngeal timing in consonant distinctions. Phonetica 34.295–303.

———. 1986. The perception of word-initial consonant length: Pattani Malay. Journal of the International Phonetic Association 16.8–16.

———. 1987. Word-initial consonant length in Pattani Malay. Proceedings of the XIth International Congress of Phonetic Sciences, 6–70. Tallinn: Academy of Sciences of the Estonian S.S.R.

———. 1991. Amplitude as a cue to word-initial consonant length: Pattani Malay. Actes du XIIème congrès international des sciences phonétiques, Vol. 3, 98–101. Aix-en-Provence: Université de Provence.

Browman, Catherine P., and Louis Goldstein. 1986. Towards an articulatory phonology. Phonology Yearbook 3.219–252.

Chaiyanara, Phaythuun M. 1983. Dialek Melayu Patani des bahasa Malaysia [The Pattani Malay dialect of the Malay language]. Kuala Lumpur: University of Malaya master's thesis.

Denes, Peter B. 1955. Effect of duration on the perception of voicing. Journal of the Acoustical Society of America 27.761–764.

Fowler, Carol A., and Elliot Saltzman. 1993. Coordination and coarticulation in speech production. Language and Speech 36.171–195.

Fry, Dennis B. 1955. Duration and intensity as physical correlates of linguistic stress. Journal of the Acoustical Society of America 27.765–768.

House, Arthur S., and Gordon Fairbanks. 1953. The influence of consonant environment upon the secondary acoustical characteristics of vowels. Journal of the Acoustical Society of America 25.105–113.

Lahiri, Aditi, and J.E. Hankamer. 1988. The timing of geminate consonants. Journal of Phonetics 16.327–338.

Lehiste, Ilse; Katherine Morton; and Marcel A.A. Tatham. 1973. An instrumental study of consonant gemination. Journal of Phonetics 1.131–148.

Liberman, Alvin M., and Ignatius G. Mattingly. 1985. The motor theory of speech perception revised. Cognition 21.1–36.

Lisker, Leigh. 1974. On time and timing in speech. Current trends in linguistics, Vol. 12, ed. by T.A. Sebeok; A.S. Abramson; D. Hymes; H. Rubenstein; E. Stankiewicz; and B. Spolsky, 2387–2418. The Hague: Mouton.

Lisker, Leigh, and Arthur S. Abramson. 1964. A cross-language study of voicing in initial stops: Acoustical measurements. Word 20.384–422.

Löfqvist, Anders; Thomas Baer; Nancy S. McGarr; and Robin Seider Story. 1989. The cricothyroid muscle in voicing control. Journal of the Acoustical Society of America 85.1314–1321.

Peterson, Gordon E., and Ilse Lehiste. 1960. Duration of syllable nuclei in English. Journal of the Acoustical Society of America 32.693–703.

Raphael, Lawrence J. 1974. The physiological control of durational differences between vowels preceding voiced and voiceless consonants in English. Journal of Phonetics 3.25–33.

————. 1981. Durations and contexts as cues to word-final cognate opposition in English. Phonetica 38.126–147.

Thavisak, Amon. 1987. ภาษามลายูถิ่นในประเทศไทย [Malay dialects in Thailand]. Nakhorn Pathom, Thailand: Institute of Language and Culture for Rural Development, Mahidol University.

The interlanguage phonology of Brunei English

Jonathan Mossop
Universiti Brunei Darussalam

This paper covers some of the phonological processes common in the interlanguage (IL) of Brunei English, together with a discussion of the respective influences of the native language (NL) and universals. As Contrastive Analysis would predict, the English IL of Bruneians has many features which can be traced directly to the NL. At the same time, most researchers these days would accept that the Contrastive Analysis Hypothesis (CAH) no longer provides a satisfactory explanation as to why certain features in the target language (TL) are found to be more difficult that others and that universals have a role to play. Much of the recent research into IL phonology has attempted to identify both the nature of universal constraints and the extent to which they interact with NL transfer. An attempt will be made here to identify transfer and developmental factors affecting the IL phonology of Brunei English and also to identify persistent features. This paper will show that while transfer can account for the major trends of the phonology of Brunei English, appeal must also be made to universal considerations to account for the relative strengths of these trends.

1. Background

In the context of Southeast Asia, there are very strong historical and cultural ties between the three English speaking countries; Singapore, Malaysia and Brunei. All three have undergone a similar colonial past and all three have an ethnic mix which is predominantly Malay and Chinese (though in differing proportions). This ethnic and historical similarity, together with present economic and cultural ties, has led to phonological systems which are close relations. (Singapore TV is available in the southern Malaysian states, while Malaysian TV can be viewed in Brunei and Brunei TV in parts of East Malaysia.) In fact, virtually all of the features of Malaysian and Singaporean English, identified by Platt & Weber (1980) and Platt, Weber & Ho (1983), are to be found also in Brunei. Nevertheless, it might be pointed out that there are also influences in Brunei quite different from the other two countries. Due to the unique economic situation in Brunei and the need for expatriate labour, there is a variety of ethnic or linguistic backgrounds among the workforce (e.g., Malay, Chinese, Filipino, Thai, Tamil, Hindi, English, Australian). As Ozog (1990) points out, these diverse backgrounds and their associated Englishes (e.g., Filipino English and Indian English) may be assumed to play some role in forming the phonology of Brunei English. Another difference between Brunei, Singapore, or Malaysian English lies in the high proportion of the local workforce that is sent overseas for training (although this trend is now decreasing since the establishment of a local university). Returning Bruneians, especially those who have sat "A" Levels and attended university in the United Kingdom, have often progressed extremely far along the basilect/acrolect continuum. As a result they provide an input to the phonological system which is proportionately greater than is the case in either Singapore or Malaysia.

2. Theoretical Considerations

In contrast to activity in other domains of language (especially morphology), research into IL phonology, until comparatively recently, has tended, as Ioup and Weinberger have remarked (1987:xi), to be either ignored or trivialized. This is the area of language where CA has traditionally been seen to have the most validity, possibly due to the motor-based nature of speech production and the natural ability people have to identify the first language (L1) source of a "foreign" accent. While admitting the very powerful role of L1 transfer, research (e.g., Brière 1966, Johansson 1973) has shown that not all deviant sounds can be predicted by CA. Factors such as the data gathering method (Nemser 1971), the sociolinguistic context (W.Dickerson 1977, Schmidt 1977, Beebe 1980), the linguistic context (L.Dickerson 1974, W.Dickerson 1976), equivalence classification (Flege & Hillenbrand 1984, Flege 1987) have all been found to affect the learner's output. A.James (1988:149) also suggests that phonological chunking can take place with phrases being produced as wholes and displaying an accuracy level in advance of other phonological structures produced by the learner. Thus, taking these factors into account, it is not surprising that traditional CA, as C.James (1980:183–4) points out, both predicts IL forms that do not occur and, at the same time, does not predict some forms that do occur.

Since the advent of Universal Grammar (UG), the focus of phonological research has been into universal tendencies and the extent to which they might interact with NL transfer. Central to this research is a concept of markedness as a scale of universal difficulty with the more unmarked or core elements being intrinsically easier than the more marked or peripheral elements. Eckman (1977) presents a theory which attempts to explain why it is that some TL forms are more difficult, through being more marked, than others. This he calls the Marked Differential Hypothesis (MDH), whereby the NL and the TL can be compared according to the following criterion:

> *Markedness* A phenomenon A in some language is more marked than B if the presence of A in a language implies the presence of B; but the presence of B does *not* imply the presence of A.

Eckman explores several areas where he claims phonological markedness can be identified. His 1981 paper proposes that there is a universal rule of Terminal Devoicing (TD) which is independent of both the NL and the TL. Since all languages allow voiceless obstruents but not all allow voiced obstruents the former are unmarked and the latter are marked. This is an implicational relationship where the presence of the latter implies the presence of the former. With respect to position, some languages (e.g., Korean) allow no voice contrast, some allow the contrast only in initial position (e.g., Corsican), some have it in initial and medial positions (e.g., German) and finally some have it in initial, medial and terminal positions (e.g., English). Thus, the presence of a medial voice contrast implies the presence of an initial contrast and the presence of a terminal contrast implies both medial and initial contrasts. Eckman uses these implicational relationships to explain why German speakers have difficulty with final voiced obstruents in English. Here the move is from a less marked position to a more marked position. On the other hand, English speakers of French do not find it difficult to articulate initial [ʒ]. Although this sound does not exist in initial position in English, it does exist in the more marked medial and terminal positions. As a result it causes no problems, as the move is from a marked position to a relatively unmarked position.

Eckman (1981) considers the situation when final obstruents are not allowed at all in the NL (e.g., Mandarin). Here he finds a schwa paragoge to be common (e.g., [tægə] for *tag* and [hizə] for *he's*) and proposes a rule of Schwa Paragoge which comes into effect when there is a NL constraint against obstruents occurring in word final position. Thus, as well as universal tendencies, the MDH must take into account the specific characteristics of both the NL and the TL.

Eckman (1987) applies the MDH to the reduction of word final consonant clusters to explain what at first sight seems like unsystematic shortening among Cantonese, Japanese and Korean speakers. He proposes an optional Consonant Cluster Reduction (CCR) rule, in which more marked features imply the presence of less marked features. The CCR rule claims that:

1. Final three consonant clusters imply the presence of two consonant clusters and final two consonant clusters imply the presence of single consonants. In each case the longer sequence is more marked.
2. Final stop-stop clusters imply the presence of, and are more marked than, fricative-stop clusters.
3. Final fricative-fricative clusters imply the presence of, and are more marked than, both fricative-stop and stop fricative clusters.

Taking these markedness conditions into account, Eckman is able to explain why certain reductions are more likely than others.

In contrast to Eckman's approach, described by A.James (1988:23) as "ad hoc", Tropf (1987) proposes an alternative explanation for universal difficulty based on sonority within the context of the syllable. Each syllable has a peak or sonority, usually located on a vowel, and the degree of sonority declines as the peripheral segments of the syllable are approached. Thus there is a hierarchical order of sonority spreading down from the vowel peak at the centre to glides, then sonorants (first liquids and then nasals) and finally obstruents (first fricatives and then plosives). The hypothesis is that the most sonorous segments are the most easily acquired while those that are the least sonorous are the most resistant to acquisition. It is claimed that sonority is a phonological-phonetic parameter which can account for forms that cannot be explained by either the constraints of the NL or the TL. Tropf found that in the German IL of Spanish speakers, the more sonorant a final target consonant was, the more likely it was to be realized in the IL.

With respect to onset clusters in a second language, Broselow (1987) proposes a vowel epenthesis rule as a way of dealing with syllable structures which would not be permissible in the NL. In the English of Egyptian speakers, words like *slide* and *floor* are realized as [silaɪd] and [filoor]. However, not all onset clusters conform to the structure of the sonority hierarchy. While the clusters in *slide* and *floor* do, the cluster in *stick* does not (fricative followed by stop). In fact the s-stop cluster is the only onset cluster, according to Broselow, to violate the sonority hierarchy and she follows Selkirk (1984) to argue in favour of the s-stop functioning at the level of a single segment. In this way she explains how her Egyptian speakers, rather than epenthesizing, prefix a vowel in words such as *study* or *ski* (realized as [istadi] and [iski]). Although Broselow does not discuss final clusters, here too the sonority hierarchy is violated by stop-s clusters, either within the root (e.g., *six*) or crossing morpheme boundaries (e.g., *cups, that's*). It could be argued, therefore, that final stop-s clusters also function phonologically as a single segment.

From the above review of markedness in IL phonology the following comments can be made about the English of native Malay speakers.

1. Since Malay does not allow a terminal voice contrast for final fricatives, the Marked Differential Hypothesis would predict this to be an area of particular difficulty for Malay speakers of English.
2. Although Malay allows final stops, these are not released and therefore the introduction of a schwa paragoge might seem a logical way of differentiating between words such as *dog* and *dock*.
3. As Malay does not allow final consonant clusters, the Consonant Cluster Reduction rule would predict first that clusters be reduced, secondly that stop-stop clusters be more prone to reduction than fricative-stop clusters, and thirdly that fricative-fricative clusters be more prone to reduction than both fricative-stop and stop-fricative clusters.
4. The Sonority Hierarchy would predict generally, that the less segments are sonorous, the more learners should experience difficulty. Vowel epenthesis in onset clusters might be predicted since written Malay generally does not allow onset clusters (an exception being the word "Brunei") although the first vowels in words like *perempuan* and *selalu* are dropped in conversational speech. Syllables which violate the hierarchy with the initial s-stop sequence may not undergo significant modification (being treated as single segmental units). Final stop-s clusters also violate the hierarchy and may be subject to less reduction than clusters obeying it.

3. Data and Methodology
First of all, it must be stressed that this paper can only be regarded as a preliminary study. The data were collected from three very different sources: school students reading word lists, university students interacting communicatively and newsreaders on television. Furthermore since the equipment to make high quality recordings was not available, any conclusions must be regarded as tentative. The criterion used to determine phonological

status was quite simply native speaker judgements by members of the English Department at UBD as to whether the speech sounded standard or non-standard.

The main source of data came from an analysis of the speech of trainee teachers at Universiti Brunei Darussalam (UBD) who were involved in peer teaching sessions as part of their training. This is the speech of English medium educated students who had studied at school as far as Form 6 and had taken, though not usually passed, the Cambridge "A" Level examinations. They were enrolled at UBD on a Certificate in Education course to train as primary teachers. For purposes of comparison and in an attempt to give some idea of the range of Brunei English, two other sources were also used. The first was data collected by two fourth year students in the BA TESL degree programme for their research projects (Nor Aziah 1991, Noraini 1991). These projects consisted of an analysis of the vowel and consonant systems of lower secondary school students. The other source was an analysis of the speech of Bruneian newscasters. Thus three distinct lects were chosen for this study; the lower mesolectal speech of school students, the upper mesolectal/lower acrolectal speech of university students and the acrolectal speech of newscasters.

While in all three cases subjects were used whose L1 is Malay, there were considerable differences between the data sources. The secondary school data were gathered from audio-taped sessions where the subjects were asked to read word lists aloud. While the lists were devised to cover a range of articulatory features, there are important phonological differences between the reading of isolated words and normal speech (e.g. elision and stress patterns). The university data were collected from video-taped recordings of 13 trainee teachers conducting peer teaching sessions. The tapes were then transcribed. Where audible, both "teacher" and "student" speech was analyzed, though specific articulatory forms could not be targeted since this was a recording of communicative interaction between speakers and not open to manipulation in any way by the researcher. The fact that examples of the more difficult articulatory sequences were extremely infrequent here may either reflect their rarity in this domain of language use or a strategy of avoidance on the part of the speakers. Furthermore, this particular domain (classroom language) is limited to specific discourse types such as questions, directives and explanations. This in turn limits the variety of syntactic forms and consequently their associated phonological features (e.g. consonant clusters involving past tense morphemes). The TV data were gathered from taping and transcribing three Bruneian newscasters whose L1 is Malay. The subjects here were reading sequences of connected discourse at considerable speed. Although certain features (e.g. elision), which were lacking in the first source of data, were in evidence here, the stress patterns are obviously different from those of interactive speech. This domain of speech employs one discourse type, the report, and as a result syntactic forms and associated phonological features are limited (e.g. consonant clusters involving the present copula and auxiliary verbs).

While there are obvious methodological problems comparing three such disparate speech types, it may be assumed that the secondary school data represents a basilectal variety of Bruneian English, while the university data, based as it is on trainee primary school teachers, represents an upper mesolectal to lower acrolectal variety. The English of the newscasters may be assumed to represent a high acrolectal variety, especially in view of the extreme formality of context. Furthermore, research (e.g. Dickerson 1977) has shown that there is a strong correlation between task formality and accuracy.

4. Analysis

In the data taken for this analysis there were no recorded instances of schwa parogoge and the only instances of vowel epenthesis occurred with the initial cluster [ʃr] as in *shriek* and *shred* and final cluster [lm] as in *whelm*. These were in evidence only in the school data. Therefore it might be concluded that universal tendencies both towards an open CV syllable structure and vowel epenthesis are not major features of this interlanguage, being precluded by both positive transfer, for syllable structure and initial clusters, and the rule of cluster reduction for final clusters. Both cluster reduction and terminal devoicing, though, are very much in evidence and will be discussed below. Some distinctive features of the vowel system will also be covered.

4.1 Consonant Cluster Modification

Probably the most striking tendency, and one which manifests itself across the three data types, is final cluster modification, which involves cluster reduction and consonant substitution. Disregarding the conjunction *and* and clusters occurring before consonants, which are both also subject to native speaker reduction, final cluster modification is at 80% in the school data, about 45% in the UBD data and at 38% in the TV data. Thus it is clearly, a major feature of Brunei English. It is also clear that this modification decreases as the acrolect is approached.

At the school level, although reduction was the dominant modification strategy, substitution was also significant. As might be expected since Malay does not allow final voiced consonants, these were generally devoiced (e.g., z->s). However other substitutions took place as well. As well as some idiosyncratic substitutions it was noted that stops were affricated (e.g., [dʒ] for [gz] as in *wags* and *jugs*. Fricative-fricative clusters were replaced by stop-fricative clusters (e.g., [gs] for [fs] in *laughs* and *coughs* and [ts] for [θs] in *paths* and *births*. Finally stop-stop clusters were replaced by stop-fricative clusters (e.g., [ps] for [pt] in *hopped* and *leapt*. If we compare these substitutions with the list provided in Eckman (1977), it is clear that the moves here are from more marked clusters to less marked clusters.

At the UBD level, the more complicated clusters, which were tested at the school level, tended to be either avoided or were precluded by the discourse mode. Cluster reduction, however, was very common and is hardly surprising since Malay does not have final consonant clusters.

When the reduced consonant clusters are examined, it becomes clear that the clusters that are consistently reduced are those with a final stop. Examples here are *first, hand, just, left, think, ask, count, fault* from the UBD data and *held, point, resident, equipment, protest, rump, camp, world* from the TV data. While this reduction is a major feature of the UBD data, it is virtually the only non-standard feature of the TV data. This reduction is consistent with Eckman's rule of CCR and also with the sonority hierarchy proposed by Tropf. As stops are the least sonorous of segments, they are the most marked and consequently likely to cause the most difficulty. Even taking native speaker elision into account, this is one of the most distinctive features of Bruneian English.

Some very common final clusters with a final stop, however, are rarely deleted in the UBD data. These clusters, although final in the word, are in the middle of common highly automatic expressions and as such, are fully pronounced. Examples here are *thank you, stand up, want you.* The final stop in *thank* here (never reduced) can be compared with the same stop in *think*, which is often reduced in the data. Possibly resyllabification is taking place here as the final stop is transferred to the vowel or glide of the following word. Another possiblity may be chunking or the existence of automatized routines. A.James (1988:149) refers to this phenomenon of chunking as follows:

> These "wholes" often manifest in their form a degree of phonetic (and phonological) TL accuracy well in advance of that typical of other phonological structures produced by the learner.

In the cases where the final cluster does not consist of consonant+stop, the picture is much more variable. In the UBD data final lateral+fricative clusters (as in *shelf, twelve* and *else*) and nasal+fricative clusters (as in *pronounce, science, balance, sentence, difference*) are sometimes reduced and sometimes not. In the TV data these clusters are generally not reduced. These final clusters are reduced less than those with a final stop and this is a fact which can be explained by markedness. In Tropf's hierarchy stops are the least sonorous of segments and therefore are the most marked. Fricatives are more sonorous and therefore less marked.

Interestingly however, final clusters which violate the sonority hierarchy by having a stop+fricative sequence tend not to be reduced or if they are both the stop and the fricative disappear. In the UBD data *six* was sometimes pronounced fully and sometimes reduced to [sɪʔ]. *Chicken pox* was also reduced to *chicken* [pɒʔ]. The stop+fricative+stop sequence in next was consistently reduced to a stop+fricative [neks]. These reductions did not take place, except for normal elision, in the TV data. From the few available examples it seems there is a reluctance to break this type of cluster, one which violates the sonority hierarchy in a similar fashion to those discussed by Broselow (1987). Although Broselow discussed the anomalous case of initial fricative+stop clusters, it would seem that the same holds for the equally exceptional final stop+fricative sequence. Rather than reduce this cluster, Bruneian speakers of English either maintain it or drop it completely to an unreleased glottal stop.

However, the vast majority of final stop+fricative clusters involves grammatical morphemes in the contracted copula and the plural. The fricative [s] in these clusters obviously differs in that it bears meaning. As far as the copula is concerned, the [s] is hardly ever dropped in the data, even when followed by a consonant. Examples here are *what's this, it's for, that's right.* The [s] in the plural was also seldom dropped in words like *weeks, cards, lots,* though there was a tendency for it to disappear, together with the stop, in more unusual lexical items such as *chopsticks* and *elephants.* The plural in nasal+fricative clusters (e.g., *things, drawings, items*) and lateral+fricative clusters (e.g., *animals, reptiles, symbols*) was also maintained. Here, although these clusters fit into the sonority hierarchy it would seem that the semantic power of the morpheme precludes any reduction. One modification did take place however, and that was with the fricative+fricative cluster in *months.* It was modified to the stop+fricative cluster of [mʌnts]. This supports Eckmann's comments about the marked nature of such a sequence.

When we consider initial clusters, Bruneian speakers of English experience few problems. Malay allows initial clusters, and although there might be a tendency to insert a vowel into loan words, this did not happen in the data. The initial clusters in words like *school, class, square* were never broken. One modification, however, that did take place was the modification of [θr] to [tr], which is hardly surprising since the fricative [θ] does not exist in Malay. This occurs in the words *three* and *throat.* In the school data this modification was recorded in 88% of the cases, in the UBD data in 71% of the cases but not at all in the TV data.

4.2 The voicing contrast and single consonants
In the school and UBD data there was a very clear tendency to devoice final the fricatives [z] and [v] which would be normally voiced in English but there were no instances of a normally voiceless consonant being voiced. Examples here of devoicing were: *these, please, close(v), use, have.* English, as Eckmann (1981) points out, is a language with voicing contrasts in initial, medial and final positions. Malay on the other hand allows voicing contrasts in initial and medial positions only. Since no languages, according to Eckmann, allow a medial voice contrast if they do not allow an initial voice contrast and a terminal contrast if they do not have a medial contrast, the MDH can be invoked to claim that English is more marked than Malay in this respect. Thus the MDH would predict that the IL of Malay speakers should show evidence of devoicing in syllable final position which is indeed is the case. It can be suggested, then, that the Terminal Devoicing

rule proposed by Eckmann is in operation here. This feature is common in the school and UBD data but not in the acrolectal TV IL. Thus, while TD is common at the lower end of the basilect-acrolect continuum it seems to be susceptible to modification towards TL norms as the acrolect is approached.

With initial consonants there were two tendencies. First, the initial voiced fricative [ð], as in *this, these, the that*, was not devoiced but rather modified to [d], right across the data. The voiceless fricative [θ], as in *thing, thirteen, throat* similarly showed a tendency, but a weaker one, to be modified to [t]. These modifications can be seen as NL transfer since neither of these fricatives exist in Malay. On the sonority hierarchy, fricatives are less marked than stops so NL transfer can be seen here to override the power of markedness. However what the data also shows is that [ð] is modified right across the data while [θ] changes only in the school speech and then only occasionally. While both are fricatives and occupy the same position on the hierarchy as presented by Tropf, it would seem plausible to suggest that the voiced fricative is more sonorous than the voiceless fricative. If so, then sonority could account for the relative persistence of the voiced form.

Devoicing is, however, only readily discernible with fricatives since final stops, both voiced and voiceless, tend to be glottalized and unreleased, as is common in Malay. As a result the voicing distinction is lost. Final [k] is unreleased throughout the data. Examples here are *sick, book, stomach, dog* (final [g]) from the UBD data and *Pacific, week, basic* from the TV data. This also happens in words where [k] is followed by a deleted stop (e.g. *district, attract, reject, effect*). Final [t] and [d] are also unreleased though not as consistently as final [k]. This is found mostly in content words such as *goat, straight, throat, period, God, good* from the UBD data and *eight, digit* from the TV data. However the final stop in function words such as *it, that* is usually articulated when it occurs medially in a phrase and is followed by a vowel. In contrast the final [k] is dropped even in the middle of a phonological word as in *stomach ache*.

4.3 Vowels and stress
Due to the fluid nature of vowel sounds, especially in rapid speech, it is both difficult and somewhat subjective, with the means available, to identify precise quantities of specific

phonemes. Nevertheless some clear tendencies do emerge from the school and UBD data. In the TV data, on the other hand, non-standard vowel pronunciation is rare, mainly occurring in conjunction with non-standard stress patterns in particular lexical items (e.g. *frigate* /ˈfrɪgət/ pronounced as /ˈfrɪˈgeɪt/.)

In the school data, vowel substitution and shortening were common while in the UBD data there was some substitution and shortening and also vowel lengthening, especially when a final syllable (usually unstressed in English) is given prominence.

Malay does not have the front vowel [æ] as in English *cat* and as might be expected, this vowel sound caused problems, generally being substituted by the front vowel [e]. Thus *cat, slap* and *grab* sounded like *cet, slep* and *greb*. However this confusion was not so clearcut in the UBD recordings. The [æ] vowel at times sounded standard, at times about half way between the [æ] and the [e] and at times is closer to the [e]. It is not normal, of course, for people to interact in *ship/sheep* type situations and so that even when there is a vowel shift we tend not to hear it if there is no possibility of confusion. In the data, words like *understand* and *hand* did not sound like *understend* or *hend*.

As Malay does not have long vowels there is a tendency for shortening to take place in Brunei English. This was widespread in both the school and UBD data. Words like *choose, shoes* and *room* were all pronounced with a shortened [uː]. Similarly the long [ɜː] in *thirteen* and *working* was also shortened. In one instance the shortened *working* is indistinguishable from a shortened form of *walking*, the vowel sound of which [ɔː] is also shortened. However the long [iː]as in *please* is not shortened in the data, with one common exception. The word *these*, [ðiːz] generally appears in the data as [dis]. The shift of the consonants together with the shortening of the vowel combine to produce a sound which sounds somewhere between *this* and *these*. Perhaps this is a strategy similar to that of the English speaking learner of French who produces a sound somewhere between *le* and *la* when unsure of gender.

Diphthongs are also a problem for Malay L1 speakers, as they are for many learners of English. The school data identifies three diphthongs [eə] as in *care*, [eɪ] as in *pay*, and [əu] as in *show* which undergo shortening. In the UBD data the diphthong in *square, chair* and *hair* was also consistently shortened. The [əʊ] diphthong is usually shortened when followed by a final consonant as in *home, coat, smoke, goat* but it is not shortened in some common words like *know* and *okay.* The diphthong [eɪ] appears relatively frequently and is generally not shortened. This is especially the case with common words like *today, okay* and *name* where the diphthong is not followed by a stop. In words such as *shape, tasting* and *straight* it is shortened to [e].

While NL transfer can be seen to account for a general tendency to shorten vowel sounds in the English IL of Bruneian Malay speakers, it would seem that some sounds are more prone to this shortening than others. Although there has not been much research in this area, it may well be possible to suggest a universal order of difficulty or markedness for vowel sounds.

Frequently, in the UBD data, vowel sounds are stressed and lengthened or, at times, transformed from a schwa into a full vowel in words of more than one syllable. NL influence can be seen here as syllables are usually stressed more or less equally in Malay. English, on the other hand, has what is known as a stress timed rhythm (Platt & Weber 1980), in which unstressed syllables are usually shorter than stressed syllables. Examples of this lengthening are the final syllables in *lastly* [i] and *table* [ə]. Here normally unstressed short syllables are stressed as they are lengthened. Long vowels too, at times become lengthened and a schwa is inserted. This occurs in words like *board* [ɔ:], *steel* [i:] and *group* [u:]. Diphthongs, normally shortened, can too be lengthened into what sounds almost like two syllables. Examples here are *late, eight, brain* [ei] and *coat, no* [əʊ]. Triphthongs, too, at times can sound as if they are broken into two syllables. Examples are *here* [ɪə] and *flower, our, hour* [əʊə]. This last modification was also present in the TV data.

This lengthening phenomenon may arise for several reasons. First there is a tendency to give equal stress across two syllable words such as *table, mammal* and *lastly.* This distorts the final unstressed vowel sound. Secondly the lengthening may be seen as a strategy to cope with the difficulty of diphthongs, triphthongs and long vowels. Instead of being shortened the vowel is lengthened and given some stress so that it is almost recognizable as a separate sound. Finally, this phenomenon may simply depend on the amount of emphasis the speaker is willing to attribute to the lexical item. An example here is the word *coat*, which appears both shortened and lengthened. Some items would appear to be stressed deliberately for emphasis (e.g. *no* and *lastly*), but with others it remains to be seen whether the increased stress is due to a desire for emphasis or articulation difficulties.

5. Conclusion

In conclusion it is claimed that transfer and universal factors combine to constrain the interlanguage phonology of Bruneian English. However this relationship is complex and other factors such as grammatical environment and chunking are also relevant. The features most resistant to modification towards the TL norm would seem to be those which are both predicted by contrastive analysis and have been identified as being relatively marked (e.g., final consonant cluster reduction and terminal devoicing). However the extent to which modifications of these features can be attributed to universal causes is probably impossible to determine, as when the L1 is less marked than the L2, modifications towards less marked positions are also modifications in the direction of the L1. However it must be reiterated that this study is only a preliminary investigation into the interlanguage phonology of Brunei English and research within a more rigorous methodological framework is now necessary in order to confirm or reject these tentative findings.

References:

Beebe, L. 1980: Sociolinguistic variation and style shifting in second language acquisition. *Language Learning* 30, 433-447.

Brière, E. 1966: An investigation of phonological interference. *Language* 42, 4, 768-796.

Broselow, E. 1987: Non-obvious transfer: on predicting epenthesis errors. In G. Ioup and S. Weinberger, editors, *Interlanguage Phonology: the acquisition of a second language sound system.* (pp. 292-304) Cambridge, MA: Newbury House.

Dickerson, L. 1974: *Internal and external patterning of phonological variability in the speech of Japenese learners of English.* Ph.D. dissertation, University of Illinois.

Dickerson, W. 1976: The psycholinguistic unity of language learning and language change. *Language Learning* 26, 215-231.

Dickerson, W. 1977: Language variation in Applied Linguistics. *ITL Review of Applied Linguistics* 35, 43-66.

Eckmann, F. 1977: Markedness and the contrastive analysis hypothesis. *Language Learning* 27, 315-330.

Eckmann, F. 1981: On the naturalness of interlanguage phonological rules. *Language Learning* 31, 195-216.

Eckmann, F. 1987: The reduction of word final consonant clusters in interlanguage. In A. James and J. Leather, editors, *Sound Patterns in Second Language Acquisition* (pp. 143-162). Dordrecht: Foris.

Flege, J. 1986: Effects of equivalence classification on the production of foreign language speech sounds. In A. James. and J. Leather, editors (pp. 9-39).

Flege, J. and Hillenbrand, J. 1984: Limits on phonetic accuracy in foreign language speech production. *Journal of the Acoustical Society of America* 76, 708-721.

Ioup, G. and Weinberger, S. 1987: Introduction. In G. Ioup and S. Weinberger, editors (pp. xi-xiv).

James, A. 1988: *The Acquisition of a Second Language Phonology: a linguistic theory of developing sound structures.* Tübingen: Gunter Narr Verlag.

James, C. 1980. *Contrastive Analysis.* London: Longman

Johansson, F. 1973: *Immigrant Swedish Phonology: A Study in Multiple Contact Analysis.* Lund, Sweden: CWK Gleerup.

Nemser, W. 1971: *An Experimental Study of Phonological Interference in the English of Hungarians.* Bloomington, Indiana: Indiana University Press.

Nor Aziah binti Hj. Mohd. Ismail 1991: *The English vowel pronunciation problems encountered by Bruneian students with specific reference to the lower secondary students of the Menglait Secondary School.* Universiti Brunei Darussalam TESL Project.

Noraini binti Ibrahim 1991: *Pronunciation problems amongst secondary school students with specific reference to English consonants.* Universiti Brunei Darussalam TESL Project.

Ozog, A. 1990: *Brunei English: A new variety?* Paper presented at 1st Extraordinary Session of the Borneo Research Council, Kuching.

Platt, J. and Weber, H. 1980: *English in Singapore and Malaysia.* Kuala Lumpur: Oxford University Press.

Platt, J., Weber, H. and Ho, M. 1983: *Singapore and Malaysia,* Amsterdam: John Benjamins.

Schmidt, R. 1977: Sociolinguistic variation and language transfer in phonology. *Working Papers in Bilingualism* 12, 79-95.

Tropf, H. 1987: Sonority as a variability factor in second language phonology. In A. James and J. Leather, editors (pp. 173-191).

Phonological variation and change in the Khmu dialects of Northern Thailand[1]

Suwilai Premsrirat
Mahidol University

Although in Thailand Khmu is just a small ethnic minority, a remnant of a much bigger group in Laos, Khmu dialects are scattered along the Thai-Lao border in Nan and Chiengrai provinces and provide an ideal subject for the study of phonological variation and the so-called "register-tone development process." Synchronic variation can often indicate diachronic change. Cross-dialectal phonetic variation has important implications for Khmu historical phonology.

The Khmu in Chiengrai emigrated from Laos across the Mae Khong river to Thailand about 40-50 years ago; the Khmu in Nan have lived in their present and nearby locations for a long time. Some of them may have moved down from old villages further north. Some knew that their ancestors came from the Luangprabang area in Laos. There are about 10 Khmu villages in Chiengrai with a population of about 3,000 speakers, whereas in Nan there are about 20 villages with about 6,000 speakers. The synchronic structures of various Khmu dialects differ from one another phonologically, lexically, and syntactically. Speakers of one dialect do not have much contact with speakers of other dialects which they call /tmɔ́ːj/, but they do have contact with the Khmu of the same dialect which they call /kúŋ táːj kúŋ héːm/ 'sister villages'. On the other hand, they have a lot of contact with local Tai speakers living in the same area who are mainly Northern Thai and Tai Lue.

This paper analyzes phonological variation in five Khmu dialects. These dialects are spoken in the following villages:

1. Huey Yen village, Chiengkhong district, and Huey Ian village, King Wiengkaen district, Chiengrai province = Dial(1)[2]

---

[1] The author would like to thank Dr. David Thomas and Dr. Robert Bauer for editing this paper, and providing helpful suggestions and comments.

[2] The data for this dialect is based on the author's *Thai-Khmu-English Dictionary*, 1993.

2. Nam Pan, Huey Moy villages, King Songkhwai district, Nan province = Dial(2a)[3] and Ban Maj Chajdan village, King Songkhwai district, Nan province = Dial(2b). These two dialects are in fact the same dialect but while the Dial(2a) may have several word structures for one word Dial(2b) has only one consistent word structure.

3. Nam Sot and Phu Kham villages, Thung Chang district, Nan province = Dial(3)

4. Pa Phae village, Wieng Sa district, Nan province = Dial (4)

5. Huey Puk and Huey Hai villages, Muang district, Nan province = Dial(5)

The phonological structure of these Khmu dialects is discussed here in terms of word and syllable structure, and segmental and suprasegmental phonemes. The data used for discussion here was mainly obtained or rechecked from the most recent field work done in February 1994. The informants for each dialect are over 35 years of age.

1. Word and syllable structures

The Khmu syllable structure comprises one or more consonants and a vowel and may be of two types, unstressed presyllable and stressed main syllable. The main syllable canon is 'C(C)V(C).

A phonological word in Khmu may have one, two, or three syllables. A word has only one strong stress, which is always on the last syllable. The phonological word structures in Khmu are :

Monosyllabic word 'C(C)V(C):
['tráːk] 'buffalo', ['raː] 'to wash', ['pɔh] 'dust'

Disyllabic word C(C)V(C) 'C(C)V(C):
[kɨm'póŋ] 'head', [lawaːŋ] 'sky'
[m̩'raŋ] 'horse', [ŋ̩'kur] 'storm'

Trisyllabic word C(C)V,C(C)V(C)'C(C)VC:
[trəˌlap'táːp] 'butterfly'
[cəˌlɛn'téŋ] 'dragonfly'

---

[3] The data for this dialect is based mainly on Preedaporn Srisakorn's *The Sound System of Khmu at Nampan in Nan*, 1984.

In general, monosyllabic and disyllabic words are common and trisyllabic words are rare. The presyllable in most of the disyllabic words is generally believed to be a fossil of affixation, a Mon-Khmer characteristic. As shown in the variation of word structures in Khmu dialects below, the unstressed presyllable is sometimes deleted either partially or entirely.

1.1. Variation of word structures in different Khmu dialects

Word structures may vary in different Khmu dialects as shown in the following table. In Dial (2b) words are monosyllabic, whereas in the other dialects they are either monosyllabic or disyllabic.

Dial(1)	Dial(2) (a)	(b)	Dial(3)	Dial(4)	Meaning
cmkɨn	cmkɨn/ mkɨn	kɨn	smkɨn	cmkɨn	'female'
hʔiər	hʔiər	ʔiər	ʔiəj	ʔiəj/jial	'chicken'
khmuʔ	khmuʔ	muʔ	khmúʔ	kamhmuʔ	'Khmu people'
ptəʔ	ptəʔ	təʔ	ktəʔ	ptəʔ	'smoke'
smʔɨr	mʔɨr	ʔɨr	bɨl	hʔɨr	'to smell'
tmrạʔ	mrạʔ	rạʔ	tmphlaʔ/ mphaʔ	tmbraʔ	'charcoal stove'
chʔaːŋ	chʔaːŋ	ʔaːŋ	sʔâːŋ	cʔaːŋ	'bone'
cmpiəŋ	mpiəŋ	piəŋ	mpiəŋ	cmpiəŋ	'straw'
hʔeʔ	hʔeʔ	ʔeʔ	ʔéʔ	hʔeʔ	'firewood'
kmaʔ	kbaʔ	maʔ	kmáʔ	kmaʔ	'rain'
kmlə̣ːt	mlə̣ːt	lə̣ːt	mpɔːt	kmlə̣ːt	'to swallow'
kmɲɛŋ	mɲɛŋ	ɲɛːŋ	smjaŋ/kmjaŋ	ɲɛːŋ	'to listen'
kntịːŋ	ntịːŋ	tịːŋ	ktiːŋ	tiːŋ	'to fall down'
kntuər	ntuər	tuər	ntûəl/j	kntuəl	'neck'
pnɨr	pdɨr	nɨr	pnɨl/j	pnɨr	'wing'
pnsɨm	nsɨm	sɨm	psɨm	psɨm	'to plant'
rŋkɔ̣ʔ	rŋkɔ̣ʔ	kɔ̣ʔ	ŋkoʔ	ŋkoʔ	'husked rice'
scaːŋ	scaːŋ	caːŋ	kacâːŋ/ kachâːŋ	sacaːŋ	'elephant'
tmʔas	mʔas	ʔas	tmbɛh	tmʔɛs	'to sneeze'
tmkɔʔ	tmkɔʔ	kɔʔ	mphláʔ/ mpáʔ	mbraʔ	'wife'

It is obvious that Dial(1) has the fuller form of disyllabic words whereas Dial(2) has variations. Most words in Dial(2a) have disyllabic structure though in many cases the initial consonant of the presyllable is lost and the presyllable becomes a syllabic nasal whereas Dial(2b) drops most of the presyllable, making monosyllabic words. Dial(3) and Dial(4) also show variation in the word structure though not as obvious and consistent as Dial(2).

1.2. Variation of word structure within Dialect (2a)

Looking at the word structure within a dialect, we see variation similar to that found between different dialects. The main differences are found in the loss of the presyllable (including the nasal syllable), the simplification of consonant cluster, some difference in vowels, and differences in pitch level. Dial(2a) provides a good illustration.

1.2.1 Loss of presyllable

In Dial(2a) some of the presyllables which are not stressed have variant forms which show various stages of syllabicity: full syllable, half syllable, deletion of the whole syllable, or keeping only the main syllable.

1 (2 syllables)		2 (1 1/2 syllable)		3 (1 syllable)	Meaning
prlɨə	~	rlɨə	~	lɨə	'fire'
cmkɨn	~	mkɨn	~	kɨn	'woman, girl'
crŋaːj	~	rŋaːj	~	ŋaːj	'to have a cold'
prthuh	~	rthuh	~	thuh	'carelessly'
prcɨː	~	rcɨː	~	cɨː	'to remember'
prnǫːj	~	rnǫːj	~	nǫːj	'fan'
tmkɔʔ	~	mkɔʔ	~	kɔʔ	'wife'
kamraŋ	~	mraŋ	~	raŋ	'horse'
hmteʔ	~	mteʔ	~	teʔ	'to howl'
rmheʔ	~	rheʔ/mheʔ	~	heʔ	'sinew, vessel'
rŋkǫʔ	~	ŋkǫʔ	~	kǫʔ	'milled rice'

Speakers of different age groups do not pronounce the words in the same way. The speakers over 30 tend to use the fuller form of disyllabic words as in columns 1 and 2 above, whereas people younger than 30 tend to use monosyllabic words dropping the presyllable as in column 3.

1.2.2 Loss of syllabic nasal

mpuːr	~	puːr	'skin'
nchịm	~	chịm	'soft'
ŋkhịːn	~	khịːn	'yesterday'
pleʔ mpiːr	~	pleʔ piːr	'pumkin'
nthẹʔ	~	thẹʔ	'below'
mɲɛŋ	~	ɲɛŋ	'to listen, believe'
nthɛh	~	thɛh	'bowl'
nsɨm	~	sɨm	'to plant'
mkɨn	~	kɨn	'woman'
ntạŋ	~	tạŋ	'brain'
mrạŋ	~	rạŋ	'horse'
nsal	~	sal	'galanga (a kind of spice)'
nlạh	~	lạh	'to be broken'
ŋkɔːt	~	kɔːt	'to cough'
mphọʔ	~	phọʔ	'ox'
mpɔŋ	~	pɔŋ	'head'
mrọʔ	~	rọʔ	'male'

1.2.3 Change in consonant clusters

Consonant clusters /tr-, thr-, cr-, chr-, sr-/ change to /kr-, khr-/ and any nasal presyllable is lost.

traːk	-->	kraːk	'buffalo'
trɔh	-->	khrɔh	'to pull out'
crɨp	-->	krɨp	'to close the lid'
chrụʔ	-->	khrụʔ	'deep'
sreʔ	-->	khreʔ	'sand'
srạʔ	-->	khrạʔ	'a kind of edible plant'
sroʔ	-->	khroʔ	'taro'
sruət	-->	khruət	'morning'
nthrịːk	-->	khrịːk	'a kind of peel eaten with betel'
nthrụːp	-->	khrụːp	'to turn upside down'
nthrịŋ	-->	khrịŋ	'horn'
nthrịː	-->	khrịː	'to demolish, collapse'
nthrọːj	-->	khrọːj	'wind'
nthrịəs	-->	khrịəs	'to comb'
knthrɔːŋ/	-->	khrɔːŋ	'back, roof'
nthrɔːŋ			

1.2.4 Change of vowel from ə to a in presyllable

pənpiːk	-->	panpiːk	'to make the water muddy'
pənseh	-->	panseh	'to cause of fall'
pəntrɨm	-->	pantrɨm	'to cause to be smooth'

pɔnkhạr	-->	pankhạr	'to cause to be straight'
pɔnlạːc	-->	panlạːc	'to loose'
pɔnlạːh	-->	panlạːh	'to cause to be broken'
pɔnpak	-->	panpak	'to cause to be broken'

1.2.5 Change of pitch level from high to low

| rɔkét | --> | rɔkèt | 'to think' |

2. Segmental phonemes

2.1 Consonants

2.1.1 Initial consonants

The general initial consonant system may be charted as follows.

		Bilabial	Alveolar	Palatal	Velar	Glottal
Stops	vl. unasp.	p	t	c	k	?
	vl. asp.	ph	th	ch	kh	
	vd.	b*	d*	ɟ*	g*	
Fricatives			s			h
Nasals	vd.	m	n	ɲ	ŋ	
	vl. (preasp.)	hm*	hn*	hɲ*	hŋ*	
Lateral	vd.		l			
	vl. (preasp.)		hl*			
Trill/Flap	vd.		r*			
	vl. (preasp.)		hr*			
Approximants	vd.	w			j	
	vl. (preasp.)	hw*			hj*	

The * marks initial consonants that do not occur in all dialects.

While the consonant inventory of most Khmu dialects is basically similar, there are also important differences. Some dialects have the series of voiced initial stops contrasting with voiceless stops, some have voiceless continuants contrasting with voiced continuants, which are more common. In the following examples Dial(4) provides examples with voiced initial stops, whereas Dial(3) and Dial(4) provide examples with voiceless continuants.

It should be noted here that in the voiced stop series, the *b* and *d* in dial(1) are clearly implosive, dial(2) and (3) have normal voiced stop, and dial(4) is a kind of prenasalized stop. An instrumental study of certain consonants may be needed.

Examples given below present variation in initial consonant of different dialects.

a) Variation in the initial stops with voiceless aspirated, voiceless unaspirated and voiced stops in contrast.

Dial(1)	Dial(2a, b)	Dial(3)	Dial(4)	Meaning
pr̥ḭʔ	phr̥ḭʔ	kɔːŋ pl̥ḭʔ/pḭʔ	briʔ	'forest'
pa̰ːr	pha̰ːr	phaːl/j	baːr/l	'two'
ka̰ːŋ	kha̰ːŋ	kaːŋ	gaːŋ	'house'
kṵːɲ	khṵːɲ	kùːn	guːɲ	'to see'
pṵːc	phṵːc	puːc/t	buːc	'rice wine'
pa̰ː	pha̰ː	paː	baː	'you (female)'
kḭː	khiː	kiː	giː	'here'
kḭt	khɨt	kɨ̆t	gɨt	'to chop'
kla̰ːŋ	khla̰ːŋ	klàːŋ	glaːŋ	'stone'
klḛʔ	khlḛʔ	klèʔ/kèʔ	gleʔ	'husband'
klɔ̰ʔ	khlɔ̰ʔ	klɔ̀ʔ/kɔ̀ʔ	glɔʔ	'hair'
kta̰h	ktha̰h	ktah	kdah	'forehead'
plṵʔ	phlṵʔ	plùʔ/pùʔ	bluʔ	'thigh'
plɔ̰ːŋ	plɔ̰ːŋ	plɔ̀ːŋ/pɔ̀ːŋ	blɔːŋ	'rattan'
pɔ̰k	phɔ̰k	pɔ̀k	bok	'to cut a tree'
pɔ̰h	phɔ̰h	pɔh	bɔh	'ash'
pr̥ḭəl	phr̥ḭəl	phɨəl/j	bɨər	'to be alive, living'
pr̥ḭəŋ	phr̥ḭəŋ	priəŋ/piəŋ	briəŋ	'other people'
pṵʔ	phṵʔ	pùʔ	buʔ	'breast feeding'
pṵŋ	phṵŋ	pùŋ	buŋ	'mud'
tḛn	thḛn	ten	den	'to sit'
ṭḭn	thḭn	tɨ̆n	din	'to stand'

b) Variations in voiced and voiceless continuants. Not only *r ~ hr ~ l ~ hl ~ h* but also *w ~ hw, N ~ hN, and m ~ hm ~ sm* are in variation in different dialects, and in some cases they are also used in free variation in the same dialect, especially in Dial(3) and Dial(4).

Dial(1)	Dial(2) (a, b)	Dial(3)	Dial(4)	Meaning
laʔ	laʔ	hláʔ	hlaʔ	'leaf'
loŋ	loŋ	hlóŋ	hloŋ	'to forget'
riəŋ	riəŋ	hlíəŋ	hriəŋ	'gut, intestine'
roːj	roːj	róːj/hóːj	hroːj	'ghost, spirit'
raːŋ	raːŋ	hláːŋ	hraːŋ	'teeth'
reʔ	reʔ	hréʔ/hléʔ/héʔ	hreʔ	'field'

wa̤ːk	waːk	wáːk	hwaːk	'earthworm'
waʔ	waʔ	wáʔ	hwaʔ	'monkey'
ntaːk	ntaːk/taːk	ntáːk	hntaːk	'tongue'
ŋaːp	ŋaːp	háːp	hŋaːp	'to yawn'
nam	nam	nám	hnam	'big'
me̤ʔ	me̤ʔ	meʔ	hme̤ʔ	'new'
smpɔ̤ːr	mpɔ̤ːr/pɔːr	-	hmpɔːr	'tamarind'
			hrjaʔ/ɦjaʔ	'cloth bag'
khmuʔ	khmuʔ/muʔ	khmúʔ	kmhmuʔ	'Khmu people'

c) Variation in the use of consonant clusters:

Dial(1)	Dial(2) (a)	Dial(2) (b)	Dial(3)	Dial(4)	Meaning
traːk	thraːk	kraːk	thráːk/tháːk	thraːk	'buffalo'
kra̤ŋ	khra̤ŋ	khra̤ŋ	khraŋ/khlaŋ/ khaŋ	graŋ	'strong'
cntra̤ŋ	ntra̤ŋ	khra̤ŋ	nthràŋ/nthàŋ	ntraŋ	'post'
cri̤əs	chri̤əs	khi̤əs	nthriəs	nciəs	'to comb'
cruʔ	chrṳʔ/trṳʔ	khrṳʔ/khṳʔ	chrùʔ	ɟruʔ	'deep'
kle̤ʔ	khle̤ʔ	khle̤ʔ	klèʔ/kèʔ	gleʔ	'husband'
klɔ̤ʔ	khlɔ̤ʔ	khlɔ̤ʔ	klɔ̀ʔ/kɔ̀ʔ	glɔʔ	'to see'

d) Variation in the initial consonant of the presyllable:

chʔa̤ːŋ	cʔa̤ːŋ	ʔa̤ːŋ	sʔáːŋ	cʔaːŋ	'bone'
cmkɨn	mkɨn	kɨn	smkɨn	cmkɨn	'female'
cmrɔ̤ʔ	mrɔ̤ʔ	rɔ̤ʔ	smphrɔ̀ʔ	cmrɔʔ	'male'
cntah	cntah	tah	sntáh/sŋtáh	cntah	'shrimp'

e) Variation in other initial consonants:

Dial(1)	Dial(2)	Dial(3)	Dial(4)	Meaning
ʔɨ̀ək	ʔɨ̀ək	jɨ̀ək	ʔɨ̀ək	'to drink'
hʔɨər	hʔɨər/ʔɨər	ʔɨəj	ʔɨəj/jɨəl	'chicken'
nɛʔ	nɛʔ	ɲɛʔ/jɛʔ	ɲɛʔ	'small'
cat	cat	ját/cát	cát	'sour'
cɨ̀əŋ	chɨəŋ	-	jɨəŋ	'foot'
hʔɨ̀r	hʔɨr/ʔɨr	ʔɨ̀l/khʔɨ̀ːj	hʔɨr	'good smell'
hʔɨ̀ə	hʔɨə/ʔɨə	jɨə/ʔɨə	hʔɨə	'sweet'

2.1.2 Final Consonants

The general final consonant system may be charted as follows.

	Labial	Alveolar	Palatal	Velar	Glottal
Stop	p	t	c*	k	ʔ
Fricative		s*			h
Nasal	m	n	ɲ*	ŋ	
Trill/Flap		r*			
Lateral		l			
Semivowel	w			j	

The * marks final consonants which do not appear in all dialects.

Among these four Khmu dialects the following final consonant correspondences have been found:

Dial(1, 2, 4)	Dial(3)
-r	-l, -j
-l	-j
-ɲ	-n, (-ɲ)
-c	-t
-s	-h

Dial(1)	Dial(2) (a, b)	Dial(3)	Dial(4)	Meaning
maːr	maːr	mâːj	maːr	'salt'
mạr	mạr	mal/maj	mar	'snake'
kntuər	ntuər	ntûəl/ntûəj	kntuəl	'neck'
cụːr	chụːr	cùːl/cùːj	cuːr	'to go down' finger nail'
kɨr	kɨr	kɨ̂j	kɨr	'thunder'
kọr	khọr	kol/koj	gor	'to scratch with'
mpiər	mpiər/piər	mpîəl/mpîəj	mpiər	'flat bamboo tray' of the animal'
pạːr	phạːr	paːl/paːj	baːr	'two'
pliər	pliər	pîəl/pîəj	mpliər/piər	'hail'
pnɨr	pdɨr/nɨr	pnɨ̂l/pnɨ̂j	pnɨr	'wing'
tiːr	tiːr	tíːl/tíːj	tiːr	'to fly'
huəl	huəl	húəl/húəj	huəl	'bear'
kuəl	khuəl	kûəl/kûəj	kuəl	'rice mortar'
pạːɲ	phạːɲ	paːɲ/paːn	baːɲ	'to get drunk'
piɲ	piɲ	piɲ/piŋ	piɲ	'to shoot a gun'
plec	plẹc	plét	plec	'to clean inner part'
tmʔas	mʔas/ʔas	tmbéh	tmʔɛs	'to sneeze'

2.1.3 Age-conditioned variants

In Nam Sot, Thung Chang district, Nan province, (Dial3) there is a clear difference in pronunciation between people over 30 years old and those under 30.

1) Initial consonants

a) The simplification of consonant clusters: *pl-*, *phl-*, *thl-*, *kl-*, and *khl-* become *p-*, *ph-*, *th-*, *k-*, *kh-* respectively as in the following example:

Over 30	Under 30	Meaning
plé?/pé?	plé?/pé?	'fruit'
mplɔːt	mpəːt	'to swallow'
pléc/péc	pét	'to clean the internal organ of animal'
pl̃ət	pĩət	'to cut short the wood'
plaː	plaː/paː	'to cook by mincing raw meat'
plɛh	pɛh	'flat taste'
phlí?	phí?	'peppery hot'
kɔːŋ phli?	kɔːŋ phi?	'forest'
phliːŋ	phiːŋ	'drum'
thlâːk	thâːk	'buffalo'
nthlaŋ	nthaŋ	'post'
nthlòh	nthòh	'to be boiled'
nthlɨŋ/nthɨŋ	nthɨŋ	'horn'
klə̀?	kə̀?	'hair'
klàːŋ/kàːŋ	klàːŋ/kàːŋ	'stone'
klép/kép	kép/kép	'shoulder'
klè?	klè?/kè?	'husband'
klíh	kíh	'to do wrong'

b) The loss of the lateral articulation leaving only the glottal fricative: *hl~ h*

Over 30	Under 30	Meaning
hlàːŋ	hlàːŋ/hàːŋ	'tooth'
hl̃əŋ/h̃əŋ	h̃əŋ	'intestine'
hliː	hiː	'to pull'
hlaː	haː	'to wash'
hlɔ́h/hɔ́h	hɔ́h	'to get up'
hlé?	hé?	'field, farm'

c) Other correspondences: *?~ j, c~ s, ch~ th~ s, k~ kh,.* and *ɲ~ j*

Over 30	Under 30	Meaning
ʔɨək	jɨək	'to drink'
calɨəŋ/calɨəŋ	calɨəŋ/salɨəŋ	'roofing grass'
canɨm	canɨm/sanɨm	'medicine'
chɨmkɨn	thɨmkɨn/simkɨn	'female'
calɛʔ/salɛʔ	salɛʔ	'to run'
chɨəŋ	sɨəŋ	'pig'
kamɲaŋ/ kamjaŋ	khamjaŋ	'to listen'

2) Final Consonants

The variation between final -*l* and -*j* , occur in words in Dial.3 which have a final -*r* in other dialects.

Dial(1)	Dial(3)		Meaning
	Over 30	Under 30	
ma̰r	mal	maj	'snake'
hʔiər	ʔiəl	ʔiəj	'chicken'
pnɨr	pənɨl	pənɨj	'wing'
mpuːr	mpûːl	mpûːj	'skin'
kntuər	ntûəl	ntûəj	'neck'
khuːl	khûːl	khûːj	'hair'
ktḛl	kətel	kətej	'stomach'
mpiər	mpîəl	mpîəj	'bamboo tray'
kuəl	kûəl	kûəl/kûəj	'rice motar'
ŋɔ̰ːr	ŋɔ̂ːl	ŋɔ̂ːj	'way'
pa̰ːr	pâːl	pâːj	'two'
kor̰	khól	khôj	'to scratch'
kwaːl	kwaːl	kwaːj	'to bark'
hur	hûl	hûj	'to blow'
tiːr	fiːl	fiːj	'to fly'
cṵːr	cùːl	cûːj	'to go down'
hɨəl	hɨ̂əl	hɨ̂əj	'to vomit'
huːr	hûːl	hûːj	'rotten'
heːl	hêːl	hêːj	'to cut grass'
haːl	hâːl	hâːj	'to peel with knife'
ŋa̰r	ŋàl	ŋàj	'cool'

It should be noted that for many people -*r, -l* and -*j* seem to be in free variation. They may prefer one sound but they are ready to change to the other two sounds if they are speaking to people who use those sounds. Final -r occurs in Dial(3) but only in the speech of older people who use it in free variation with -l.

For other final consonants, final *-ɲ* has also been found corresponding to *-n* or *-ŋ*

samêɲ	samên	'star'
p̂iɲ/p̂iŋ	p̂iŋ	'to shoot'
kûːɲ	kûːn	'to see'
kêɲ	kên	'to stab'

2.2 Vowels

The Khmu vowel system is rather simple. Most dialects have a nine vowel system in which length is contrastive, and there are three diphthongs. Only some dialects have the long central back vowel ʌː.

		Front	Unrounded Central	Back	Rounded Back
High	i iː		ɨ ɨː		u uː
Mid	e ' eː		ə əː		o oː
Low	ɛ ɛː		a aː	*ʌː	ɔ ɔː
	iə		iə		uə

3. Suprasegmental phonemes

Suprasegmental phonemes in Khmu are rather complex. Both within dialects and between dialects of Khmu they are very complex.

Using register, based on Henderson (1952), as a framework in which to explain Khmu suprasegmental features, we can arrive at the solution.

Register (also called register complex) refers to the linguistic phenomenon that several suprasegmental features tend to work together as a complex group rather than as individual features. In Mon-Khmer languages these clustering features tend to include voice quality, pitch, voicing of the initial consonant, vowel height, and vowel gliding. The voice quality ranges from breathy to clear (modal) to creaky. The pitch ranges from high to mid to low. The voicing refers to voiced and voiceless initial consonants. The vowel height refers to close or open vowels. The vowel gliding refers to onglide, plain, and offglide. The tension refers to tenseness and laxness. The register complex affects the whole syllable not just the vowel. Normally one or two features of the register complex will become more prominent in one language.

The four Khmu dialects discussed plus Dial(5) provide examples for discussion here. They contain most of the suprasegmental features just mentioned. However, different features have been exploited by different dialects. The voicing contrast is exploited by Dial(4), while voice quality is exploited by Dial (1) and (2), and in Dial (2) some initial stops are aspirated. Dial(3) and Dial(5) contrast high and low pitches.

Dial(1)*	Dial(2a,b)	Dial(3)	Dial(4)	Dial(5)	Meaning
cạŋ	chạŋ	càŋ	ɟaŋ	càŋ	'to weigh'
caŋ	caŋ	cáŋ	caŋ	cáŋ	'to be astringent'
kṵːɲ	khṵːɲ	kùːn	gṵːɲ	kùːɲ	'to see'
kuːɲ	kuːɲ	kúːn	kuːɲ	kúːɲ	'elder male relative'
ŋɔ̰ʔ	ŋɔ̰ʔ	ŋɔ̀ʔ	ŋɔʔ	ŋɔ̀ʔ	'to fear'
ŋɔʔ	ŋɔʔ	ŋɔ́ʔ	hŋɔʔ/hɔʔ	ŋɔ́ʔ	'paddy rice'
pṵːc	phṵːc	pùːc/pùːt	buːc	pùːc	'rice wine'
puːc	puːc	púːc/púːt	puːc	púːc	'to take off'
cạm	chạm	càm	ɟam	càm	'to soak in water'
cam	cam	cám	cam	cám	'a kind of trap'
klạːŋ	khlạːŋ	klàːŋ	glaːŋ	klàːŋ	'stone, pebble'
klaːŋ	klaːŋ	kláːŋ	klaːŋ	kláːŋ	'eagle'
lạʔ	lạʔ	-	laʔ	làʔ	'to go for pleasure'
laʔ	laʔ	hláʔ	hlaʔ	láʔ	'leaf'
pạːt	phạːt	pàːt	baːt	pàːt	'to sharpen wood'
paːt	paːt	páːt	paːt	páːt	'to slice (meat)'
pạk	phạk	pàk	bak	pàk	'to ride'
pak	pak	pák	pak	pák	'to break'
plɔ̰ːŋ	plɔ̰ːŋ	plɔ̀ːŋ/pɔ̀ːŋ	blɔːŋ	plɔ̀ːŋ	'rattan'
plɔːŋ	plɔːŋ	plɔ́ːŋ/pɔ́ːŋ	plɔːŋ	plɔ́ːŋ	'calf of leg'
pɔ̰k	phɔ̰k	pòk	bok	pòk	'to cut a tree'
pok	pok	pók	pok	pók	'to take a bite'
pɔ̰ʔ	phɔ̰ʔ	pɔ̀ʔ	bɔʔ	pɔ̀ʔ	'to carry a baby with piece of cloth'
pɔʔ	pɔʔ	-	pɔʔ	pɔ́ʔ	'to sweep'
pṵŋ	phṵŋ	pùŋ	buŋ	pùŋ	'mud'
puŋ	puŋ	púŋ	puŋ	púŋ	'to blow (instrument)'
pṵːm	phṵːm	pùːm	buːm	pùːm	'to chew'
puːm	puːm	púːm	puːm	púːm	'to fart'
rạːŋ	rạːŋ	laːŋ	raːŋ	ràːŋ	'flower'
raːŋ	raːŋ	hláːŋ/haːŋ	hraːŋ	ráːŋ	'tooth'
tạr	thạr	salɛʔ	dar	tàr	'to run'

tar	tar	-	tar	tár	'rattan band for carrying basket'
wạːk	wạːk	wàːk	waːk	wàːk	'earthworm'
waːk	waːk	-	hwaːk	wáːk	'to be chipped'
wạt	wạt	wàt	wat	wàt	'to pierce'
wat	wat	wát	hwat	wát	'to throw'

Dial(5) has been added here to show another dialect of Khmu which is very close to Dial(1) but in Dial(5) pitch is contrastive while Dial(1) voice quality is contrastive. The difference between Dial(1) and Dial(5) is quite obvious from auditory impression as well as from the speakers' intuition.

The variation of suprasegmental features in different Khmu dialects indicates an aspect of historical development of Khmu phonology. Huffman's hypothesis of stages of register complex in 15 Mon-Khmer languages (1976) can be partly applied in explaining the stages of phonological change or the register-tone development process in Khmu.

Dial(4), with voicing contrast in the initial consonant, shows the early stage of the development. The voiced and voiceless initial consonants with no vowel difference show this dialect is a conservative type of dialect.

Dial(1) and Dial(2), with voice quality contrast, indicate that the initial consonant has lost the voicing and the whole syllable is associated with the register complex especially laxness and tenseness. It is noticeable that the laxness or breathiness is stronger in words with initial stops. Initial stops in Dial(2) are also associated with aspiration as well as the laxness.

Dial(3) and Dial(5), with pitch contrast, show that the initial consonants have lost the voicing contrast. Acoustic studies have found that voiced consonants are associated with low pitch, whereas voiceless consonants are associated with high pitch, and in Khmu this is the normal interdialectal correspondence. Dial(5) has obviously two contrastive tones, whereas Dial(3) has two contrastive tones with the tendency to develop a four tone system. Dial(5) is similar to Dial(1) in terms of syllable structure, choice of lexicon, and final consonants, etc. However, for the suprasegmental feature it has developed a contrastive tone system, whereas Dial(1) has developed a contrastive register system.

As a result, some dialects of Khmu, such as Dial(3) and Dial(5), have become tone languages. The presyllable is reduced in one way or another, phonation is less prominent or even disappears; but the pitch differences can be heard clearly. These are high and low tones with a tendency to develop a four tone system in Dial(3). Other dialects are at different stages of the process. Dial(1) has developed a tense-lax register system in the same way as Dial(2a,b), except that the latter has added aspiration to the initial stop of the lax/breathy register syllable. Dial(4) is the most conservative by retaining the voicing contrast. It is a non-tonal non-register language.

BIBLIOGRAPHY

Chambers, J.K and Peter Trudgill. 1980. *Dialectology.* Cambridge University Press.

Cholthissa Ong-arj. 1988. A phonology of Khmu Lue at Nan Province. M.A. Thesis. Mahidol University.

Delcros, H. 1966. Petit dictionnaire du language des Khmu' de la region de Xieng Khouang. Mimeo. Vientiane.

Diffloth, Gérard. 1973. "Austro-Asiatic Languages", Encyclopaedia Britanica. 480-484.

Dorian, Nancy. ed. 1989. *Investing Obsolescence.* Cambridge University Press, Cambridge.

Ferlus, M. 1977. L'infixe instrumental rn en khamou et sa trace en vietnamien. Cahiers de Linguistique, *AO* 2:51-55.

Fisiak, Jacek, ed. 1988. *Historical Dialectology.* Mouton de Gruyter, Berlin.

Henderson, Eugénie J.A. "The main features of Cambodian Pronunciation" *BSOAS* 14.1 (1952):149-174.

Hombert, Jean-Marie. 1978. Consonant Types, Vowel Quality, and Tone. In *Tone: A Linguistic Survey* edited by Victoria A Fromkin, Academic Press, Inc.

Huffman, Franklin E. "The Register Problem in Fifteen Mon-Khmer languages", *AS* 5.1 (1974): 25-37.

Lebar, Frank. 1965. "The Khamu." *Final Report to National Research Council, Bangkok.* Human Relations Area Files—Yale University, 1-8.

Lindell, Kristina. Svantesson, Jan-Olof and Damrong Tayanin. 1981. "Phonology of Kammu Dialects." *Cahiers de Linguistique, AO* 9: 45-71.

Matisoff, James A. 1973. Tonogenesis in Southeast Asia. In *Consonant Types of Tone.* edited by Jarry M. Hyman, Southern California. Occasional Papers in Linguistics No. 1.

Pittman, Richard S. "The Explanatory Potential of Voice-register Phonology" *MKS VII*: 201-229.

Preedaporn Srisakorn. 1984. The Sound System of Khmu at Nampan in Nan. M.A. Thesis. Mahidol University.

Proschan, Frank. *Khmu Verbal Art in America: The Poetic of Khmu Verse,* Ph.D. Dissertation, The University of Austin at Texas.

Smalley, William A. 1961. *Outline of Khmu? Structure.* New Haven : American Oriental Society.

Suwilai Premsrirat. 1986. "Aspects of Inter-Clausal Relations in Khmu." Davidson, ed, *Essays in Honour of H.L Shorto,* London, School of Oreintal and African Studies.

Suwilai Premsrirat. 1993.*Thai-Khmu-English Dictionary,* Mahidol University.

Suwilai Premsrirat. *Khmu, A Minority Language of Thailand.* (A Khmu Grammar and A Study of Thai and Khmu Cutting Words) Papers in South-East Asian Linguistics No. 10, Pacific Linguistics Series A-No. 75.

Suwilai Premsrirat.1986. "World view in Khmu." *Thammasat University Journal.* 15, No. 1 94-133.

Svantesson, Jan-Olof.1983. *Kammu Phonology and Morphology.* Travaux de L'institut de Linguistique de Lund.

Thomas, David D. and Robert R. Headley Jr. "More on Mon-Khmer subgroupings", *Lingua* 25.4 (1970) : 398-418.

Thongkum, Theraphan L. 1982. "Register without Tongue-Root in Nyah-Kur (Chao Bon)." *Paper presented at the XVth International conference on Sino-Tibetan languages and linguistics,* Beijing, China, August 17-19.

The metrical structure of Thai in a non-linear perspective

Apiluck Tumtavitikul
Kasetsart University

1. Syllables in Autosegmental and Metrical Phonology

Syllables and stress patterns have been considered suprasegments, being external to segmental features of consonants and vowels. In a more recent approach to phonological analysis, the autosegmental approach (Goldsmith 1976, 1990), the distinction between segments and suprasegments is, more or less, neutralized to autosegments. That is, consonants and vowels, phonetic features, and tones are all viewed as autosegments on their own separate tiers. Although autosegments are independent of one another, they are geometrically linked to one another by association lines which express simultaneity in time-- Linked elements jointly represent a sound.

While Clements and Keyser (1985) see syllables as elements on their own syllable tier in a multi-linear representation, Goldsmith (1990) takes a syllable to be a 'hierarchical structure organized on the skeletal tier.' Syllables themselves constitute a phonological plane of metrical structure, upon which stress assignment is based. For example,

(1)

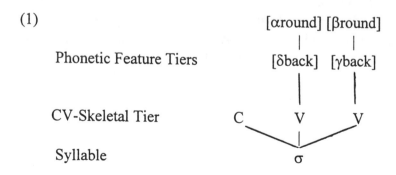

Phonetic Feature Tiers $[\alpha\text{round}]$ $[\beta\text{round}]$
$[\delta\text{back}]$ $[\gamma\text{back}]$

CV-Skeletal Tier C V V

Syllable σ

2. Syllable Organization

The 'hierarchical' internal structure of a syllable according to Goldsmith, consists of two major constituents: onset and rime; with nucleus and coda as the subconstituents of the rime. The internal structure of the syllable on the syllable plane can be charted as follows:

(2)

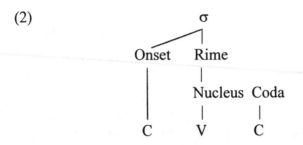

For a complex nucleus, the nucleus node branches as in (3) below:

(3)   Nucleus
                                          / \
                                          V V

This internal structure of the syllable is psychologically real and is well attested cross-linguistically in phenomena, e.g., language games, speech errors, etc. These constituents and subconstituents of the syllables are evidenced in Thai language games, Kham Phùán (Surintramont 1973) where rimes are permuted, and in a form of reduplication in Thai (Luksaneeya-nawin 1986) where the syllable nucleus behaves differently from the syllable coda in reduplication. For example,

(4)a. Kham Phùán (Surintramont 1973): rimes permutation

Where tones as autosegments may or may not move with the 'melodic' segments of the rime. Thus, [duu năŋ] > [daŋ nùú] or [dăŋ nuu].

b. Special Reduplication (Luksaneeyanawin 1986): vowel ablaut

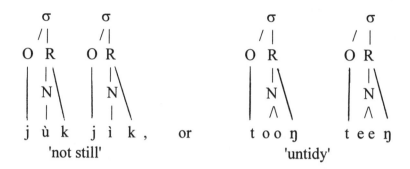

'not still'   or   'untidy'

Whereas Kham Phùán takes a larger unit of rime permutation regardless of the internal structure of the rime itself, the special reduplication in (4)b looks at the subconstituent of the rime, the syllable nucleus. Both phenomena are good evidence of the reality of the internal structure of the syllable for Thai speakers.

A notion that has been given much weight in Goldsmith (1990) is the 'extrasyllabicity' which is an extra element of the internal structure of the syllable. Such an element is a consonant in either initial or final position of a syllable which, if it is not syllabified during the word-formation process, will be deleted on the phonetic form. At word-final position, such a segment has been traditionally called an 'appendix' or a 'termination' (1990:107). Extrasyllabic segments are evidenced in Thai and may be said to be comparable to [tua kà?ran] in Thai (to be discussed in section 4.2 below).

3. Syllable Weight, Stress, and Metrical Structure

Metrical Phonology (tree theory) analyzes stress patterns as hierarchical representations of relative prominence of syllables and higher constituents in the metrical structure (metrical tree).

In general, stress assignment is based on rhythm and/or syllable weight which looks at the rime structure. While rhythm alternates stress at regular intervals, syllable weight distinction, which is in general binary, i.e. light and heavy, counts moras in the rimes. Heavy syllables are those with branching rimes whereas light syllables are single moraic with non-branching rimes (cf. (5) & (6) below). In a quantity sensitive language, heavy syllables are the ones that attract stresses.

(5) Light syllables are of the form;

Rime
|
V

(6) Heavy syllables may take one of the following internal structures of the rime:

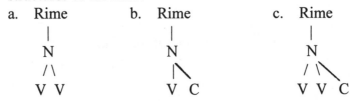

a. Rime   b. Rime   c. Rime
     | | |
    N   N   N
   /\   / \   / \
  V V   V C   V V C

Syllable weight is crucial to stress assignment in Thai (to be discussed in sections 4 & 5 below).

Metrical Theory, developed from Liberman & Prince (1977) and Prince (1980) (cf. Goldsmith 1990), sees three main hierarchical constituents in the metrical tree;
a. *The syllable, which is the lowest level constituent, with internal structure of the rime being crucial to stress attraction.*
b. *The metrical foot, which is a higher level constituent, constisting of a strong and one or more weak syllables.* A foot may be degenerate, i.e., dominating a single syllable.
c. *The word, which is the highest level, consisting of a strong foot and one or more weak feet.*

For example, (from Luangthongkum 1977)

(7)

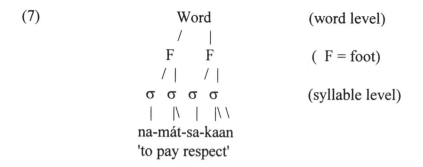

Where a strong node denoted by a vertical line at either F or W-level represents prominence.

4. Thai Syllables

Surface structures of Thai syllables can be summarized as follows,

(8) $C_1(C_2) \{V(V)(C_3)\}$

That is, all the following structures are possible phonetic forms;

(9)a. $C_1(C_2)V$ b. $C_1(C_2)VV$
   c. $C_1(C_2)VC_3$ d. $C_1(C_2)VVC_3$

With the following constraints,

(10) Syllable Structure Constraints

    a. $C_2 = \{l, r, w\}$, and
        if $C_2 = [w]$, then $C_1 = [k, k^h]$ (Luksaneeyanawin 1993)

    b.*$[\alpha \text{ son}] [\alpha \text{ son}]$

i.e., in a cluster onset, the consonants cannot both be [+son] or both be [-son]. For example, *pt, *rl, or *kk are all ill-formed. The language does not allow a sequence of stops or approximants in the onset position.

    c. $C_3 = \{m, n, ŋ, w, j, p, t, k, ʔ\}$

4.1 Cluster Onsets

Two types of cluster onsets are observed;

a. *True Cluster*

In a true cluster, the consonants in the onset position cannot be separated (Tumtavitikul 1992). For example,

(11) trii 'three' > trai-jaaŋ, *tàʔraijaaŋ

  klaaŋ 'middle' > *kàʔlaaŋ

  pràp 'fine' > *pàʔràp

Such clusters have the internal structure as in (12) below,

(12)
```
              σ
             /|
            O  R
            |
            C
           /\
          t  r ...
```

With a multiple-mapping between 'melodic' segments and C-segment on the onset position such that vowel insertion will create association line-crossing and thus, is prohibited. The result is an unbreakable cluster onset.

b. *CC-cluster*

A CC-cluster is a complex onset where the two consonants can be separated due to the following internal structure,

(13)
```
              σ
             /|
            O  R
           /\
          C C
          | |
          t  r ...
```

for example,

(14) trùət 'check' > tamrùət 'policeman'
      pràap 'raid'   > bamràap (p > b)
      tràt   'speak' > damràt   (t > d)

Such cluster onsets consist of two C-slots, each mapping to a 'melodic' segment in a one-to-one fashion, thus the cluster is breakable without violating the association line-crossing constraint.

4.2 Complex Coda

A complex coda consists of one or more 'extrasyllabic' segments which are not linked to the syllable underlyingly, nevertheless form a part of the lexical entry. The extrasyllabic segment will surface only if it is syllabified in the word-formation process, otherwise it will be deleted on the surface. An extrasyllabic segment is denoted by parentheses ( ). A single extrasyllabic segment is comparable to [tua kàʔran] in the Thai grammar. For example,

(15)a. /yák(s)/ > [yák]   'giant'
                  > [yáksàá], [yáksìí]
     b. /phátʰ(n)/ > [phát]   'progress'
                    > [pháttʰáʔnaa]

and (15)a. can be charted as follows;

(16)a.   σ   σ
            / | / |
           O R   O R
           | |\ | |\
           C V C C   >   C V C C
           | | | | | | | |
          / y á k s /   [y á k s]   > [yák]
                                         ↓
                                         ø

b.
```
     σ              σ                          σ           σ
    /|             /|                         /|          /|
   O R    +      O R          >            O R         O R
   | |\           /\                        | |\       / ∧
   C V C C        V V                       C V C C    V V
   | | | |        | |                       | | | |    | |
  / y á k s /   / a a /                    [y á k s    a a]
                                           [yáksàá]
                              >
```

4.3 Syllable Reduction
Two types of syllable reduction are observed:

a. *Vowel Reduction*
Vowel reduction mainly occurs in unstressed CVʔ surface
syllables. The reduction mainly takes place in the form of a >
ə , or i > I . A final glottal deletion always precedes
vowel reduction which is most often accompanied by tone
neutralization to Mid. For example,

(17)a. rátt̪ʰàʔbaan   >   ratt̪ʰàbaan   'government'
                       >   ratt̪ʰabaan
                       >   ratt̪ʰəbaan

     b. raac̠ʰíʔnii   >   raac̠ʰínii   'queen'
                       >   raac̠ʰinii
                       >   raac̠ʰInii

b. *Vowel Deletion*
Vowel deletion is a further step beyond vowel reduction, which
often occurs with surface CVʔ with a fricative onset. For
example,

(18) sàʔtìʔ   >   sàtìʔ   'mental, mind'
               >   satìʔ
               >   sətìʔ
               >   s̪tìʔ

It is noted that all word-final CV? syllables are inherently stressed (Luksaneeyanawin 1993). This matter will be taken up under Stress Assignment. (18) can be charted as;

```
(19)  σ      σ                σ                    σ
      /|     / |              /|                   / |
      O R    O R              O R                  O R
      | |\   | |\             | |\                 | |\
      C V C  C VC    >        C V C...    >         C  V  C ...
      | | |  | | |            | | |                 ⧸⧸'
      s à ?  t ì ?            s à ?...              s       ...
                               ↓↓
                              ø ø                  [s̩]
```

Syllable reduction may have introduced a new surface structure into the language, namely a syllabic consonant, e.g., [s̩]. Another possible surface form which vowel deletion may have brought into the language is the surface cluster onset [st] as in (20) below;

```
(20)    σ        σ                  σ          σ
       /|       /|                 /|         /|
       O R      O R                O R        O R
       | ↓      | |\               ⧸----7     | |\
       C ø      C V C    >         C          C V C
       |        | | |              |          | | |
       s        t ì ?              s          t ì ?    >  [stì?]
```

Whether we like it or not, either (19) or (20) or both surface forms are indicative of an ongoing process of language change in modern Thai. For more examples,

(21) s̩nàps̩nŭn   < sà?nàp-sà?nŭn   'support'
     kìtçʰkaan   < kìtcà?kaan ; (cʰ < c)   'business'
     s̩tʰàában   < sà?tʰàában   'institution'

4.4 Surface and Underlying CV-Syllables

It is clear from 4.3 that Thai does have surface CV-syllables from syllable reduction, which is a late phonetic process of glottal deletion, vowel reduction or deletion, and tone neutralization.

(22) Glottal Deletion (Phonetic Implementation Rule)

$$? \quad > \quad ø \quad / \quad \text{CV} \_]\sigma_x \quad (\sigma_x = \text{unstressed syllable}) $$

(23) Vowel Reduction (Phonetic Implementation Rule)

$$ V \quad > \quad ə \quad / \quad C \_]\sigma_x \quad (\sigma_x = \text{unstressed syllable}) $$
$$ | $$
$$ \text{[-high]} $$

Underlying CV-syllables are more controversial. Gandour (1974) suggests that there are no underlying CV-syllables in Thai. His suggestion is based mainly on the arguments concerning surface vs. underlying glottal stop in Thai. We would like to propose here that there are underlying CV-syllables in Thai, in fact we would like to suggest that all surface CV?'s are from underlying /CV/ where the glottal final comes from a glottal insertion rule (24).

(24) Glottal Insertion (Post-Lexical Rule)

$$ ø \quad > \quad ? \quad / \quad \text{CV} \_]\sigma $$

The justification for glottal insertion is as follows:
a. /b, d/ *are Thai phonemes which occur only syllable-initially. It is not unusual to have /?/ restricted in the same manner since /b, d, ?/ do behave similarly with respect to tone assignments in syllable onset position.*
b. *For* CVV[-son] *syllables, only /p, t, k/ occur at syllable coda, but a glottal final with long vowel is absent (as noted by Gandour 1974).* Such a gap cannot be explained if there is an underlying /?/ at syllable-final in a CV? syllable.
c. *An underlying /CV/ helps count syllable weight such that*

surface (not word-final) CV? *can be counted as light syllables.*
Thus, stress assignment in Thai can be simplified to depend
mainly on syllable quantity.

5. Stress Assignments in Thai

Luksaneeyanawin (1983, 1993) has given the following
generalizations for stress assignments in Thai:

(25) Stress Assignments in Mono-Morphemic Polysyllabic
Words (Luksaneeyanawin 1983, 1993):
a. Thai distinguishes two types of syllables: linker syllables
(i.e., [Ca] syllables) and non-linker syllables of all other types.
b. Thai recognizes double stress in a word: primary and
secondary. The last syllable always receives primary stress
and secondary stress is sometimes suppressed in casual or fast
speech.
c. Between linker and non-linker syllables in all other positions
(non-final in a word), non-linker syllables attract stresses.
d. In a 2-4 syllable-word, stress patterns usually follow the
patterns below:

$$- \quad | \qquad \qquad (- = \text{unstressed}, \ | = \text{stressed})$$
$$| \ - \ |$$
$$- \ | \ - \ |$$

e. However, if in a 3-syllable word, the 1st syllable is a linker
and the 2nd is a non-linker, the stress pattern is as follows,

$$- \ | \ |$$

f. Also, in a 4-syllable word where the 1st syllable is a non-
linker but the 2nd is a linker syllable, the stress pattern is:

$$| \ - \ - \ |$$

g. In the case where both the 1st and 2nd syllables are
non-linker syllables, the degree of syllable weight gives
precedence to stress assignment-- the heavier the rime, the
more likely it is to attract stress.
  The degree of syllable weight is given as follows:

$$\begin{Bmatrix} CV(V)[\text{-son}] \\ CV(V)[\text{+nas}] \end{Bmatrix} > CVV, \text{ and}$$

$$CV(V)[\text{+nas}] > CV(V)[\text{-son}] > CV?$$

For word-compounds, the generalizations in (25) do not apply; stress assignment is rather determined by 'the morphological derivation of the compounds'. For example, (from Luksaneeyanawin 1993:287)

(26)a. [náam sôm]   'orange juice'   - |
       [náam sôm kʰán] 'fresh orange juice'   - | |

   b. [kàp kʰáàw]   'dish'   - |
      [túù kàp kʰáàw]   'kitchen cabinet' | - |

What we attempt to do in this paper is to account for the generalizations given in (25) for mono-morphemic polysyllabic words as well as for word-compounds by a single set of rules in metrical phonology.

5.1 Thai Metrical Structure

As discussed earlier in sections 3 and 4.1, we distinguish two types of Thai syllables according to rime-projection: light and heavy. All surface (not word-final) CVʔ-syllables are considered 'light' from an underlying /CV/. By this, we distinguish stress assignment in emphatic words as optional (emphatic rule) where each and every syllable of the word emphasized is stressed.

With the above convention, stress assignments in Thai can be derived from the metrical tree with the following tree-building rules;

(27) Thai Metrical Tree:

a. Count syllable weight according to rime-projection. An exception is a word-final CV-syllable which, by its position, is inherently 'heavy' despite its internal structure.
b. Build right-headed metrical feet with a leftward spreading unbounded foot tree for each foot.

c. Build right-headed word-tree with a leftward spreading unbounded word.

For word-compounds, (27) cyclically applies in the lexicon as a stress assignment rule in word-formation. For example,

(28)

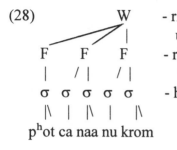

- right-headed, right-to-left spreading unbounded word
- right-headed, right-to-left spreading unbounded foot
- heavy/light syllables

pʰot ca naa nu krom   'dictionary'

Stress pattern: | - | - | ; where the last syllable receives primary stress.

By Glottal Insertion (GI, (24)), we have [phótcàʔnaanúʔkrom].

(29)

```
        W
        |
        F
       / |
      σ   σ
      |   |
     ka  tʰa          'frying pan'
```

Stress pattern: - |

With the application of GI (24), we have [kàʔtʰáʔ]. In casual speech, Glottal Deletion (GD, (22)) and Vowel Reduction (VR, (23)) apply yielding [kətʰáʔ].

66

(30)a.

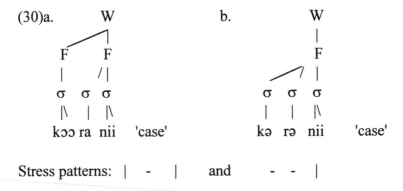

Stress patterns: | - | and   - - |

(30)a is comparable to the stress pattern given by
Luangthongkum's (1977) careful speech style and (30)b is
comparable to her casual speech pattern. It is noted that (30)b
can be derived from (30)a by secondary-stress suppression.
The metrical tree in (30)a assigns primary stress to the last
syllable [nii] and secondary stress to the first syllable [kɔɔ]. If
secondary-stress suppression applies, we have a vowel
shortening rule (31) shortening the syllable. When stress
assignment reapplies, (30)b is derived with the application of
vowel reduction (23).

(31) Vowel Shortening
         VV   >   V / [-stress σ]
i.e., a long vowel in an unstressed syllable is shortened.

    If the word-compounds are reanalyzed as monomorphemic
polysyllabic words, that is, indivisible unit words, the same
metrical rules given in (27) apply. However, in the case that
the compounds are perceived as compounds, (27) applies in
cyclical applications in lexical phonology. For example,
(32)

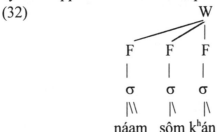

Stress pattern: -   - |

With Vowel Shortening (VS (31)), we have [nám sôm kʰán].

In (32) the compound is reanalyzed as one polysyllabic word.
If the compound is taken as a compound from morpheme
concatenation, we then have (33) below,

(33)   [W   W] w   Word Cmpounding

```
              [      W            W  ] w      Word Cmpounding
                    /|            |
                  F   F           F
                  |   |           |
                  σ   σ           σ
                 /|\  /\          /\
               náam sôm         kʰán
```

With Foot-Percolation, (27) reapplies yielding,

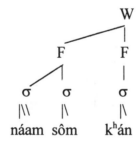

```
                        W
                      /  |
                    F     F
                   /|     |
                  σ  σ    σ
                 /|\ /\   /\
              náam sôm  kʰán
```

Stress pattern: - | |

In the same manner, we may have [túù kàp kʰáàw] with the
stress pattern; - - |, or we may have [túù kàp kʰáàw] with the
pattern; | - |, being word-compound stress pattern. Hence, we
have both monomorphemic polysyllabic words as well as
word-compounds accounted for by one single set of rules in
metrical phonology.

5.2 Evidence

If we truly have the rules for building Thai metrical trees, (27) should not only account for stress assignments, but also other phenomena related to the metrical structure, e.g., syllable reduction, syllable deletion, foot deletion, etc.

a. *Syllable Reduction*
For syllable reduction, (27) predicts that all unstressed syllables, either those dominated by weak nodes at the foot-level, i.e., [CV?] syllables, or those subject to secondary-stress suppression, i.e., those dominated by strong nodes at the foot-level but by weak nodes at the word-level, are susceptible to syllable reduction. While [CV?] syllables are almost always reduced in casual speech, secondary-stress suppression is optional.

(34) sà?trɔɔbəəríì   >   sətrɔɔbəəríì, or sətrɔɔbəríì
     'strawberry'   - | | | - | - |
                                          (2nd stress suppression)

GD (22) and VR (23) apply to [sà?] in both cases, but secondary-stress suppression only applies to the latter not the former in (34) and VS (31) applies to [bəə] yielding [bə]. It is noted that [sà?] may have gone all the way to become [s̩] or [st]-cluster in both cases.

b. *Syllable and Foot Deletion*
Both syllable and foot deletions are good testing grounds for the metrical constituents proposed in (27) for Thai. For example,

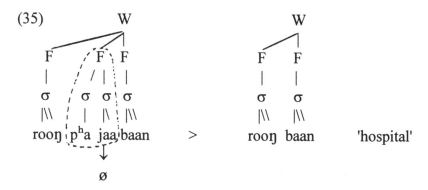

The metrical foot [pʰajaa] deletes as a constituent in (35).

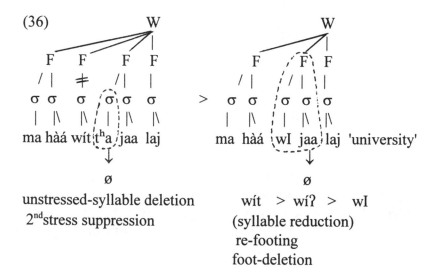

unstressed-syllable deletion
2ⁿᵈstress suppression

wít > wíʔ > wI
(syllable reduction)
re-footing
foot-deletion

The final phonetic reduced form is [mahàálaj].

In (36) there are both unstressed-syllable deletion and
foot-deletion. It is noticeable that secondary-stress
suppression chooses a non-branching foot, i.e. a degenerate
foot. This is not at all surprising given the principle of heavy
and light contrast at the syllable level in (5) and (6). The same
principle seems to be operative at the foot level in this case and
also in (34).   However, secondary-stress supression also
applies to a branching foot when no degenerate foot carrying a

secondary stress is available. In this case, stress assignment is subject to Foot Constraint (37) below:

(37) Foot Constraint

*   F
    ⁻ ⁻ ⁻/＊
      σ

That is, there can be no foot-tree without a strong node dominating a strong syllable. For example, (from Luangthongkum 1977)

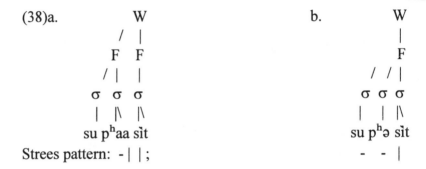

(38)a.   W   b.   W

            / | |

         F F   F

        / | | / / |

     σ σ σ   σ σ σ

     | \ \\ | | \\

    su pʰaa sìt   su pʰə sìt

Strees pattern: - | | ;   - - |

The casual speech style (38)b is derived from the careful speech style (38)a via secondary-stress suppression followed by vowel shortening (31), re-footing due to cyclical application of stress asignment (27) which is subject to Foot Constraint (37), and followed by vowel reduction (23) as shown in (39) below;

(39)   W   W   W

     / | ≠ | |

   F F   F F   F

  /≠ | >   / | >   / / |

  σ σ σ   σ σ σ   σ σ σ

  | \ \\ | | \\ | | \\

su pʰaa sìt   su pʰa sìt   su pʰə sìt

2ⁿᵈ stress suppression Vowel Shortening (31) Stress Rules (27)
                        Foot Constraint (37)   Vowel Reduction
                                                    (23)

6. Concluding Remarks

What we have introduced in this paper is an analysis of the metrical structure of Thai in a non-linear perspective. Previous works, e.g., Luangthongkum (1977) and Luksaneeyanawin (1983, 1993) have been tremendously helpful in laying out the generalizations in the language with respect to rhythms and word accents. We hope that in future research non-linear phonology will play a significant role in the analysis of Thai metrical structure beyond the word level.

REFERENCES

Clements, G. N., and Keyser, S. J. (1985). *CV Phonology: A Generative Theory of the Syllable*. Cambridge, Mass.: MIT.

Gandour, J. (1974). The Glottal Stop in Siamese: Predictability in Phonological Description. *University of California at Los Angeles Working Papers in Phonetics* 27.84-91.

Goldsmith, J. A. (1976). An Overview of Autosegmental Phonology. *Linguistic Analysis* 2.1.23-67.

_____. (1990). *Autosegmental and Metrical Phonology*. Cambridge, Mass.: Basil Blackwell.

Luangthongkum, T. (1977). *Rhythym in Thai*. Ph.D. Diss., University of Edinburgh.

Luksaneeyanawin, S. (1983). *Intonation in Thai*. Ph.D. Diss., University of Edinburgh.

_____ . (1986). Some Semantic Functions of Reduplicatives in Thai. *Satthasaat læœ Phasaasaat*. Bangkok: Tech-Press Service.

_____. (1993). Speech Computing and Speech Technology in Thailand. *Proceedings of the Symposium on Natural Language Processing in Thailand*, 17-21 March, 1993, Chulalongkorn University.

Surintramont, A. (1973). Some Aspects of Underlying Syllable Structure in Thai: Evidence from Khamphuan-- A Thai Word Game. *Studies in Linguistic Science* 3.1.121-42.

Tumtavitikul, A. (1992). *Consonant Onsets and Tones in Thai*. Ph.D. Diss., University of Texas at Austin. (Distributed by UMI, Ann Arbor, Michigan).

Toward a comprehensive theory of noun categorization, with special reference to Thai

Christopher I. Beckwith
Indiana University

1.   Introduction

In order to review the current standard typological model of noun categorization (Dixon, 1982, 1986), or to develop a new theory, it is necessary to define the limits of the category. This paper focuses on class nouns (henceforth CLNs), a subcategory of compounds.

Compound nouns may be constructed in several ways, such as synonym or polar compounds, additive compounds, verb-noun compounds, and so on. CLNs are compound nouns formed from two elements in which one element---normally a noun or nominal stem---represents a class, and one element---frequently, but by no means always, a nominal---functions as a qualifier; in any case, the head of the compound must be a noun. For example, consider *way* in English *railway, byway, passageway, leeway, freeway, expressway, highway, throughway, runway, tramway, subway,* and so on, the class term (henceforth CLT) –*way* is the head of the compound and of the class WAY.[1] The sense of class is perhaps easier to understand if the English CLT *woman* in the CLNs *businesswoman, saleswoman, policewoman,* and so on, which belong to the class WOMAN, is compared to the English suffix –*ess* in *waitress, stewardess, actress, songstress,* and *mistress,* which belong to a FEMALE HUMAN or WOMAN class. In other words, the CLTs of English CLNs function morphologically and semantically not only as taxonomic class heads but also like English gender suffixes, with the difference that the number and kinds of classes that may occur in CLNs are practically unlimited.

It has been said of Thai that the categorization of CLTs and classifiers (henceforth CLFs) is "not entirely coherent" (DeLancey 1986:441), and that semantically the two types "overlap to a considerable degree" and "are clearly distinct only as syntactic categories" (DeLancey 1986:442). This paper, which is based partly on theoretical results deriving from a study of noun categorization in Tibetan (Beckwith 1994), addresses the issue of these apparently fuzzy boundaries by investigating the internal structure of Thai class nouns, which appear to straddle the line between grammaticized and non-grammaticized (or lexical) noun categorization.[2]

2.   Analysis

Most Thai CLNs have the surface morphological structure N + Attribute, which is normal for a left-headedness language. Classifier agreement is based, as in other classifier languages, on salient characteristics of the real-world referents of the nouns classified.[3] The classifiers assigned will thus be the same for taxonomically subordinate-level nouns and for the basic level head of those same nouns. For example, consider the examples in (1), nouns with the CLT *ŋuu* 'snake'.

(1)a   *ŋuukhiaw*   *nỳŋ*   *tua*
        greensnake   1   CLF[animal, animal-shaped]
        'one greensnake'
        (khiaw 'green')

(1)b   *ŋuulyam*   *nỳŋ*   *tua*
        python   1   CLF[animal, animal-shaped]
        'one python'
        (lyam 'python')

(1)c   *ŋuuhàw*   *nỳŋ*   *tua*
        cobra   1   CLF[animal, animal-shaped]
        'one cobra'
        (hàw 'to bark')

The type of CLN in (1) is clearly taxonomic in the classic sense of Rosch (1977). Since *ŋuu* is the internal lexical head of such CLNs, I will refer to it as a 'taxonomic CLT', and to such nouns as 'taxonomic CLNs', following Iguchi (1994).[4]

Some CLNs in Thai, including several mentioned by DeLancey (1986:438-442), clearly differ from these taxonomic CLNs in their semantic structure. Consider the examples in (2), with the CLT *duaŋ* 'CLF for round shining things'.

(2)a   *duaŋcan*   *nỳŋ*   *duaŋ*
        'moon'   1   CLF[round & shining]
        'one moon'
        (can 'moon')

(2)b   *duaŋtaa*   *nỳŋ*   *duaŋ*
        'eye'   1   CLF[round & shining]
        'one eye'
        (*taa* 'eye')

(2)c   *duaŋfaj*   *nỳŋ*   *duaŋ*
        'light'   1   CLF[round & shining]
        'one (round) light'
        (*faj* 'fire')

The examples in (2), and all other CLNs formed with *duaŋ*, take *duaŋ* as their CLF. Since the lexical heads of these CLNs are in each example clearly the second term, which is morphologically the attribute, *duaŋ* functions here not as a taxonomic CLT but as a classifying CLT. Since CLTs, unlike CLFs, are bound forms, I will refer to this kind of CLT as a 'gender CLT', and this kind of noun as a 'gender CLN', following Iguchi (1994).

Since the second term in such examples functions as internal lexical head of the CLN and takes the CLF agreement both internally (with its classifying CLT, *duaŋ*) and externally in full specifier phrases (with the classifier *duaŋ*), there are actually two CLTs in such nouns, the first term (*duaŋ*) being a gender CLT and the second a taxonomic CLT. Since the salient characteristics of a noun---or, in the case of a CLN, of its identifiable lexical head---determine CLF assignment, the head of the CLN in each of the examples in (2) is the second term. Although, taxonomically speaking, the second terms are all basic level nouns and might be expected to have considerable variation in classifier assignment, that does not happen with these particular basic level nouns because they have already been classed together by their common morphological head, the gender CLT *duaŋ*, which as a CLF classifies each taxonomic CLT within each noun in (2). Thus, rather than variation there is instead full gender concord in the specifier phrase, as shown in the examples in (2).

Let us turn now to CLNs formed with the honorific noun *phrá?* 'lord, god, priest, Buddha image'. This noun itself takes the CLF *?oŋ* for honorific beings, but consider the CLNs in (3) and the CLFs they are normally assigned.

(3)a *phrá?cân*   *nŷŋ*   *?oŋ*
      god/ruler/king   1   CLF[body (honorific)]
      'one god/ruler/king'

(3)b *phrá?can*   *nŷŋ*   *duaŋ*
      moon   1   CLF[round & shining]
      'one moon'

(3)c *phrá?aathid*   *nŷŋ*   *duaŋ*
      sun   1   CLF[round & shining]
      'one sun'

(3)d *phrá?râadchawaŋ*   *nŷŋ*   *lăŋ*
      royal palace   1   CLF[building]
      'one royal.palace'

Although example (3)a might lead one to suspect the honorific classifier *?oŋ* agrees with the honorific CLT *phrá?*, in fact both *?oŋ* and *phrá?* are in agreement with the second term, *cân*, which is the lexical head of the CLN, as in examples (3)b-d. It is manifest that in each example in (3) the CLF assignment is based not on the first term, *phrá?*, but on the second term. Thus, as in example (2), the morphological head is not the lexical head.

Consider now the examples in (4), CLNs that include

the CLT *máj* 'wood, stick'.

(4)a   *májdɔ̀ɔg*   *nỳŋ*   *tôn*
       flowering plant   1   CLF[stalk]
       'one flowering plant (a plant known to bear flowers)'

(4)b   *májkhìid*   *nỳŋ*   *kâan*
       matchstick   1   CLF[stick-like things]
       'one match'

(4)c   *májkhìid*   *nỳŋ*   *klàg*
       matchstick   1   CLF[box]
       'one box of matches'

(4)d   *dɔ̀ɔgmáj*   *nỳŋ*   *dɔ̀ɔg*
       flower   1   CLF[flower]
       'one (specific) flower'

(4)e   *bajmáj*   *nỳŋ*   *baj*
       leaf   1   CLF[leaf]
       'one leaf'

(4)f   *tônmáj*   *nỳŋ*   *tôn*
       tree   1   CLF[stalk]
       'one tree'

Examples (4)a-c are regular taxonomic CLNs, where the morphological head is the lexical head. Examples (4)d-f are clearly different. From a taxonomic viewpoint, *máj*, the second term, represents a higher taxonomic level than the first term; *máj* is thus undoubtedly a taxonomic CLT, not a gender CLT. It does not classify the first term in these CLNs, it tells where the first term belongs in a taxonomic hierarchy. Although the first terms in examples (4)d-f are all CLFs, they are also nominal CLT stems used to form subordinate level taxonomic nouns. Therefore, here they function not as gender CLTs but as taxonomic CLTs---and the lexical heads---of these CLNs. Accordingly they take the classifier agreement. Since they do also exist as separate classifiers, like *duaŋ* they assign themselves as classifiers of their CLNs.

There are, however, numerous cases where the CLN has been lexicalized at the word level and analyzing the constituents of the CLN will not work. Consider the examples in (5).

(5)a   *khrŷaŋdontrii*   *nỳŋ*   *khrŷaŋ*
       musical.instrument   1   CLF[instrument]
       'one musical instrument'
       (*dontrii* 'music')

(5)b   *khrŷaŋbin*   *nỳŋ*   *lam*
       flying.machine 1   CLF[cylindrical]
       'one airplane'

(5)c   *klûajmáj*   *nỳŋ*   *dɔ̀ɔg*
       orchid   1   CLF[flower]
       'one orchid'

Example (5)a is a typical taxonomic CLN where the CLF appears to agree with itself as the lexical head. Example (5)b is not at all transparent. While it is morphologically identifiable as a CLN, it is not lexically analyzable with respect to its CLF assignment, which is probably due to another word for airplane, *ryabin* 'flying boat', because words with *rya* 'boat' as CLT head take *lam* as classifier; words for airplane thus take the same classifier.[5] Unless one knows this connection, however, the reason for the assignment of the classifier *lam* to *khrŷaŋbin* is not clear. Even more opaque is example (5)c, which is morphologically a CLN built on the taxonomic CLT *klûaj* 'banana', with the qualifier *máj* 'wood'. The meaning 'orchid' for this CLN is not derivable from the constituents, which are therefore not analyzable. One simply must know what it means (i.e., what it refers to) in order to assign a CLF.

CLF agreement is thus not with nouns or CLTs themselves, but with selected salient characteristics of their real-world referents,[6] whether or not the agreement is mappable onto the lexical head of a given CLN. This accounts for the often considerable variation in CLF usage that has been much discussed in the literature (Becker 1986, Erbaugh 1986, Lakoff 1986, 1987, Lehman 1990, Tai & Wang 1991). This variation is generally cognitively motivated. In a recent study of Japanese classifier selection, for example, adult speakers tended to agree on classifier choices for the same noun when provided with specific situations in which the real word object would be perceived.[7] In other words, CLF assignment and CLF categories are essentially independent of linguistic form.

3. Conclusion

With respect to Thai class nouns, then, it seems that the semantic categories of folk taxonomy, a non-grammaticized system of noun categorization, do not extend into or overlap with the categories of grammaticized noun categorization systems, although the two types of categorization are tied together both by morphology and by the fact that each categorizes the other. It would seem that grammaticized systems of noun categorization are motivated by specific features of the particular nominal systems in which the noun categorization appears. Although the *number* of semantic categories within a given noun categorization system is constrained to some extent by pragmatic considerations, there is no formal restriction on the *kinds* of semantic categories that may be found in a given language as a whole. Thus there is, for example, no formal constraint on the development of animacy-type noun categorization in a language which has mostly classifier-type noun categorization. However, the different types tend to occur in different areas of the language, as in Thai, where natural gender occurs in the pronominal system rather than in the classifier system. Dixon's model (1982, 1986) proposes a one-to-one correspondence between language types and types of grammaticized noun categorization. It appears, instead, that there is a close correspondence between grammatical function (or grammatical category) and type of grammaticized noun categorization system.

Paradoxically, however, assignment of specific classifiers to specific nouns is unconnected to any grammatical function. Classifiers refer directly to the real world features of the thing named by the noun, and to the situation or manner in which the thing is perceived; classifier categories, too, are based on real-world referents. It is this direct accessing of the real world, cutting through all other layers of language, which makes classifier categorization so intriguing. If ethologists and psychologists are able to determine through experiment what the categorization systems of various primate species are like, and then compare them to known human classifier systems, it is quite possible that something valuable might be learned about the primordial cognitive system of early humans.

Notes

1   The variety of qualifier elements can be surprising. In this by no means exhaustive list of examples built on *way*, the qualifier terms include nouns, a verb, adjectives, prepositions, and a prefix.

2. Other studies of Thai compounding have focused on syntactic models of compound formation (Warotamasikkhadit 1970, Placzek 1978). Keiko Iguchi, one of my graduate students, is writing a thesis dealing with class nouns' internal structure and semantic classes.

3   Typically physical characteristics or 'kinesthetic image schemas' (Johnson 1987, Lakoff 1987).

4. My usage of the term 'taxonomic' in several earlier papers is unfortunate. I hope the present paper will rectify it to some extent.

5. One Thai colleague suggested I find out which classifier Karen speakers use for the dragonfly, a common airplane-shaped animal, since Thai classifies all animals with *tua*, regardless of the shape. In my subsequent visit with Thai friends to a Karen village west of Chiang Mai, we saw some

dragonflies and asked a speaker of Sgaw Karen how they are classified. He replied with the classifier for flat things, /plə/; a speaker of Plang Karen, in which dialect it is pronounced /plo/, confirmed this. (Tones are not marked.)

6. This has often been stated (for example, Placzek 1978:8), but I owe the proper appreciation of the insight to Megumi Yui, one of my graduate students.

7. Unpublished research paper by Megumi Yui.

References

Becker, A.L. 1986. The figure a classifier makes: describing a particular Burmese classifier. *Noun classes and categorization*, ed. by Colette Craig, 327-343. Amsterdam: John Benjamins.

Beckwith, Christopher I. 1994. Categorization in Tibetan. Unpublished paper presented in Madison before the American Oriental Society.

Craig, Colette (ed.) 1986. *Noun classes and categorization*. Amsterdam: John Benjamins.

DeLancey, Scott. 1986. Toward a history of Tai classifier systems. *Noun classes and categorization*, ed. by Colette Craig, 437-452. Amsterdam: John Benjamins.

Dixon, R.M.W. 1982. *Where have all the adjectives gone? and other essays in semantics and syntax*. Berlin: Mouton.

Dixon, R.M.W. 1986. Noun classes and noun classification in typological perspective. *Noun classes and categorization*, ed. by Colette Craig, 105-112. Amsterdam: John Benjamins..

Erbaugh, Mary S. 1986. Taking stock: the development of Chinese noun classifiers historically and in young children. *Noun classes and categorization*, ed. by Colette Craig, 399-436. Amsterdam: John Benjamins.

Iguchi, Keiko. 1994. Re-examination of the structure of nominal compounds: two basic types of class terms in class nouns. Unpublished research paper.

Johnson, Mark. 1987. *The body in the mind: the bodily basis of meaning, imagination, and reason.* Chicago: University of Chicago Press.

Lakoff, George. 1986. Classifiers as a reflection of mind. *Noun classes and categorization,* ed. by Colette Craig, 13-5. Amsterdam: John Benjamins.

Lakoff, George. 1987. *Women, fire, and dangerous things.* Chicago: University of Chicago Press.

Lehman, F.K. 1990. Outline of a formal syntax of numerical expressions, with special reference to the phenomenn of numeral classifiers. *Linguistics of the Tibeto-Burman area* 13.1: 89-120.

Placzek, James Anthony. 1978. Classifiers in standard Thai: a study of semantic relations between headwords and classifiers. Unpublished M.A. thesis. Vancouver: University of British Columbia.

Rosch, Eleanor. 1977. Classification of real-world objects: origin and representation in cognition. *Thinking: readings in cognitive scienc,* ed. by P.N. Johnson-Laird and P.C. Willson, 212-222. Cambridge: Cambridge University Press.

Tai, James and Liangqing Wang. 1991. A semantic study of the classifier tiao 條 . *Journal of the Chinese language teachers' association* 25.1: 35-56.

Warotamasikkhadit, Udom. 1970. *Thai syntax.* The Hague: Mouton.

The status of 'auxiliary verbs' in Thai[1]

Kitima Indrambarya
Kasetsart University

1. Introduction

This paper looks into the syntactic category of words such as *cà?* 'will, *khəəy* 'ever', and *khɔ̀nkhâaŋ* 'rather' which are referred to as preverbs by Kullavanijaya (1968), as modals by Noss (1964) and Sriphen (1982), and as auxiliaries in Panupong (1970), Ekniyom (1981) and Savetamalya (1987). The list of 'auxiliary' words to be tested here includes only those which precede verbs, and thus exclude words such as *yùu* which occur in a postverb position.

Working within the lexicase dependency framework, Savetamalya (1987) proposes a dependency analysis of auxiliaries as main verbs, in which the regent verb is the head of the construction (cf. Starosta 1977:73; 1988). In this paper, I point out certain characteristics of these 'auxiliaries' which are not accounted for in Savetamalya (1987) and test the syntactic status of these words. I then propose a more limited set of auxiliary verbs in Thai.

This paper is divided into six sections. The first section provides an introduction. The second section discusses phenomena not accounted for by Savetamalya (1987). The third section discusses the test used to identify the syntactic category of 'auxiliary verbs'. The fourth section presents the results. The fifth section discusses possible solutions to the problem raised. The final section presents a conclusion.

2. Problems

Savetamalya (1987:21), who works within the lexicase dependency grammar, identifies auxiliary verbs as words signifying the meanings of mood, aspect, intention, and obligation. She analyzes auxiliary verbs as extension intransitive verbs expecting a non-finite verb complement.

intransitive verbs expecting a non-finite verb complement. However, they differ from other verbs of this class both in their semantic limitations and in their ability to command any non-auxiliary verbs within the same finite domain.[2] For example, the auxiliary intransitive verb ʔàat 'may' precedes and commands the non-auxiliary intransitive verb khít₂ 'to think', as in (1a), but not vice versa, as in (1b). The requirement that the auxiliary verb ʔàat requires a non-finite verb dependent is shown by the implied contextual feature [4[-fint]] in the lexical matrix of ʔàat.

(1a)

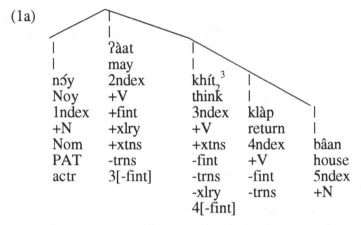

nɔ́y	ʔàat	khít₂[3]		
Noy	may	think		
1ndex	2ndex	3ndex	klàp	
+N	+V	+V	return	
Nom	+fint	+xtns	4ndex	bâan
PAT	+xlry	-fint	+V	house
actr	+xtns	-trns	-fint	5ndex
	-trns	-xlry	-trns	+N
	3[-fint]	4[-fint]		

'Noy may consider returning home.'

(1b) *nɔ́y khít₂ ʔàat klàp bâan
      Noy think may   return house
                  +V   +V
                  -xlry +xlry

'Noy thinks (she) may return home.'

Even though Savetamalya's analysis provides a nice account of the dependency relationship between auxiliary verbs and other verbs in Thai, the verb dependency analysis encounters the following problems. First of all, some of these words (e.g. khɔ̂nkhâaŋ 'rather') may also precede sentence-final adverbs, for example, the frequency adverb bɔ̀y 'often' in (2a) and the resultative adverb dii 'good' in (3a). By the definition of auxiliary verbs, they should cooccur with a non-finite verb dependent, rather than an adverb dependent. In these examples, the requirement for a non-finite verb complement is not satisfied and yet these sentences are acceptable.

(2a)

kháw	pay	thîi	nân	khɔ̂nkhâaŋ
he	go	at	there	rather
1ndex	2ndex	3ndex	4ndex	5ndex
+N	+V			+V
Nom	+fint			+xlry
PAT	-xlry			+xtns
actr	-trns			-trns
				$?([+V])^4$
				?[-fint]

bɔ̀y
often
6ndex
+Adv
+dgre

'He went there rather often.'

(3a)

kháw	phûut	khɔ̂y	dii	khîn
he	speak	rather	good	up
1ndex	2ndex	3ndex	4ndex	5ndex
+N	+V	+V	+Adv	+Adv
Nom	+fint	+xlry	+rslt	+path
PAT	-trns	+xtns		+slnt
actr	-xlry	-trns		
		$?([+V])$		
		?[-fint]		

'He gradually spoke better.'

Moreover, examples (2a) and (3a) above and (4a) and (5a) below also illustrate the fact that non-auxiliary intransitive verbs such as *pay*₃ 'to go', *phûut* 'to speak', *phayayaam* 'to try' and *tàtsĭncay* 'to decide' may precede the supposed non-finite auxiliary verbs *khɔ̂nkhâaŋ* 'rather', *khɔ̂y* 'gradually', *càʔ* 'will' and *tɔ̂ŋ* 'must' within the same finite domain. This fact violates the requirement that auxiliary verbs precede and command other non-finite verbs, rather than vice versa (cf. Savetamalya 1987:21) and raises a question about the status of auxiliary verbs in Thai.

(4a)

kôy	phayayaam	cà?	khăay
Koy	try	will	sell
1ndex	2ndex	3ndex	4ndex
+N	+V	+V	+V
Nom	+fint	+xlry	+trns
PAT	+xtns	+xtns	-fint
actr	-trns	-fint	
	-xlry	-trns	
	3[-fint]	4[-fint]	

càkkayaan
bicycle
5ndex
+N

'Koy tried to sell her bicycle.'

(5a)

nát	tàtsĭncay₁	tôŋ	klàp₄	bâan
Nat	decide	must	return	house
1ndex	2ndex	3ndex	4ndex	5ndex
+N	+V	+V	+V	+N
Nom	+fint	+xlry	+lctn	
PAT	+xtns	+xtns	-fint	
actr	-trns	-fint	-trns	
	-xlry	-trns		
	3[-fint]	4[-fint]		

'Nat decided that she must return home.'

Having discussed problems in the verbal analysis of auxiliaries, I will attempt to reexamine the syntactic categories of these 'auxiliary verbs' by testing the position in which the negation adverb *mây* 'not' occupies with relation to these putative 'auxiliary verbs' in a root predicate clause. Specifically, when these words occur after a subject, as opposed to at the end of a clause, do they precede or follow the negation word *mây*?

3. The Root Predicate with Negation Word *mây*

In Thai, the negation adverb *mây* 'not' may precede a verb or a sentence-final adverb. Even though *mây* may not differentiate verbs from adverbs when they occur after another verb, as shown in (6) and (7), this adverb *mây* may distinguish verbs from adverbs when it precedes the forms in question in a root predicate clause. A root predicate clause refers to a simple clause which contains only one predicate.

Mây before an adverb occurring sentence-finally:

(6)

kháw	pay	thîi	nân	mây	bɔ̀y
he	go	at	there	NEG	often
	+V				+Adv

'He does not go there often.'

Mây before an embedded verb:

(7)

kháw	kradòot	mây	khâam	rúa
he	jump	NEG	cross	fence
	+V		+V	

'He jumped but did not make it over the fence.'

In a root predicate clause, only a verb may occur in construction with the negation adverb *mây,* as shown in (8a), (8b), and (8c). Both root predicate nouns and root predicate prepositions occur in construction with *mâychây* 'not true', rather than with *mây* 'not'. An adverb, on the other hand, may not occur at all as a root predicate in a sentence, as shown in (8d) and cannot occur with the negation word *mây* in (8e).

Negation in root clauses:

(8a)

kháw	mây/*mâychây	pay
he	NEG	go
		+V
		-trns

'He is not going.'

(8b)

náŋsɨ̌	níi	*mây/mâychây	khɔ̌ɔŋ	thəə
book	this	NEG	POSS	you
			+N	
			+prdc	

'This book is not yours.'

(8c) náŋsɨ̌   níi   *mây/mâychây   sǎmràp   thəə
    book   this   NEG   for   you
                                     +P
                                     +prdc

'This book is not for you.'

(8d) *kháw   wáy   náŋsɨ̌   thîi   nîi[5]
    he   lying   book   at   here
              +Adv
              -prdc

'He left a book lying here.'

(8e) *kháw   mây/mâychây   wáy   náŋsɨ̌
    he   NEG   lying   book
                                +Adv
                                -prdc

thîi   nîi
at   here

'He did not leave a book here.'

Thus, in a root clause containing a subject, if these 'auxiliary verbs' may follow the negation word *mây*, they are identified as verbs, at least when occurring in that environment. This conclusion is based on the fact that every verb may be preceded by the negation word *mây*.[6]

If these 'auxiliary verbs' can only precede but never follow *mây*, they are analyzed as adverbs.[7] Since these adverbs may occur with any verb subject to pragmatic considerations, they are not subcategorized by verbs and hence are adjuncts.

4. Results

Figure 1 shows that words which can only precede but never follow *mây* in the post-subject position are regarded as adverbs. Eight words which may follow *mây*, namely *ʔàat* 'may', *hɘ̌ncàʔ* 'to seem', *khɔ̌y* 'gradually', *khəəy* 'ever', *khuan* 'should', *nâa* 'likely', *mua* 'to be absorbed in' and *tɔ̂ŋ* 'must' are shown to be verbs by this negation test.

words	before *mây*	After mây	Result
ʔàat 'may'	+	+	V
cà ʔ 'will'	+	-	Adv
chák 'begin to'	+	-	Adv
cuan 'almost'	+	-	Adv
hɛ̆ncà ʔ 'seem'	+	+	V
kamlaŋ 'in progress'	+	-	Adv
kə̀ət 'happen'	+	-	Adv
khəəy 'ever'	+	+	V
khoŋ 'may'	+	-	Adv
khɔ̂nkhâaŋ 'rather'	+	-	Adv
khɔ̂y 'gradually'	-	+	V
khuan 'should'	+	+	V
kìap 'almost'	+	-	Adv
kɔ̂ɔ 'also'	+	-	Adv
mák 'often'	+	-	Adv
mua 'be absorbed in'	-	+	V
nâa 'likely'	-	+	V
phɔ̂ŋ 'just'	+	-	Adv
thɛ̂ɛp 'almost'	+	-	Adv
tɔ̂ŋ 'must'	+	+	V
yaŋ 'still'	+	-	Adv
yɔ̂m 'apt to'	+	-	Adv

Figure 1: Application of the Position of Negation Test
to putative 'Auxiliary Verbs' in the Post-subject Position

However, concluding that words which may follow *mây* are
verbs leaves unresolved problems with the forms *khɔ̂y*
'gradually' and *tɔ̂ŋ* 'must', as shown earlier in (3a) and (5a).
That is, both of them may be preceded and commanded by the
non-auxiliary verbs *phûut* 'to speak' and *tàtsĭncay*, 'to decide,'
respectively. Moreover, the form *khɔ̂y* in (3a) is followed by an
adverb rather than a non-finite verb, as it should be if it were an
auxiliary verb. The following section presents possible
solutions.

5. Possible Solutions and Discussion

Two possible solutions to account for the forms *khɔ̌y* 'gradually' and *tɔ̂ŋ* 'must' in (3a) and (5a) are: 1) *khɔ̌y* and *tɔ̂ŋ* might be treated as adverbs like *cà?* 'will' and *khɔ̂nkhâaŋ* 'rather', so that they may follow any non-auxiliary verbs and so that *khɔ̌y* may precede an adverb without any violation of constraints on the distribution of auxiliary verbs, or; 2) the forms *khɔ̌y* and *tɔ̂ŋ* might be analyzed as belonging to two distinct lexical entries: *khɔ̌y₁* 'gradually' and *tɔ̂ŋ₁* 'must' would then be auxiliary verbs while *khɔ̌y₂* 'gradually' and *tɔ̂ŋ₂* 'must' would be adverbs.

The first alternative would contradict the test result shown in figure 1, which suggests that they are verbs since they may follow the negation word *mây*. Morever, by considering these two words to be adverbs, one would lose the important and otherwise absolute generalization about verbs. That is, not only verbs but also adverbs would be able to occur as a predicate in a root clause.

In the second alternative, because there would be two separate lexical items for each of the forms *khɔ̌y* and *tɔ̂ŋ*, there would be no contradiction in the result of the negation test. Moreover, one could then explain why examples (3a) and (5a) are acceptable. That is, there exist the verbs *tɔ̂ŋ₁* and *khɔ̌y₁*, which may follow *mây* in a post-subject position and there are adverbs *tɔ̂ŋ₂* and *khɔ̌y₂* which modify the following verbs or adverbs. Hence these adverbs *tɔ̂ŋ₂* and *khɔ̌y₂* may follow non-auxiliary verbs and precede both verbs and adverbs which they modify, as exemplified in (3a) and (5a).

This study favors this second possibility based on evidence from the following 'grammatically significant environment criterion' in lexicase. The grammatically significant environment criterion plays an important role in separating a form which occurs in separate syntactic environments into distinct lexical items and syntactic subclasses. While the form *khɔ̌y* may occur in both environments a and b, the form *khəəy* can occur only in the environment a. Hence, the form *khɔ̌y* in the two environments must belong to two lexical items and syntactic subclasses.

(9a) kháw   khɔ̌y₁   phûut   dii   khîn
      he   gradually   speak   good   up
             +V   +V
             +xlry   -fint

'He gradually spoke better.'

(9b) kháw   phûut   khɔ̌y₂   dii   khîn
      he   speak   gradually   good   up
             +V   +Adv

'He spoke gradually better.'

(10a) kháw   khəəy   phûut   dii   kwàa   níi
      he   ever   speak   good   than   this
             +V   +V
             +xlry   -fint

'He once spoke better than this.'

(10b) *kháw   phûut   khəəy   dii   kwàa   níi
       he   speak   ever   good   than   this
              +V   +V
                      +xlry

'He spoke ever better than this.'

Considering some of the words expressing mood and aspect to be adverbs, rather than auxiliary verbs as in Savetamalya's analysis, enables us to explain the following: 1) why forms such as *khɔ̌nkhâaŋ* 'rather' and *khɔ̌y₂* 'gradually' may precede frequency adverbs, as in (2b), and resultative adverbs, as in (3b); and 2) why *càʔ* 'will', which has long been a puzzle, and *tɔ̂ŋ₂* 'must' may directly follow and be commanded by non-auxiliary verbs, as in (4b) and (5b). In other words, analyzing these words as adverbs rather than auxiliary verbs solves the problem of their occurrence after a non-auxiliary verb and before an adverb. *Khɔ̌nkhâaŋ* 'rather', *khɔ̌y₂* 'gradually', *càʔ* 'will', and *tɔ̂ŋ₂* 'must' are adverbs, which precede verbs and adverbs over which they have semantic scope. Since they are not grammatically required by their regent, these adverbs are adjuct dependents of any words they precede and modify.

(2b) kháw   pay   thîi   nân   khɔ̀nkhâaŋ
      he   go   at   there   rather
      1ndex   2ndex   3ndex   4ndex   5ndex
              +V   +Adv
              +fint
              -trns

bɔ̀y
often
6ndex
+Adv
+dgre
5([+Adv])

'He went there rather often.'

(3b) kháw   phûut   khɔ̂y₂   dii   khîn
      he   speak   rather   good   up
      1ndex   2ndex   3ndex   4ndex   5ndex
      +N   +V   +Adv   +Adv   +Adv
      Nom   +fint   +rslt   +path
      PAT   -trns   3([+Adv]) +slnt
      actr

'He gradually spoke better.'

(4b) kɔ̂y   phayayaam cà?   khǎay   càkkayaan
      Koy   try   will   sell   bicycle
      1ndex   2ndex   3ndex 4ndex   5ndex
      +N   +V   +Adv   +trns   +N
      Nom   +fint   -fint
      PAT   +xtns   3([+Adv])
      actr   -trns
              -xlry
              4[-fint]

'Koy tried to sell her bicycle.'

(5b)

nát	tàtsĭncay	tɔ̂ŋ₂	klàp	bâan
Nat	decide	must	return	house
1ndex	2ndex	3ndex	4ndex	5ndex
+N	+V	+Adv	+lctn	+N
Nom	+fint		-fint	
PAT	+xtns		-trns	
actr	-trns		3([+Adv])	
	-xlry			
	4[-fint]			

'Nat decided that she must return home.'

Maintaining Savetamalya's (1987) dependency analysis of auxiliary verbs, I illustrate in example (11) with a lexicase stemma and lexical matrices how a true auxiliary verb precedes and commands other verbs, while an adverb is always subordinate to a following verb or adverb. I will also adopt Savetamalya's (1987) coocurrence restriction for true auxiliary verbs in Thai and for forms which are identified in this study as adverbs signifying mood and aspect.

(11)

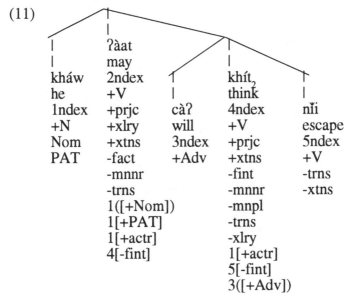

'He may consider escaping.'

In (11), the auxiliary verb *ʔàat* 'may' precedes and cap-commands the non-auxiliary verb *khít* 'to think'. Since the adverb *càʔ* 'will' may occur with any verb and has the following verb *khít* 'to think' in its scope, it is an adjunct dependent of *khít* 'to think'.

I will further claim that the following four auxiliary verbs are prime auxiliaries: *ʔàat* 'may', *hĕncàʔ* 'to seem', *khuan* 'should', and *nâa* 'likely'. That is, they are lexically finite (Starosta 1977:83; Pagotto 1987:482; Savetamalya 1987:26). Example (12a) shows that a prime auxiliary verb may precede and command another non-finite non-prime auxiliary verb. Examples (12b) and (12c) show that a prime auxiliary verb may not be preceded and commanded by other verbs. Moreover, both sentences are unacceptable because the requirement for a non-finite verb dependent is not satisfied.

(12a)

chán	ʔàat$_1$	càʔ	tɔ̂ŋ$_1$	pay
I	may	will	must	go
1ndex	2ndex	3ndex	4ndex	5ndex
+N	+V	+Adv	+V	+V
Nom	+fint		+xlry	-fint
PAT	+prim		-prim	
actr	+xlry		-fint	
	4[-fint]		3([+Adv])	
			5[-fint]	

chiaŋmày
Chiangmai
6ndex
+N

'I may have to go to Chiangmai.'

(12b) *chán   tôŋ₁   ʔàat₁   cà?   pay
       I   must   may   will   go
       1ndex   2ndex   3ndex   4ndex   5ndex
       Nom   +V   +V   +Adv   +V
       PAT   +fint   +fint   -fint
       actr   +xlry   +prim   3([+Adv])
                   -prim   +xlry
                   ?[-fint] 5[-fint]

       chiaŋmày
       Chiangmai
       6ndex
       +N

       'I must may go to Chiangmai.'

(12c) *chán   ʔàat₁   cà?   khuan₁   pay
       I   may   will   should   go
       1ndex   2ndex   3ndex   4ndex   5ndex
       +N   +V   +Adv   +V   +V
       Nom   +fint   +fint   -fint
       PAT   +prim   +prim
       actr   +xlry   +xlry
                   ?[-fint]   5[-fint]
                                       3([+Adv])

       chiaŋmày
       Chiangmai
       6ndex
       +N

       'I may should go to Chiangmai tomorrow.'[8]

6. Summary

This study finds that words which are referred to as 'auxiliary verbs' in Thai are in fact belong to two syntactic category: adverbs and verbs. Those words which may precede an adverb and follow a non-auxiliary verb are adverbs. The others, which are limited in number, are true auxiliary verbs.

In summary, I support Savetamalya's dependency analysis of auxiliary verbs but limit the number of auxiliary verbs in Thai. There are eight auxiliary verbs, namely *ʔàat* 'may', *hĕncàʔ* 'to seem', *khuan*₁ 'should', *nâa* 'likely', *khǝǝy* 'ever' *khɔ̂y*₁ 'gradually', *mua* 'absorb in', and *tɔ̂ŋ*₁ 'must', the first four of which are prime auxiliary verbs. The following is the list of words in Savetamalya (1987) which have been reanalyzed as adverbs in this study.

càʔ	'will'	*kìap*	'almost'
chák '	begin to'	*kɔ̂ɔ*	'also'
cuan	'almost'	*mák*	'often'
kamlaŋ	'in progress'	*phɔ̂ŋ*	'just'
kǝ̀ǝt	'happen'	*thêɛp*	'almost'
khoŋ '	may'	*tɔŋ*₂	'must'
khɔ̂nkhâaŋ	'rather'	*yaŋ*	'still'
khɔ̂ɔy₂	'gradually'	*yɔ̂m*	'apt to'

Because the test employed in this study to identify the syntactic categories of these words is limited to the position of the negation word in a root clause, in conjunction with the grammatically significant environment cirteria, the conclusions presented here are tentative and would benefit from supporting study.

NOTES

[1] I am grateful to Professor Stanley Starosta and Professor William O'Grady for their valuable comments and critism on the earlier draft of this paper. Any remaining mistakes are naturally mine.

[2] Within the lexicase framework, the notion 'command' is defined as an indirect syntactic relationship between words. X commands Y iff:
(a) X cap-commands Y, or
(b) X cap-commands Z and Z commands Y.
Cap-command: X cap-commands Y if X is the regent of Y.

[3] The number of subscript reflects the number of homophonous forms for forms which are found to belong to more than one lexical items.

[4] Note the difference between the parentheses and brackets on a word class contextual feature and on other kinds of contextual features. The parentheses for a contextual feature referring to word classes, such as [ʔ([+V])], indicate simply that the word permits a verb as its dependent,

and say nothing about the dependent being an adjunct or a complement. The square brackets on a contextual feature such as [?[-fint]], on the other hand, indicate that the regent requires a non-finite complement, in contrast with the parentheses on [?([-fint])] which indicate that a non-finite verb is an adjunct, since it is allowed but not required.

[5] When I conducted the research for this paper, all of the Thais I have checked with agree that the sentence is totally unacceptable. However, to my surprise, at the SEALS IV conference, a small number of Thai liguists argued that this sentence is acceptable. They did not, however, provide the context within which acceptable usage may occur.

[6] The only exception to this claim is the copula verb *khɨɨ* 'to be' which may not occur with any negation words (cf. Warotamasikkhadit 1976:233).

[7] This hypothesis is based on the fact that all verbs except *khɨɨ* may follow the negation word *mây*.

[8] Note that the English translation is wrong for exactly the same reason.

ABBREVIATIONS

actr	actor	P	Preposition
Adv	Adverb	PAT	Patient
fact	fact	POSS	Possessive
fint	finite	prdc	predicate
mnnr	manner	prjc	projection
mnpl	manipulative	rslt	resultative
N	Noun	slnt	salient
ndex	index	trns	transitive
NEG	Negation	V	Verb
	Marker	xlry	auxiliary
Nom	Nominative	xtns	extension

REFERENCES

Ekniyom, Piansiri. 1981. An Internal Reconstruction of Auxiliaries in Thai. University of Hawai'i Working Papers in Linguistics.

Indrambarya, Kitima. 1994. Subcategorization of Verbs in Thai: A Lexicase Dependency Approach. University of Hawai'i Ph.D. Dissertation.

Kullavanijaya, Pranee. 1968. A Study of Preverbs in Thai. University of Hawai'i M.A. Thesis.

Noss, Richard. 1964. Thai Reference Grammar. Washington D.C.: Foreign Service Institute.

Pagotto, Louise. 1987. Verb Subcategorization and Verb Derivation in Marshallese: A Lexicase Anaysis. University of Hawai'i Ph.D. Dissertation.

Panupong, Vichin. 1970. Inter-sentence relations in Modern Conversational Thai. Siam Society: Bangkok.

Savetamalya, Saranya. 1987. A Reanalysis of Auxiliaries in Thai. University of Hawai'i Working Papers in Linguistics. 19.1.1-44.

Sriphen, Salee. 1982. The Thai Verb Phrase. Univesity of Michigan Ph.D. Dissertation.

Starosta, Stanley. 1977. Affix Hobbling. University of Hawai'i Working Papers in Linguistics. 9.1.61-158.

_____. 1985. The Great AUX Cataclysm. University of Hawai'i Working Papers in Linguistics. 17.2.95-114.

_____. 1988. The Case for Lexicase: An Outline of Lexicase Grammatical Theory. Pinter Publishers.

_____. 1992. Lexicase revisited. draft (August 18, 1992), a revision and extension of 'lexicase', an article submitted to the Encyclopedia of Language and Linguistics, Pergamon Press, Edinburgh.

The acquisition of syntax/pragmatics by a Cambodian and English speaking two-year-old child

B. Jean Longmire
School of Education
University of the Pacific

Introduction. The acquisition of Khmer by children is interesting linguistically for several reasons. Phonologically, little if any language acquisition research has been done on languages which, like Khmer, stress the second syllable in two syllable words. Cambodian parents, as if to emphasize the importance to Khmer of the last part of a word, address their infants using a baby talk characterized by the deletion of this first syllable, and often the reduction of syllable initial consonant clusters. Given the phonological prominence of the second syllable and the reduction of onset consonant clusters in the speech of Cambodian parents to children, it is not surprising that Cambodian children, learning to speak, begin by producing words which are thus reduced. (See Longmire 1994 for more on Cambodian baby talk and phonological reduction.) Khmer is also interesting in that, like Japanese, pragmatic and sociolinguistic considerations pervade the language. (See Clancy, 1985, for a discussion of this regarding Japanese.) Thus, for example, Cambodian children need to acquire mastery of a vocabulary which conveys their social relationship with hearers and addressees. Learning how to refer to oneself and to others, then, presents a problem for a child. Sentence final particles signal other subtle pragmatic information such as questioning, doubt, disgust, emphasis, etc. Syntactically, the acquisition of Khmer is interesting not just for the acquisition of aspect, deixis, head first constructions, and so on, but also for the intersection of syntax and pragmatics. Indeed, the difficulty in teasing apart that which is pragmatic and that which is syntactic in languages such as Khmer may shed light on the weakness of so many studies in child language acquisition, and that is the failure to recognize that all language is learned in context and that the context is an oral one. Finally, it is interesting to study the acquisition of both Cambodian and English by a child. The differences between these two languages make it easier to see the hypotheses the child is making about each language when the child incorrectly applies the rules of one language in speaking the other. Because the social and linguistic context in which one language is spoken may differ from that of the other, one can also see the effect of this on the differing pragmatic strategies the child uses to initiate a conversation or to make a contribution to an on-going one. In this paper I will look at the pragmatic context in which a Cambodian-English speaking child learns her languages and how this affects her understanding and acquisition of pragmatics and syntax.

Methodology. The data for this study come from a three year longitudinal study of the language development of the oldest daughter of a Cambodian and English speaking couple living in America. Cambodian was the predominant language in the environment of this child until, at the age of three, she entered an American preschool. Thus, the hypotheses this child made about both English and Cambodian were initially based on her growing understanding of the way Cambodian is structured. To conduct this study, I, along with this child's' parents, have audiotaped and videotaped the child approximately every two weeks from the time this child was born. Transcripts of these tapes have been written in Khmer and English, and the examples I will use here come from these transcripts. For this paper, I will look at the child's development of language from a mean length of utterance (MLU) around 1.5 in Cambodian and 1.0 in English, to a MLU of 2.5 in Cambodian to 2.0 in English. This is when the child was between 1;9.23 (one year, nine months, 23 days) to the age of 2;5.0.

Pragmatics versus syntax. In a paper entitled "Discourse Analysis of Japanese and Thai", Robert Jones and Eleanor Jorden asked the question, "Do 'sentences' occur in Thai speech?" (1976, p.13) Given the difficulty of identifying sentences in oral discourse in a Southeast Asian language, it is no wonder that they questioned whether the sentence was a justifiable linguistic unit of oral discourse. As they pointed out, historically the sentence is closely tied to "literary norms and the convention of writing." (p. 15) Because children learn language from oral discourse, because so much of child language acquisition research is aimed at providing evidence for one particular linguistic theory or another, and because the prevailing linguistic theories are sentence-based and thus research in language acquisition is often focused on what a child knows about the structure of sentences, the question of what is a sentence in oral discourse is an important one. Charles N. Li and Sandra A. Thompson (1976) claimed that "the notion of topic may be as basic as that of subject in grammatical descriptions". (p. 459) They distinguished languages according to whether the structure of sentences favored "a description in which the grammatical relation *subject-predicate* plays a major role" or the structure of sentences favored "a description in which the grammatical relation *topic-comment* plays a major role". (p. 459) Thus, they contrasted the subject-predicate construction of a sentence with the topic-comment construction of a sentence. Languages which favor topic-comment constructions were considered topic-prominent languages. Feng-Fu Tsao (1979), in his book *A Functional Study of Topic in Chinese: The First Step Towards Discourse Analysis,* argues that "to place topic in contrast with subject is very misleading because they essentially belong to different levels of grammatical organization". (p. 37) In Tsao's view, topic-comment structures are discourse level structures. He points out that the topic extends its semantic domain over several sentences, playing a major role in such phenomena as pronominalization and coreferential NP deletion, but topics play no role in sentence-level phenomena like reflexivization and verb serialization. (p. 261) Of course, discourse level phenomena are often found in sentences. Word final particles in Khmer often signal how previous utterances are viewed and what the speaker expects in utterances to follow (e.g., an answer). There is no doubt, however, that topic plays a major role in determining what can be deleted from a following comment and even whether the subject of the following sentence or comment can be placed in sentence final position. Of interest in this paper is the question of how the environment of a child might lead the child to an understanding of topic/comment structures and how early a child begins to produce them. Certainly, one would think, nothing is more fundamental in language acquisition than the ability to understand or initiate a topic.

Establishing topic. True child-adult discourse in Khmer, where both adult and child contribute to the topic nominated, begins with joint attention to an object or person in the environment. Usually, a deictic word is involved. An example of of this from my data occurs when Sopha's mother tried to get Sopha to "read" a Garfield comic strip in the Sunday newspaper with her. Sopha, age 1;9.23, gets down after a second or two and goes to the window. The conversation is as follows:

child	niə niə pə niə
	here here pa here
mother	na koun? əi ke?
	Where, child? What is it?
child	ba
	(unclear but interpreted by mother below)
mother	cma: ɔt kəːɲ pʰɔɽ
	cat not-see-too (I don't see)

Here the mother requests the topic from her daughter, getting a syllable of the word "cat" and, given the previous context of the Garfield cartoon, she supplies the full word "cmaa" and makes a comment regarding the cat, i.e., that she can't see one. Two month's later, the child is supplying nouns with her deictic words. It is clear also that she has equated "this" and "nih" and the meaning "here". For example, at the age of 2;0.7, she is removing silly putty from a container and talking to herself. She says:

> -n- cake
> thisa cake
> nii-a cake
> da-a cake

She seems to be trying out various words and sounds that fit in initial position. On the next day, we find her sitting in a high chair trying to get her father to give her a small Christmas tree ornament, a bear beating on a drum. She and her father interact:

Child	bear nih (three times) (=bear here/this)
	papa (=father)
	bear nih (two times)
Father	mui na: koun (=one which, child)
	na:
	mui na:
Child	Babbles
Father	nih? (=here/this)
	naɤ̣ (He hands the ornament to his
	daughter)

(a minute later)

Father	əi ke nih aː nih? (=what this? this?)
	əi ke koun? (=what this, child)
Child	bear
Father	bear leŋ əi?
Child	biŋ kə kau (sound in tune like" jingle bell"
	but it is unclear)
Father	hn?
	leŋ klaun? (The father is guessing that she
	said something like: he plays like a clown.)
Child	klaun? (repeats what her father said)
Father	Bear vai sko (=bear plays drum)

In this interaction, we can not only see how the father requested further information in order to clarify the topic (and retrieve the object), but how he then engaged his child in an exchange: first getting her to name the topic (what's this, child? bear) and then encouraging her to provide a comment (plays drum). This little routine, identifying a topic and then demanding comments about that topic, occurs again and again. One can see it not only in events where the child labels an object she picks up, and then the parents demand a comment, but also in story-book reading where the parent or the child identifies a picture and the parents demand comments about the picture. An example of this occurred when Sopha was 2;3.15. Both her mother and father helped her to identify the topic. When she did this, they elicited comments:

M əi ke?	(What's that?)
C kʰi mau	(Mickey Mouse)

M tvə ʔəi ?	(Do what?)
M tvə ʔəi nih?	(Do what here?)
M Mickey Mouse tvə ʔəi?	(Mickey Mouse do what?)
F Mickey Mouse tvə ʔəi koun?	(Mickey Mouse do what, child?)
C təː haəl tɨk	(Do swim.)
F haəl tɨk	(Swim.)
C Fish haəl tɨk	(Fish swim.)
F haəl tɨk nɨw aenaː?	(Swim be where?)
C haəl kau	(Swim outside.)
F haəl nɨw krau	(Swim be outside.)
F haəl tvə mec tɨw	(Swim do how?)
C haəl əpcəŋ	(Swim like this.)

Notice here how, after the topic (Mickey Mouse) was initially identified, the parents omitted the subject of the comment-sentence, but then they felt compelled to put the topic back into the topic-comment construction when the child didn't seem to understand the question. They then omitted the subject when the child responded correctly. When the child announced the next topic (fish) and made a comment about it, the parents demanded further comment, in every instance without a subject in the comment-sentences. Thus, the parents model topic-chaining and subject deletion in discourse.

Sopha's growing ability to establish a topic and make a comment about it can also be seen in her nomination of the topic "fish" in the previous example. More typically, however, she continued to fill the topic slot with the deictic word *nih* "here/this". Sopha's English ability was also growing, although her mean length of utterance in English was smaller than in Cambodian, and her hypotheses about how English is structured were greatly influenced by Cambodian. Whereas with even a small 1.5 MLU Sopha could initiate a conversation in Cambodian with *nih*, usually causing her parents to ask her for clarification of the topic, e.g., ʔɑv ʔəː? What's that?", or to make a comment about the topic. In English, however, this conversation-initiating ploy failed. For example, when she ran around the house one day, stopping here and there to say "This!", noone reacted, and she soon stopped this as a way to elicit comments. In English, she equated *nih* with "this" and she would construct topic-identifying utterances in the form: dis ABC; dis train;

dis tape; disa cake and even mixed language utterances in the form: diꞩ boŋ duck "this brother duck" (example from age 2;3.27). She always paused slightly between this/dis/diꞩ. In Cambodian, she made subjectless comments if the topic was already established. For example, at the age of 2;8.2, in a conversation with me which took place while we were examining the book *Peter Pan*, the following interaction took place:

> Me: Who's that?
>   Captain Hook.
>   That's Captain Hook!
> Sopha: ɔt miɛn dai (not have hand)

When I responded by translating the Cambodian to "doesn't have a hand", she corrected her response to:

> itꞩ nat miɛn dai (itsa not have hand)

A few pages later when we came upon another picture of Captain Hook, she announced:

> nih ɔt miɛn dai
> this/here not have hand

When we then saw a picture of Peter Pan and Captain Hook with swords standing on a plank above the water, she said:

> nih tiw vai
> this/here go fight

and when we had turned to the book *Snow White*, and we came upon the picture of the prince kissing Snow White, she announced:

> nih cʰup cʰɯ haay
> this/here stop ill finish
> This not ill anymore

The comment part of this construction also developed in English, beginning initially with noun phrases in constructions like "Thisa alligator.", and developing into constructions like:

> ðɪꞩ lion roar
> ðɪꞩ baby cry
> ʊꞩ fall down

The last utterance was made after she demonstrated "falling down". The idea that the construction would, perhaps, be clearer or more complete with a topic marker can be seen in her trying out an utterance she must have heard at the baby-sitter's house. The utterance was:

> wadajúsei or wat-n-júsei

What do you say?

where the -n- in wat-n-júsei seemed a syllable which, perhaps even to her, was unclear. She was playing with a doll house one day (age 2;6.2) when the following interaction occurred:

Sopha:	wadəjúsei
	wat-n-júsei
	wat-n-júsei
	maʔ wadjúsei
Mother:	mɛc koun ? (What, child?)
Sopha:	wadəjúsei
Mother:	əi ke? (What's that?)
Sopha:	wat'əjúsei
Mother:	tʰaː mɛc?
Sopha:	watjúsei
Mother:	What what?
Sopha:	diˌs wadʒúsei
Mother:	What do you think?
Sopha:	diˌs wadʒúsei !

Subjects in Comments. Throughout this period of language acquisition, from 1;10 to 2;10, Sopha often placed subjects in sentence final position. Indeed, her parents often remarked that Sopha talked "backwards". An example of this is in the conversation below. Sopha (age 2;0.8) is playing with the bear ornament when she says:

Sopha:	ʔo ʔoː	(oh oh)
	baʔ haəy	(break already)
Mother	nɛəʔnaː tʰaː baʔ	(Who break it?)
Sopha:	tʰaː beibi	(Do baby (I))
Mother	beibi tʰaː baʔ	(Baby(you) do break)

Here Sopha places the subject "baby" meaning herself after the verb "do". Her mother corrects her utterance, placing the subject in first position. It does happen in Cambodian that subjects which are not identical to the topic of the discourse can be placed in sentence final position, but it is unlikely that Sopha has this level of understanding of discourse. Two things may be confusing her: first, the tendency to repeat the topic (or is the second occurance a subject?) in sentences like

"What do tigers say?" which, in Cambodian, is "kla tʰaː mec klə" (tiger say how tiger). This kind of question, what do animals do or what do animals say, is found in a familiar child-adult routine. Second, a vocative may begin or end a phrase, as in sopʰa mo nih sopʰa (Sopha, come here, Sopha). This may be the reason Sopha (2;0.8) has the following conversation with her mother:

Mother:	cam maʔ jɔːʔ aoy (let mother take give)
Sopha:	(fusses)
Mother	taə ai ke (question: what that (you want))
Sopha	fɪʃi (fish)
	daʔ mami (put mommy)
	daʔ mami (put mommy)

This last utterance "put mommy" was clearly a request for her mother to put fish on her plate, but there was no pause or tone change between "daʔ" and "mam". In other words, it had the intonation of a sentence final subject instead of a vocative. In both cases, the topic was different from the noun phrase put in sentence final position. In the first, the topic was the bear, and baby was placed at the end. In the second, the topic was fish and mommy was placed at the end. Finally, we have the inversion which occurred in English when she was 3;1.18. I bring it up because, although it occurred later than our other data here, it seems related to what she is doing with subjects which are not the same as the topic. In this case, Sopha and I were drawing a birthday cake and she announced

Sopha:	I want uhm candle.
Me:	What color?
Sopha:	uhm color this one
Me:	OK. How many?
Sopha:	Three
	and uh blow it
Me:	You want...blow?
Sopha:	plaː (flame)
Me:	Oh, OK, fire, you want the flames.
Sopha:	Yeah, and blow you
	Blow you candle

Why did the inversion occur here? Is it because the topic is candle and she feels "you" must then be down-graded? This is still unclear.

Other head + modifier constructions. If one can say that topic-comment structures are similar to other structures with a head followed by a modifier, then it should be made clear here that Sopha was also producing some other structures of this type. Given the consummate interest of a two-year-old, especially a two-year-old with a baby brother, in things that belong to her, it is not strange to see possessive constructions appearing rather early. In Cambodian, Sopha produced:

Possessive
pʰteəh beibi (2;2.17)
house baby (my)

pʰteəh sopʰa (2;2.17)
house Sopha
(my house)

dɔp pa bɔŋ təə (2;4.15)
glass father older/my isn't it
(my daddy's glass, isn't it) or
(your glass)

pah mama bear (2;10.0)
belonging mama bear
(mama bear's)

kɔr for bear (2;10.0)
bicycle belonging bear
(bear's bicycle)

As you can see, she began to equate the Cambodian word *pɑh* as in *rɪbɑh* (belong) with "for". Thus, when she was identifying things belonging to baby bear in the Goldilocks story, she looked at a picture of baby bear hanging above baby bear's bed and said: this for baby bear.

At the same time as she was producing these possessive constructions, she also called a fish-shaped magnet used to stick things to the refrigerator door a "sticker fish", a picture of a female clown a "clown mommy" and slippers under the bed of one of the bears in the story of

Goldilocks "shoe funny".   Thus, in both English and Khmer, she was using head + modifier constructions.

In conclusion, I believe we can see in all of this how a child comes to use topic-comment structures, beginning first with a simple deictic marker for the topic, gradually adding to this a comment in the form of a noun phrase, and finally using a verb phrase in comment position. I believe we can also see in this how parents, through scaffolding, aid their children in understanding the need for a clear topic and a series of comments. For those of us who teach Asian languages, often adopting methodology which is used in the teaching of European languages, we might want to consider a methodology which is less sentence centered. Tsao (1979) suggested paragraph-centered teaching. Perhaps, that is a little too literary. Instead, we may want to include in our methodology the kind of identifying topics and calling for comments which these Cambodian parents have engaged their child in.

Clancy, Patricia M. 1985. The acquisition of Japanese. The crosslinguistic study of language acquisition. Volume 1: The data, ed by Dan Isaac Slobin, 373-524. Hillsdale: Lawrence Erlbaum Associates.

Jones, Robert B. and Eleanor H. Jorden. June 1976. Discourse analysis of Japanese and Thai. Part I: Thai discourse. Final report. Contract No. OEC-0-72-1786.Washington,D.C: U.S. Department of Health, Education, and Welfare. Office of Education. Institute of International Studies. Division of Foreign Studies.

Longmire, B. Jean. In press. Cambodian caretaker speech and teaching routines. Papers from the Second Annual Meeting of the Southeast Asian Linguistics Society, ed. Karen Adams. Tempe, Az: Program for Southeast Asian Studies. Arizona State University.

Tsao, Feng-Fu. 1979. A functional study of topic in
   Chinese: The first step towards discourse analysis.
   Taipei: Student Book Co., Ltd.

The 4306 forms of the Nimboran verbal paradigm

Hein Steinhauer
Leiden University

1.1   By most linguists it is taken for granted that the linguistic situation in New Guinea and surrounding islands is the most complex in the world. For budgetary, political, and geophysical reasons, and because of the anti-descriptive trend in linguistics during the last thirty years, deplorably few linguists did work in New Guinea and/or in languages of New Guinea. This is especially true of the western half of the island, the Indonesian province of Irian Jaya.

One of the rare exceptions was Johannes Cornelis Anceaux (1920-1988), professor in Austronesian and Papuan linguistics at Leiden University (1971-1986), and a language officer of the Dutch colonial administration in New Guinea (1954-1962). One of his major studies is a detailed description of the morphologically highly complex Nimboran language. This language is spoken in the Jayapura district, Nimboran subdistrict, in an area west of Lake Sentani around the town of Nggeniém[1] by an estimated number of speakers of 3.000 (Anceaux 1965: xv and 1; Wurm & Hattori 1983: map 3)[2]. The language belongs to the Trans New Guinea Phylum, Nimboran Stock-Level Family (Silzer & Heikkinen Clouse 1991: 29 and 69, Wurm & Hattori 1981: map 3).

Since Anceaux' study Nimboran has been the target of a SIL couple (May 1978, May 1981, May & May 1981), but their scope has so far been limited to phonology and anthropology. As far as I know, Anceaux' description of Nimboran morphology (which is practically exclusively verbal) remains therefore the latest account of that aspect of the language.

1.2   Anceaux' approach is basically didactic. Step by step the various morphological categories and classes of categories ("orders"), pertinent to the structure of the Nimboran verb, are introduced and discussed, culminating in the paradigm of 62 pages of the verb *nggedóu-* 'to draw' (pp.185-246)[3]. The approach is typically word-based, with statements such as: "Opposed to the series: *suándu* - I will water (here), etc. etc. we find the following forms: *sáondáru*[4] - I will water them (here), *sáondáre* - you will water them here ... *saóindiarám* - you and I (you and we) will water them (here) ... All these new forms belong to a productive category whose members have in common the semantic element "the action is connected with a plural object". Formally, the members are characterized by an element *-de-* that immediately follows the root-morpheme and takes the form *-da-* whenever it is immediately followed by the Tense morpheme" (pp.105-106).

In this way Anceaux introduces in the fifty sections on "The Productive Categories of the Verb-system" (pp.56-122) the following categories (in this order):

1) singular actor categories: 1st person, 2d person, 3d person masculine and 3d person neutral (= non-masculine);
2) tense categories: future, present, past and recent past;
3) position categories, coined 1 to 5;
4) combinations of 2) and 3);
5) further position categories, coined 6 to 16;
6) further actor categories: 1st+2d person singular, 1st+2d person dual;
7) root-morpheme categories: singular, dual;
8) plural actor categories: 1st person exclusive, 1st person inclusive, 3d person;
9) the plural root-morpheme;
10) combinations of 5) and 8);
11) iterative vs. momentary categories;
12) object categories: masculine, plural;
13) the category of the durative;
14) combinations of 13) and 11), and of 13) and 2);
15) the "infinitive" and "final infinitive" categories;
16) The so called "secondary" verbal categories.

Subsequently (pp.123-164) "blockading" categories and words are discussed, which comprise recurrent and unique, lexically or phonemically conditioned, formal exceptions in the expression of the categorial meaning of some of the productive morphological categories.

Finally, Anceaux introduces two additional verbal categories: feminine object and 2d person plural actor, which are relevant only for a (very) restricted number of stems (pp.165-166).[5]

1.3 Anceaux does not give an explicit systematic survey of the structure of the Nimboran verbal paradigm, but this can be derived from his combined statements and especially from the sample paradigm of *nggedóu-*. Below I will present a systematized overview of the Nimboran verbal system, based on a rearrangement and reinterpretation of Anceaux' data and comments.

The multidimensional character of the verbal paradigm makes that the possible combinations of categories can best be schematized in a series of charts. In section 2 of this paper I shall discuss the positional deictic categories expressed in the verb, and in section 3 the possible combinations of these categories with other categories. In section 4 the formal build up of the verbs will be discussed.

2 One of the most salient aspects of the Nimboran verbal paradigm is the elaborate system of what Anceaux calls position categories. In an earlier paper (Steinhauer, to appear) I have tried to systematize the oppositions between these categories, which by Anceaux are described in a rather impressionistic way. The result is illustrated in chart 1. In this chart the 16 position categories are divided into two groups: those which indicate the presence of a movement (of the agent and/or of the patient), and those which do not ([+move] and [-move] in the chart). The [+move] categories are not available for actions which do not involve a change of place. For verbs which do, the [-move] categories seem to express that the movement starts at the indicated position.[6]

Both [+move] and [-move] categories are subdivided into two sets: those which involve the position of the speaker ([+S]), and those which do not ([-S]). Relevant positions are further defined by elevational features: [+H], higher than the place of the speaker; [+L], lower than the place of the speaker; [-H,-L], at the same level as the place of the speaker. All these positions are implicitly visible ([+vis]) and opposed to what is far away and not visible ([-vis]). It is understood that [-H] includes positions which are [+L] and [-H,-L], whereas [-L] includes [+H] and [-H,-L]. The numbers in the chart correspond with Anceaux' numbering of the positional categories.

	[+S]	[-S]
[-move]	(1)	(2) [+H] (3) [+L] (4) [-H,-L] (5) [-vis]
[+move]	from [+S] to ...	from ... to ...
	(6) [+H] (7) [-H,-L] (8) [+L] (9) [-vis]	(13) [-H]/[-vis] [+H] (14) [+L] [-H,-L]
	from ... to [+S]	(15) [+vis] [-vis]
	(10) [+H]/[-vis] (11) [+L] (12) [-H,-L]	(16) [-L]/[-vis] [-H]

Chart 1: The system of the 16 position categories.

3.1   The first major distinction to be made for the verbal paradigm as a whole is one between {+indicative}[7] vs. {-indicative} forms. The latter comprise only two other categories, *viz.* what is called by Anceaux the "infinitive" and the "final infinitive". The "final infinitive" has the categorial meaning 'in order to ...'. The "infinitive" is used as an adjective (translated as a passive perfect participle), a coarse imperative, or indeed a kind of infinitive occurring in contexts such as *like to ---*, *refuse to ---*.

3.2 In contradistinction to the {-indicative} forms, the {+indicative} forms always contain subject markers, and are used as heads of predicates. Their subdivision is illustrated in chart 2. There the possible combinations of the positional and other categories are presented in abbreviated semantic terms. Abbreviations and symbols used in this chart are as follows:
(i) ±act., ±stat., ±plur., durat., momt., iter., unsp., masc.:
±active, ±stative, ±plural, momentary, iterative, unspecified, masculine;
(ii) 1-16: the 16 position categories of chart 1;
(iii) P(ast), R(ecent) P(ast), Pr(esent), F(uture);
(iv) "system n": a system of n categorial oppositions for subject agreement marking (to be discussed below);
(v) } and {: one of the embraced items should be selected.

3.3 The categories which are labelled {-active} in chart 2 are coined "secondary" verbal categories by Anceaux. He distinguishes three such categories alongside the "infinitives" and what by default would be "primary" categories. The latter are called {+active} in chart 2: their subject markers are agents, whereas the subject markers of the {-active} forms are patients. Anceaux' first and second "secondary" categories have the categorial meanings 'to get into the state caused by the action' or 'to get into the state (denoted by the lexical meaning)', and 'to be in the state caused by the action' or 'to be in the state (denoted by the lexical meaning)'. They are labelled {-stative} and {+stative} in the chart. Anceaux' third "secondary" category appears to consist of variant forms for the '3d person plural inanimate' of the second "secondary" verbal paradigm.[8]
    As chart 2 shows, {-active} categories have forms for the 1st to 5th position only. Apparently, the passive categorial meaning of the {-active} forms collides with the meanings of the 6th to 16th position categories, which imply movement and action (cf. chart 1).
    Obviously only transitive verbs have both {+active} and {-active} forms. Anceaux indicates that {-active} forms are typical of adjectives (p.120). Although he is less explicit about intransitive

verbs, it may be inferred that these have a paradigm of exclusively {+active} forms.

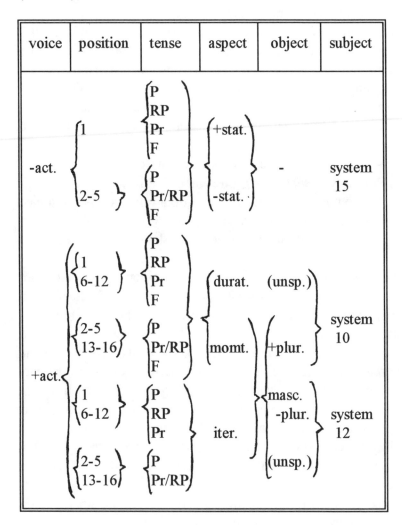

Chart 2: Combinations of {+indicative} verbal categories.

3.4   Both {+active} and {-active} forms have tense oppositions: {past}, {recent past}, {present} and {future}. The {future} indicates that "the action will take place in the future, or begins in the present and will continue in the future, or takes place in the present and is directed towards the future ... [Furthermore it is] used to indicate that the actor intends or wants to perform the action, or that the speaker wants the action to take place" (p.59); the {present} indicates that "the action takes place in the present or is completed in the present" (loc.cit.), while it is also "used in all those cases in which the time of the action is unimportant or is left out of account" (p.60); the {past} indicates that "the action took place in the past" (loc.cit.), though it supposedly does not overlap with the {recent past} which covers events which happened earlier today or yesterday, as well as past events between an earlier past event and the present (cf. p.60).

As is shown in chart 2 the opposition {present} vs. {recent past} is systematically neutralized for all position categories which do not involve the position of the speaker ([-S] in chart 1). No obvious semantic explanation for this phenomenon forces itself upon us.

3.5   For the {+active} forms Anceaux distinguishes the following aspectual (combinations of) categories: "momentary", "iterative", "durative momentary" and "durative iterative". The {iterative} indicates "repeatedness of the action"; sometimes ... "successiveness of the action" (if the actor is plural)" (p.98), while for the {momentary} category "the action is continuous, uninterrupted, or confined to one moment" (loc.cit.). Apparently the {iterative} cannot be combined with {future} tense. Perhaps the {iterative} requires repeated evidence up to the time of speaking, but further research is necessary to corroborate such a hypothesis or to find another explanation.

By distinguishing "durative momentary" and "durative iterative" categories, the combinations of the durative aspect and the tense categories are defective: Anceaux' "durative momentary" aspect only occurs in the {present}, while his "durative iterative" aspect is found in the {present}, {past} and {recent past}. Although formally this analysis seems to be justifiable, semantically it is counter-intuitive: events which are conceptually more complicated (iterative) than other events (momentary) are not likely to show a higher degree of subcategorization. The opposite is indeed the case for Anceaux' non-durative "iterative" and "momentary" categories.

Therefore it seems to me that for the durative no distinction between momentary and iterative should be made. This conclusion is in fact corroborated by Anceaux himself, when he remarks that "the Momentary forms ... also have the meaning of "continuation of an action in the future" [while] the Present forms of the Iterative of the Durative ... have the meaning "continuation in the present of an action, begun in the past ... [whereas the] Past and Recent Past forms of the Iterative of the Durative can be used to denote a continual action in the past without any element of repetition being present" (p.111). In other words, iterativity is at best a possible interpretation of the more general durative meaning ('continued presence of the action', vs. mere 'presence of the action' for the non-durative categories).

Apparently, such an iterative interpretation is precluded for what Anceaux therefore identifies as the "durative *momentary* present". Given, however, the possible meaning "continuation of the action in the future",[9] and the fact that the notions of iterativity and future cannot be combined, it seems likely that this "durative momentary present" should be interpreted as the {durative} {future}. This reinterpretation is reflected in chart 2.

As a consequence of this reanalysis, I distinguish a ternary aspectual opposition for the {+active} forms with regular distribution of tenses, replacing Anceaux' double binary opposition with defective tense distribution.

3.6   The {momentary} and {iterative} categories in chart 2 can be combined with one of the two object categories, *viz.* {plural object} and {masculine non-plural object}. The latter choice indicates that the object consists of "one or two male beings, not identical with the speaker or the person addressed" (p.104), while {plural object} indeed indicates that the object is plural, again excluding the speaker and the addressee. The object may be left unspecified. This is obviously the only option with intransitive verbs. With transitive verbs it is the unmarked option: the actual object may be any number of men, women or things (cf. p.107). With the {durative} category the object is always unspecified.

3.7 Each possible combination of {+indicative) categories discussed so far, should be combined with some subject agreement category.[10] Three subsystems for subject agreement marking are distinguished. They differ in the structure of the non-singular categories and are in complementary distribution. The most elaborate system ("system 15" in chart 2) is found with the {-active} categories of the paradigm. It is difficult to explain why this should be so. The least elaborate system ("system 10") is characteristic for those {+active} verbal categories which indicate what can be called an "extended referential scope", to wit {durative} verbs and verbs with a {plural object}. "System 12" finally, is found with the other {+active} categories.

	system 10 {+active} "extended reference"	system 12 {+active} (other)	system 15 {-active}
singular dual plural	-	1 3	1 2 3
+singular -singular	1 2 1+2 3	2 1+2	1+2

Chart 3: Combinations of number and person
in the subject agreement marking systems.

In all three systems, number of subject and person/gender are separate morphological categories. Gender is only relevant for the third person. The other persons distinguished are {first person subject}, {second person subject} and {first + second person subject}. The possible combinations of number and person are illustrated in chart 3.

It should be noted that {+singular} for the {first + second person subject} indicates the minimal number of speech participants needed to qualify as such, i.e. one speaker and one addressee.

Chart 4 illustrates the gender distinctions with the third person subject in the three subsystems. As with the object marking categories {(+)masculine} has to be read as referring to male beings only (p. 58, 84), whereas {-masculine} ("neutral" in Anceaux' terminology) refers to not exclusively male beings. Anceaux' "Feminine Object" as an additional verbal category in {+active} verb forms of *some* lexical stems is defined as referring to an object consisting of "one or two beings of the female sex" (p.165). This neutralization of singular and dual parallels the {masculine non-plural object} category discussed above. However, it is unclear how "feminine" in the 3d person dual forms of "system 15" has to be interpreted: as referring to two female beings or to at least one female being and something else (male or inanimate)?[11]

system	number	gender oppositions		
10	±singular	+masculine	-masculine	
12	singular dual	+masculine	-masculine	
	plural	-		
15	singular	+masculine	-masculine	
	dual	masculine	feminine	-animate
	plural	+animate		-animate

Chart 4: Gender oppositions for third person subject agreement

It should be noted by the way that the high degree of specification for gender of the 3d person dual in "system 15" as compared to singular and plural subject is counterevidence to one of Greenberg's language universals, *viz.* Universal 37 in Greenberg

1966 (p.95), which reads: "A language never has more gender categories in nonsingular numbers than in the singular".[12]

4.1.1 As to the formal aspects of the {+indicative} verbs in Nimboran, their general shape is *root + suffixes*. For a phonologically defined number of verbs the root comes in different shapes. No general rule can be given for the formal relations between these forms, but they are functionally distinctive. Maximally four forms are distinguished: one for forms other than {+active} forms, i.e. for {-active} forms and {-indicative} forms, and three for {+active} forms, corresponding with subject number. An example is the verb 'to put':

> *káong* {+active} {dual subject}
> *kuáng* {+active} {singular subject}
> *kaóing* {+active} {plural subject}
> *kóng* {-active} and {-indicative}

Verb forms with "extended reference" (i.e. those which are {durative} or have a {plural object} only {+singular subject} and {-singular subject} are distinguished. The {plural subject} forms for the root is used for {-singular subject} in these cases.

Verbs which lack one or more of these root forms use the form for the {dual subject} instead, e.g. the verb 'to draw':

> *nggedóu* 1. {+active} {dual subject}
>   2. {-active}, and {-indicative}
> *nggedúo* {+active} {singular subject}
> *nggedói* {+active} {plural subject}

For lists of root forms subject to such modification I refer to Anceaux (1965:86-91, 93-97, 113-114) and Steinhauer (1994).

The {-indicative} verbs forms are the only verb forms without suffixes. Anceaux' "infinitive" consists of the mere root, his "final infinitive" is derived from the latter through partial reduplication. For particulars I refer to Anceaux (1965:114-117) and again to Steinhauer (1994).

4.1.2 The semantic differences between the {+active} and {-active} sections of the {+indicative} paradigm are matched by striking formal differences. I shall therefore discuss the possible strings of suffixes for the {-active} and {+active} forms separately.

It should be stressed that fronting of vowels in all suffixes is (one of) the formal exponent(s) of the {-active} {+stative} and of the {+active} {durative} categories, as well as of those position categories which involve a movement over a large distance or downwards (i.e. position categories 8, 9, 12, 15 and 16).[13] In fact this difference in suffix vowels is the only difference between {+stative} and {-stative} forms, and between the position categories 7 and 8, and 14 and 16. Below I shall discuss suffixes in their *unfronted* shape only (except when they are inherently fronted). This also pertains to suffixes containing the vowel *a* but which can be followed by a suffix string consisting of at least two vowels separated by a consonant, in which case this *a* is also fronted to *e* (whether the other suffix vowels are fronted or not).

Some of the suffixes to be discussed below are potentially stressed. This is indicated by an acute on the relevant vowel. The last potentially stressed suffix will receive the main stress of the word. A secondary stress will then be on the verb root. If there is no potentially stressed suffix present, main stress is on the verb root.

4.2.1 The {+active} paradigm has the following order of suffixes. Suffixes of the same order are mutually exclusive. Order classes (slots) are marked by Roman numbers.

I   {dual subject}: -*ke*- (-*k*- before -*r*).
II   {durative} aspect: -*tem*- (-*te*- if followed by -*m*);
      {masculine non-plural object}: -*rá*-;
      {plural object}: -*dá*-;
III   {plural subject}: an infix -*i*- after the first consonant
          of the first suffix, provided this consonant is dental (*t, d,*
          n, s).
IV   {first + second person subject} {singular subject}:
          -*maN*-;[14]

V position category 3 {momentary} {present/recent past}, and position category 3 {durative} {future}: *-ke-*

VI the position categories (subject to fusion, see VIII):
(1) 0 (zero), (2) *-bá-*, (3) *-ngá-*, (4) *-sá-*, (5) *-ná-*,
(6) *-be-*, (7) *-se-*, (8) *-se-*, (9) *-ne-*, (10) *-keN-*,
(11) *-báN-*, (12) *-sáN-*, (13) *-bená-*, (14) *-sená-*,
(15) *-kené-*, (16) *-sené-*;

VII aspect categories:
{momentary}{present/recent past} position categories [-S] [+move]: *-ná-* (*-né-* when fronted);
{momentary} in other combinations: 0 (zero);
{iterative} the exponent of which fuses with the segmental exponents of the position categories of VI resulting in the following forms:
(1) *-ká-*, (2) *-beká-*, (3) *-nggá-*, (4) *-ská-*,
(5) *-nenggá-*, (6) *-beká-*, (7) *-ská-*, (8) *-ské-*,
(9) *-nenggé-*, (10) *-nggeN-*, (11) *-bekáN-*,
(12) *-skáN-*(13) *-benenggá-*, (14) *-senenggá-*,
(15) *-kenenggé-*, (16) *-senenggé-*;
{durative}, non-future: as {iterative};

VIII tense categories:
-k- {past};
-p- {recent past};
-t- {present};
{future} {durative} position categories [+S];
{present/recent past} other than {momentary}, position categories [-S] [-move];

0 {future} {durative} position categories [-S];
{present/recent past} {momentary}, position categories [-S] [-move];

-r- {future} {momentary} position category [+S] [-move], specified object;
{future} {momentary} position categories [-S];

-d- {future} {momentary} position category [+S] [-move], unspecified object;
{future} {momentary} position categories [+S] [+move];

IX   person/gender categories of subject (subject to fusion with the preceding suffix):

-u   first person;

-e   second person;

-ám   first + second person;

-um   third person, non-masculine, other than plural;

-am   other third persons;

when the tense marker is 0, the latter three suffixes fuse with the preceding vowel: *-á-* + *-um* > *-óm*; *-á-* + *-am* > *-ám*; *-á-* + *-ám* > *-ám* (with the fronted pendants *-é-* + *-ym* > *-yém*; *-é-* + *-im* > *-ém*; *-é-* + *-ím* > *-ém*).

4.2.2 In the {-active} section of the paradigm the following order of suffixes is found. This holds for both {+stative} and {-stative} verb forms, which - as indicated above - only differ in the frontness of their suffix vowels.

I   *-k-*   third person subject, -animate, dual;

II   *-de-*   first + second person subject, singular;

-ra-   singular subject other than first + second person;
third person subject, -animate, non-singular;

-dia-   all other dual and plural cq. -singular subjects;

III   *-maN-*   first + second person subject;
first person subject, plural;
second person subject, plural.

(NB different from {+active} *-maN-* (which has a narrower semantic scope) this {-active} *-maN-* is not subject to fronting if followed by two syllables separated by a consonant).

IV   *-ke-*   position category 3 {present/recent past}

V   the [-move] position categories:
(1) *0*, (2) *-bá-*, (3) *-ngá-*, (4) *-sá-*, (5) *-ná-*;

VI   tense categories:
{past}: *-k-;* {recent past}: *-p-;* {present}: *-t-*
{future}: *-r-* (*-d-* after *-maN-*); {present/recent past}: *0*

VII   subject agreement categories:

-u   first person, plural, position categories [+S];
first person, position categories [-S],
{present/recent past};

-ú	first person (other combinations);
-e	second person, plural, position categories [+S];
	second person, position categories [-S],
	{present/recent past};
-é	second person (other combinations);
-úm	third person, -masculine, singular;
	third person, feminine, dual;
-ám	third person (other combinations);
	first + second person.

4.2.3 As the lists in 4.2.1 and 4.2.2 illustrate, the {+active} and {-active} differ in stress placement and morphophonology, while formally similar suffixes have different functions. Both systems of categories, oppositions and suffixes, with their cumulative, extended, fused and overlapping exponence, are indicative for the ±activeness of the respective sections of the total verbal paradigm.

Notes

1. ng is used for Anceaux' velar nasal.
2. Silzer & Heikkinen (1991:69 and map VII) estimate the number of speakers to be 3500.
3. Reference is always made to Anceaux 1965.
4. In Anceaux' notation the last stressed syllable indicates main stress. A possible second stressed syllable carries a secondary stress. (Main) stress is phonemic.
5. It should be added though, that these categories are also pertinent to the "first" and "second secondary verb categories" (see below).
6. This is suggested by the two examples presented (Anceaux 1965:64).
7. Braces are used for morphological categories and corresponding sections of the paradigm. Binary oppositions are presented as privative. This does not imply a definite commitment as to the exact semantic nature of these oppositions. As positive member of each binary opposition I

    chose the one whose appropriate referents are most easily marked off.

8. I have disregarded variant forms in my calculations for the title of this paper.
9. Anceaux himself presents this formulation as one of the meanings of the future category. See the quotation above.
10. Anceaux' term "actor category" is adequate only for the {+active} part of the paradigm: the corresponding suffixes in the {-active} refer to the object of the action.
11. Anceaux does not indicate how a heterosexual couple would be referred to. Apart from that, it remains a task for ethno-metaphysics and ethno-sexuology to define the borders between animateness and inanimateness, and to establish which animate entities are male or female.
12. For another counterexample see Steinhauer 1985.
13. *ú, ó, é, á, u, a* are fronted to *ý, yé, í, i, y, e*. Only unstressed *e* and *i* remain unchanged. Other vowels do not occur in the suffixes. For details I refer to Steinhauer (to appear) and Voorhoeve (to appear).
14. *N* is a morphophoneme whose (nasal) realization is conditioned by assimilation to the following consonant. It represents a velar nasal before vowels.

References

Anceaux, J.C. 1965. The Nimboran Language. Phonology and Morphology. Verhandelingen van het Koninklijk Instituut voor Taal-, Land- en Volkenkunde 44. 's-Gravenhage: Martinus Nijhoff.

Greenberg, J.H. 1966. Some universals of grammar with particular reference to the order of meaningful elements. Universals of Language, 2nd edn. ed. by J.H. Greenberg, 73-113. Cambridge Massachusetts: MIT Press.

May, Kevin. 1978. Nimboran language survey report on a visit to Imeno and Sermai Atas villages. (Ms.)

May, Kevin. 1981. Nimboran kinship and marriage. Irian 9/2. 1-26

May, Kevin & Wendy May. 1981. Nimboran phonology revisited. Irian 9/1.9-38

Silzer, Peter J. & Heljä Heikkinen Clouse. 1991. Index of Irian Jaya Languages. Second Edition, special publication of Irian Bulletin of Irian Jaya, Jayapura

Steinhauer, Hein. 1985. Number in Biak: counterevidence to two alleged language universals. Bijdragen tot de Taal-, Land- en Volkenkunde 141/4.462-485

Steinhauer, Hein. to appear. Conceptualization of space in Nimboran.

Steinhauer, Hein. 1994. Struktur Verba Bahasa Nimboran. Contribution to the Kongres Linguistik Nasional I, Palembang.

Voorhoeve, C.L. to appear. Conceptualization of Space in Nimboran: some supplementary Remarks.

Wurm, S.A. & Shirô Hattori (eds) 1981. Language Atlas of the Pacific Area. Part I. New Guinea Area, Oceania, Australia. Pacific Linguistics, Series C, No. 66

Are there any coordinate Serial Verb constructions in Thai?

Supriya Wilawan
Thammasat University

1.   Introduction. The primary purpose of this paper is to demonstrate that within a lexicase analysis, a type of dependency grammar, the syntactic patterns called coordinate serial verb constructions, consisting of chains of verbs without any overt grammatical markers, when their syntactic characteristics are carefully examined, should be analyzed as either a construction with the lexically incorporated object intransitive verbs or an infinitive coordinate construction without an overt conjunction. The plan of this article is as follows. Section 2 is a brief introduction to the definitions of the term serial verb construction (SVC) and coordination and a review of previous work. Section 3 is a lexicase analysis of the so-called coordinate SVCs. In section 4 a summary of the paper is presented.

2.   Brief introduction of the definitions and a review of previous work. What are coordinate SVCs? There have been attempts to define the term 'SVC' but there is no agreement on the definition. In order to reduce the confusion, the SVCs in this paper have the following characteristics.

a. All verbs occurring in these serial verb constructions can occur as the sole single verb in a sentence without reverence to any particular context.

b. There is no conjunction [1] to separate the verbs in sequence.

---

[1] 'Conjunction' here refers to a coordinate conjunction. In a lexicase analysis, coordinate conjunctions are words which form an exocentric

c. Only the first verb in a serial verb construction ('V1') can take a nominative NP as its clausemate subject.

d. The actor of the second verb of a serial verb construction ('V2') is co-indexed with the subject of the first verb.

The coordinate construction, according to lexicase grammar, is exocentric. An exocentric construction is one which has two or more obligatory members. From the strict X-bar constraints imposed on lexicase grammar, a coordinate construction must have two or more phrases and at least one conjunction (Starosta 1988:247). However, there are some languages which use a coordinate construction without an overt conjunction. To accommodate this fact, lexicase grammar provisionally also allows an exocentric construction with an implicit conjunction (cf. Sak-Humphry 1992:72 and Wilawan 1993).

There are analyses of the coordinate serial verb constructions in several languages but there is only one analysis of Thai proposed by Marybeth Clark in 1992 (cf. Sebba 1987 and Schiller 1991). Clark proposed the following definition for serial verbs, limiting her definition to languages of mainland Southeast Asia:

1. Concatenated verbs represent coordinate statements referring to related events and expressed as a single proposition, i.e. with a single finite verb and where each participant occurs overtly only once;

2. A serializing verb is not predictable in the feature matrix of the finite (main) verb or of other verbs with which it serializes;

---

construction with two or more phrases of the same type (Starosta 1988:52, 107).

3. The subject of a serializing verb is coreferential with the subject of the finite verb but is never present in the construction (as stated in 1), i.e., a serializing verb is nonfinite;

4. The non-finite serial verbs are in a coordinate relationship with the finite verb and with each other if there is more than one serializing verb, but no coordinating marker is present;

5. An inner argument—Patient object, Locus (inner locative or dative), inner Correspondent— may intervene between serial verbs. When the same object is implied by more than one serial verb, it occurs only once (again, as in 1), the occurrence being not necessarily with the first transitive verb but depending on particular language preferences;

6. The time of a serial verb is either after or simultaneous with the time of the preceding verb.

Clark's analysis has two problems. First, her analysis is not explicit since she did not propose any formal syntactic structure for the SVCs. The second problem is that her examples do not accurately represent the claims she has made about the coordinate SVCs. Consider the examples in Clark's work as restated:

(1) kèp khrîangmII hôOp krapǎw
     pack tool   carry suitcase

     pay hǎakin
     go   search-eat

     'They would pack their tools and carry their suitcases to make a living.'

(2) náamphú? baang hÈng th@?thá?
     fountain some clss clumsy

     mây   ngaam
     not   pretty

tôOngtaatôOngcay
pleasant

'Some of the water fountains are clumsy and unpleasant to the eyes.'

In her definition of SVCs, Clark stated that a serializing verb is an adjunct, not a complement. An adjunct may occur freely with any head, subject to pragmatic considerations, while head words may differ in their ability to co—occur with a particular complement. However, the example given above seems to indicate that the second verb is a complement rather than an adjunct of V1. If we can replace V1 with verbs which have a similar meaning, then V2 is an adjunct. However, when the verb ruapruam 'to gather, to collect' is substituted for the verb kèp 'pack', the sentence (3) becomes unacceptable.

(3)   kèp/?rûapruam   khrîangmII
        pack/gather   tool

        hôOp   krapăw
        carry   suitcase

'(They would) pack/gather their tools and carry their suitcases (to make a living).'

This indicates that hôOp is a lexically licensed complement of kèp, so that V2 is a complement of V1 kep. We can see that there are some problems in the coordinate serial verb analysis proposed by Clark.

3. **Lexicase analysis.** Contrary to the serial verb analysis proposed by Clark, I argue that verbs in the construction covered in Clark's studies should be analyzed as either lexically incorporated object intransitive verbs or a head of an infinitival coordinate construction.

3.1.   Lexically incorporated object intransitive verbs.   The syntactic characertistics of the verbs will be used as evidence to support the lexicase anaysis.

3.1.1. V2 as subordinate, not coordinate. Contrary to Clark's claim that SVC is a coordinate construction, I argue that the second verb in the series is subordinate.

Consider the following example:

(4)   kháw yiing nók tòk
        he   shoot bird take

        plaa thúkwan
        fish everyday

        'He shoots birds and fishes everyday.'

At first glance, this sentence appears to consist of two transitive verbs, two noun dependents and two intransitive verbs. We cannot reverse the order of these verbs and their dependents.

(5)?   kháw tòk   plaa ying
        he   take fish shoot

        nók thúkwan
        bird everyday

        'He fishes and shoots birds everyday'.

This indicates that it is not a coordinate construction and that V2 and its dependent is a subordinate dependent of V1 since we can reverse the order of the verbs in the coordinate construction .

3.1.2. V2 as complement not adjunct. Unlike Clark's claim about the so-called coordinate SVCs, I argue that V2 in this construction is a complement of the head verb. Lexicase theory makes the standard dependency grammar distinction between complements and adjuncts (Starosta 1988).

Adjuncts are optional while complements are obligatory. However this criteria is not easy to apply to languages like Thai, where subjects and objects are freely omissible in context for all verbs. A head variation test then is needed. Head words may differ in their ability to co-occur with a particular complement, while an adjunct may occur freely with any head (subject to pragmatic consideration). In the following examples, the head variation indicates that V2 is a complement of a head verb since we cannot replace V1 with any verbs.

(6) kháw   dàk/?hǎa/*lôo   nók
     he   trap/seek/lure   bird

     tòk   plaa   thúkwan
     take   fish   everyday

'He traps/seeks/lures birds and fishes everyday.'

3.1.3. Vs as lexically incorporated object intransitive verbs. Since it is established that this construction is not a coordination but subordiantion, we would expect that we should be able to topicalize a noun phrase (NP) after V2. In Thai the NP after the nonfinite complement verb can be topicalized (cf. Wilawan 1993:64). However, this is not the case.

(7)* plaa   ná?   nuan   ying
     fish   Top   Nuan   shoot

     nók   tòk
     bird   take

*'The fish, Nuan shot the bird and caught.'

Then does this construction really contain two transitive verbs and their dependents? The syntactic properties of verbs and NPs indicate rather that the two verbs are not transitive but rather must be analyzed as two intransitive verbs with lexically incorporated objects, derived into compound intransitive verbs forming single lexical units. This conclusion is based on the fact that neither the nouns nor the verbs in this construction can take any additional dependents. With a number and classifier modifying the nouns, the sentence is unacceptable.

(8)?   nuan ying nók lǎay
        Nuan shoot bird many

        tua   tòk   plaa hâa tua
        clss take fish five clss

        'Nuan shot many birds and caught five fishes.'

With a relative clause modifying each noun, the sentence is also unacceptable.

(9)*   nuan ying nók   thîi tOng
        Nuan shoot bird that Tong

        kliat tòk   plaa thîi yùu
        hate take fish that be

        nay   lamthaan
        in   creek

        'Nuan shot the birds that Tong hated and caught the fish that were in the creek.'

We can see that these nouns have syntactic properties that are different from those of an ordinary noun. They do not allow any noun modifier such as a classifier, a number, or a relative clause, to follow. These nouns are incorporated into verbs as a unit forming an intransitive verb rather than a transitive verb with a noun dependent. The lexicalization analysis then explains the fact that we cannot topicalize a noun after the verb. Because an intransitive verb behaves as a compound unit, breaking it by topicalizing a noun is impossible.

3.1.4.   V2 as a non-finite verb.   The second verb in this construction is analyzed as a non-finite verb since the nominative NP is not allowed. In lexicase grammar, nonfinite verbs are defined as verbs with which overt grammatical subjects may not occur (cf. Starosta 1988).

(10)*   nuan ying nók kháw tòk
        Nuan shoot bird he   take

        plaa thúkwan
        fish everyday

'Nuan shoots birds and he fishes everyday.'

I propose the following structure for this type of construction :

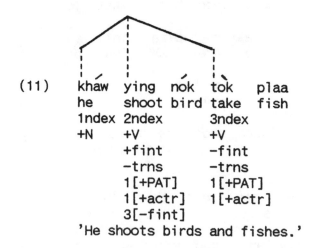

(11)   kháw   ying nók tòk   plaa
       he   shoot bird take fish
       1ndex 2ndex   3ndex
       +N   +V   +V
              +fint   -fint
              -trns   -trns
              1[+PAT]   1[+PAT]
              1[+actr]   1[+actr]
              3[-fint]

'He shoots birds and fishes.'

The standard complement control rule applies to get the interpretation of this sentence. A Patient, he, of a matrix verb is also interpreted as an implied actor of a nonfinite verb in the lower clause.

There are quite a number of phrases that
have the same syntactic characteristics as
the example given by Clark (1992). For
example:

(12)   khoncháy [sák   phaa
        maid   wash   clothes

        láang   chaam]   thúkwan
        clean   dish   everyday

        'A   maid   washes   clothes   and
washes dishes every day.'

(13)   naythun khon nán   cáang
        investor clss that   hire

        chaawbâan [tat tonmáay
        villager   cut tree

        thamlaay pàa]
        destroy   forest

        'That   investor   hires   villagers
to destroy the forest.'

3.2.   Non-finite coordinate transitive
verb.   Now consider the following example:

(14)   khonráay khâa cáwkhOOngbâan
        robber   kill owner of house

        khomkhǐIn   luukcâang kOOn
        rape   maid   before

        'The robber killed the owner of
the house and raped the maid before...'

At first glance, this sentence does not
look different from example (4). Again it
seems to consist of two transitive verbs
and two noun dependents. However, the
syntactic characteristics of the verbs in
this sentence are not similar to the ones
in example (4). Because of its syntactic
characteristics, I propose that the second

verb in example (14) should be analyzed as a head of a non-finite coordinate clause. There is evidence for this conclusion.

3.2.1. V2 as a non-finite verb. The second verb in this construction is analyzed as an infinitival verb since the presence of nominative NP creates an unacceptable sentence:

(15)* khonráay kháa cáawkhŌŌngbâan
     robber kill owner of house

     kháw   khŏmkhǐIn lûukcâang
     he   rape   maid

'The robber killed the owner of the house and he raped the maid.'

3.2.2. Coordinate not subordinate construction. In a finite and nonfinite coordinate construction in Thai, we can reverse the order of verbs and their dependents (subject to pragmatic constraints) (cf. Wilawan 1993:63). Reversing the order of verbs in example (14) also creates an acceptable sentence:

(17) khonráay khŏmkhǐIn lûukcâang
     robber   rape   maid

     kháa   cáawkhŎŎngbâan kŎŎn
     kill   owner of house before

'The robber raped the maid and killed the owner of the house before...'

Thus, this seems to indicate that it is a coordinate, not a subordinate, construction. In addition, in Thai, there is a constraint on topicalized coordinate structures which is corresponds to the Coordination Structure Constraint proposed by John Ross (Ross 1967). That is, no element can be moved out of a coordinate structure. We cannot topicalize or cleft the NP in the finite or nonfinite coordinate construction (cf.

Wilawan 1993). Topicalizing an NP after
V2 in example (14) creates an unacceptable
sentence as in:
(17)* lûukcáang ná? khonráay khâa
maid Top robber kill

 cáawkhŎOngbâan khòmkhĬIn
 owner of house rape

    *'The maid, the robber killed
the owner of the house and raped.'

It could be argued that example (14) may
consist of two lexically incorporated
object intransitive verbs. However, this
is not the case since the NPs can take the
modifers and the relative clauses as
illustrated in the following examples.
(18) khonráay khâa cáwkhŎOngbâan
 robber kill owner of house

 nìng khon khòmkhĬIn lûukcâang
 one clss rape maid

 sŎOng khon
 two clss

    'The robber killed one owner of the
house and raped two maids.'

(19) khonráay khâa cáwkhŎOngbâan
 robber kill owner of house

 thîi nuan rúucǎk khòmkhĬI
 who Nuan know rape

 lûukcâang thîi ph@ng maa
 maid who just come

    'The robber killed the owner of the
house that Nuan knew and raped the maid
who just came.'

Thus, these sentences are considered as
coordinate constructions because they have

140

syntactic characteristics of coordination.
We can reverse the order of tthe verbs and
an NP after V2 cannot be topicalized. The
second verb in this exocentric structure
is analyzed as a nonfinite verb. The
presence of an NP subject is not
acceptable. Similar syntactic structures
can be found in Mandarin Chinese (cf.
Wilawan 1993:175). I propose the
following dependency syntactic structure.
The horizontal line indicates an
exocentric construction.

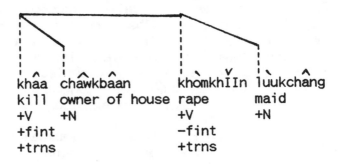

khâa chǎwkbâan khòmkhǐIn lûukchǎng
kill owner of house rape maid
+V +N +V +N
+fint -fint
+trns +trns

4. Summary. In this paper, I have
presented the lexicase analysis of the so-
called coordinate SVCs. Because of the
syntactic characteristics of the verbs in
this construction, I argue that the second
verb in the series should be analyzed as
either a lexically incorporated object
intransitive verb or a head of a
coordinate nonfinite construction.

References

Clark, Marybeth. 1992. Serialization in mainland Southeast Asia. Paper presented at the Third International Symposium on Language and Linguistics. Bangkok: Chulalongkorn University Press.

Ross, John. 1967. Constraints on variables in syntax. MIT doctoral dissertation.

Sak-Humphry, Chhany. 1992. The syntax of nouns and noun phrases in dated pre-Angkorian inscriptions. University of Hawai'i master's thesis.

Sebba, Mark. 1987. The syntax of serial verbs. Amsterdam: Benjamin.

Schiller, Eric. 1991. An autolexical account of subordinating serial verb constructions. University of Chicago doctoral dissertation.

Starosta, Stanley. 1988. The case for lexicase. London: Pinter Publishers.

Starosta, Stanley, Siew-ai Ng, Koenraad Kuiper, and Zhi-qian Wu. 1992. VR compounding in a WP perspective. Paper presented at the First International Conference on Chinese Linguistics, University of Singapore. Singapore.

Wilawan, Supriya. 1993. Reanalysis of the so-called serial verb constructions in Thai, Khmer, Mandarin Chinese and Yoruba. University of Hawai'i doctoral dissertation.

Changing to the new world:
high-tech verbalization in Thai

Nitaya Kanchanawan
Ramkhamhaeng University

1. Introduction.

The relationship between Thailand and England began in the Ayudhaya period (1350-1767). However, during that time the Portuguese and other Westerners, i.e. the French, were more familiar to the Thais than the English. Thus, not many English loanwords are found in the old documents from that time. Even in the reign of King Rama I of the Bangkok Period (1782-1809) there was no contact from any Englishman. Then in the reign of King Rama II (1809-1824) there was an official contact from England. Thus, English loanwords started to appear in various documents. The loanwords increased in the reigns of King Rama III (1824-1851) and King Rama IV or King Mongkut (1851-1868) due to more contact with Englishmen and Americans. King Rama IV himself studied English and was able to use it fluently (Changkhwanyuen 1983).

Unlike in other Asian countries where Christian missionaries had access only to the lower classes, in Thailand missionaries made a distinct impression on the ruling classes. They, however, were more interested in the missionaries' knowledge of Western sciences and modern technology than Christianity. They realized also that, in order to better pursue their scientific interest, they had to be proficient in English.

King Mongkut's successors, King Chulalongkorn (Rama V, reign 1868-1910) and King Vajiravudh (Rama VI, reign 1910-1925), were more confident in dealing with Western powers than their forefathers had been. They realized that the adoption of Western ways and the utilization of Western techniques were the tools of modernization (Masavisut et al 1986).

Today with the invasion of radio, telephone, television, video tape, fax machine, cable TV, satellite TV, computer network, and finally Thailand's own satellite, Thaicom[1], the Thais cannot escape high-tech terms in everyday life. Thailand is now in the world communications systems. The problem is how to cope with them in the Thai language.

2. Early Adaptation

Before the appointment of the word-coining committees of the Thai Royal Institute there were 3 ways of adaptation: loan blending, loan translation, and word building (Prugsapramool 1989).

2.1 Loan Blending
Loan blending is a compound word consisting of partly Thai and partly English. Either a Thai word or an English word may serve as the main part. English word may be the whole word with original meaning. For example:

เครื่องแบ็ตเตอรี่   khruangbattery[2] (/khrîaŋ/ = implement),

เครื่องไดนะโม   khruangdynamo, khruangradio,

ลูกบอลลูน   lukballoon (/lûuk/ = rounded thing),

หม้อแบ็ตเตอรี่   mobattery (/mɔ̂ɔ/ = pot), mometer,

โรงแฟกเตอรี่   rongfactory (/rooŋ/ = factory),

Otherwise it may be a part of the original word, for example:

ถุงเมล์   thungmail (/thǔŋ/ = bag, mail is cut from mail-bag),

คณะฟุตบอล   khanafootball (/kháná/ = group, football is cut from football team),

รถสติม   rotsteam (/rót/ = car, steam is cut from steam car).

2.2 Loan Translation

Loan translation is a direct translation, either word for word or with some adaptation. For example:

แรงม้า   raengma 'horsepower' (/rææŋ/ = power, /máa/ = horse),

รถยนตร์   rotyon 'motor car' (/rót/ = car, /yon/ = machine),

รถไอ   rot-ai 'steam car' (/rót/ = car, /ʔai/ = steam),

ทางรถไฟ   thangrotfai 'railway' (/thaaŋ/ = way , /rót/ = car, /fai/ = fire) (/rótfai/ = train),

รถไฟฟ้า   rotfaifa 'electric car' (/rót/ = car , /fai/ = fire, /fáa/ = sky) (/faifáa/ = electricity) .

2.3 Word Building

Word building is an interpretation of new things or ideas, for example:

แผ่นเสียง   phaensiang 'disk' (/phæ̀n/ = thin piece thing, /sǐaŋ/ = sound),

แรงไฟ   raengfai 'volt' (/ræǽng/ = power, /fai/ = fire, electricity),

ลูกสวรรค์   luksawan 'balloon' (/lûuk/ = rounded thing, /sàwǎn/ = heaven),

ตู้เย็น   tuyen 'refrigerator' (/tûu/ = cabinet, /yen/ = cool).

Besides the meaning-oriented adaptation mentioned above, another way to use loanwords is sound-oriented adaptation. The English sounds are equated to Thai sounds of familiar words which are not necessarily related to the original words, for example:

สเตแท่น   satethaen 'station' (/sàtee/ sounds like a kind of food, /thæ̂n/ = stand, platform),

กะปิต้น kapitan 'captain' (/kàpì/ sounds like shrimp paste and /tan/ sound like a Thai words meaning being clogged up, not hollow, dead end).

ตะแล็ปแก็ป talaepkaep 'telegraph' (there are many Thai words beginning with /tà/; /lǽp/ and /kǽp/ are easy to pronounce) .

Both ways of adaptation reflect the Thai ways of thinking in that they think of the new technology in terms of the familiar things in their own culture, either Thai things or Thai sounds. If they cannot equate the new things to anything in Thai they choose to adapt the foreign sounds to the Thai sounds.

3. The Royal Institute Rules

From the very start of word-coining the work has been unofficially carried out by Thai scholars including members of the Royal family and the kings themselves.

When Prince Wanwaithayakon came back from Europe in 1919, word-coining was coming into vogue, due mainly to the necessity of establishing a Thai version of the Civil and Commercial Code after the English draft of each Book of the Code was ready. At the change of Regime in 1932 he became active in coining words. He started a newspaper and felt that it was necessary to coin new words. In his opinion, to get to the people one cannot use English words which have not penetrated into the system of thought. If one can get hold of a Thai word it would be better, but if not, one can have recourse to Pali and Sanskrit words which have come into the Thai language (Wanwaitayakon 1970).

Therefore the general word-coining rules of The Royal Institute go like this (Royal Institute 1992):
1) Find a Thai word first. If no Thai word is appropriate then,
2) Find Pali and Sanskrit words already used in Thai. If not then,

3) Write the original word in Thai using another set of Royal Institute Rules.

So far the Royal Institute prefers "formal" Thai words, and sometimes remote Pali and Sanskrit words are used. Moreover, the original words are usually avoided. This practice causes some conflicts on the part of the modern language users, especially those in the high-tech world.

4. The Cataract of High-Tech Terms

When English loanwords started to penetrate into the Thai language almost 200 years ago, they were not for the general public . Only a few persons who got involved with the official documents understood those remote words. Even in the prime of Prince Wanwaithayakon only the elites and the scholars knew those words. The general public accepted whatever they were told. They rarely or never heard or used the original words. For example, they were told that 'telephone' is /thoorásàp/ ('thoorá' = 'far', 'sàp' = 'sound', both from Pali-Sanskrit). They accepted it, no questions asked. When the sounds of the original words were adapted to the Thai system they were accepted as Thai words. For example, 'pipe' became แป๊ป /pǽp/, 'litre'

became ลิตร /lít/, 'dinosaur' became ไดโนเสาร์ /dainoosǎo/,

'brandy' became บรั่นดี /bàràndii/, 'pound' became ปอนด์

/pɔɔn/, etc.

However, in the last few years the power of communication has taken people around the world closer to one another. With the coming of fax machines, cellular phones, computer networks, and satellite TV, Bangkok is as close to Los Angeles as to the neighboring Thai cities, or maybe closer. The new words, whether they are high-tech terms or not, are no longer obscure. They came ready with the concepts, which may be international. The Thais can use high-tech terms like computer, fax, video etc. right away.

148

5. Conflict between Popular Practice and Conventional Practice

In this case, popular practice means the way the general public uses loanwords. Conventional practice means the way the Royal Institute uses them. The general public in this case means only people who are exposed to high-tech terms, at least those who know how to use an ATM.

While the Royal Institute prefers Thai or Pali-Sanskrit words that general public prefers the original words, i.e. English. The big reason is that the new words are familiar to them and can be understood immediately . They always complain that words from the Royal Institute have to be translated again from "Indian" (Pali-Sankrit) into Thai . To them Pali and Sanskrit are also foreign languages. Gone are the days when education is conducted in Buddhist monasteries where the students also study Pali and Sanskrit.

For example, while 'television' is easily accepted as โทรทัศน์ /thooráthát/ (word coined from Pali-Sanskrit) and is still widely used, 'fax' is partly accepted as โทรสาร thoorásǎan/ (/thoorá/ = 'far', /sǎan/ = 'message'). The original word 'fax' is also widely used. The word 'video' is hardly accepted as วีดิทัศน์ /wiidìthát/, forming up the same way as /thooráthát/ (/thoorá/ = 'far', /thát/ = 'picture', /wiidì/ 'enjoyment, pleasure').

Not only do the general public prefer the original words but also they choose the shorter and more compact ones. For example, English ลิฟท์ 'lift' is chosen instead of American 'elevator'.

However, when it comes to the problems of 'formal' versus 'informal' Thai words, the Royal Institute seems to win, because their words are more polite and convey more precise meanings. For example, กดลง /kòt loŋ/ won over ดันลง /dan loŋ/ for 'push down' because of its politeness (/dan/ has sexual implication in Thai) .

6. Conflicts within the Popular Practice

Although the general public has discovered to its horror that a /mɔɔsides/ is in fact a /mɔrsedis/ 'Mercedes,' they do not change the word because they got used to the name now.

Some people, however, are annoyed to hear that 'label' is pronounced ลาเบล /laa-beel/ and 'erase' อีราส /ʔii-ráat/ where /aa/ is pronounced as in 'car'. Strangely enough, many Thai computer scientists or scientists still stick to the Thai pronunciation rules, i.e. one vowel for one sound.

The big conflict within this group is that some pronounce the words American or English ways, while some pronounce them the Thai way.

7. Differences between Thai and English sounds.[3]

Table 1. Comparision of Thai and English consonant sounds

	ENGLISH	THAI [4]	ROMANIZATION [5]
1)	bib	บีบ	bip
2)	church	ชัช	chat
3)	deed	ดีด	dit
4)	fife	ไฟ	fai
5)	gag	กัก	kak
6)	hat	หัด	hat
7)	which	วิด	wit
8)	judge	จัด	chat
9)	kick	คิก	khik

10)	lid ,needle	ลิด, ดาล	li̱t, da̱n
11)	mum	มัม	ma̱m
12)	no	โน	no
13)	thing	ทิ้ง	thing
		งาน	nga̱n
14)	pop	พบ, ภพ	pho̱p, pho̱p
15)	roar	รอ	ro
16)	sauce	ศาสตร์	sa̱t
17)	ship, dish	ชัช	cha̱t
18)	tight	ทบ, บท	tho̱p, bo̱t
19)	thin	ทิน	thi̱n
20)	this	ดิส	di̱t
21)	valve	วาว	wao
22)	with	วิด	wi̱t
23)	yes	ญาติ	ya̱t
24)	zebra	ซิบ	si̱p
25)	vision	ชัน	cha̱n
26)		ปา	*pa*
27)		ตา	*ta*
28)		กา	*ka*

REMARKS

1. The final in Thai is unreleased as indicated by underlining.

2. Thai /ch/ is equated to English /č/ (in *church*), /ǰ/ (in *judge*), /š/ (in *ship*), and /ž/ (in *vision*).

3. Thai /d/ is equated to English /d/ (in *deed*) and /ð/ (in *this*).

4. Thai /p/, /t/, /k/ may be equated to the second member of the English clusters /sp/, /st/, /sk/ respectively.

5. Thai /w/ is equated to English /hw/ (in *which*) , /v/ (in *valve*) and /w/ (in *with*).

6. Thai /s/ is equated to English /s/ (in *sauce*) and /z/ (in *zebra*).

7. Thai /th/ is equated to English /t/ (in *tight*) and /θ/ (in *thin*).

Table 2. Comparision of Thai and English vowel sounds.[3]

	ENGLISH	THAI	ROMANIZATION
1)	pat	แพทย์	phaet
2)	pay	เผ	phe
3)	care	แคร์	khae
4)	father	ฟ้า	fa
5)	pet	เพชร	phet
6)	bee	บี	bi
7)	pit	พิศ	phit
8)	by	ใบ	bai
9)	pier	เปีย	pia
10)	pot	พจน์	phot
11)	toe	โท	tho
12)	caught	คอด	khot
13)	noise	น้อย	noi
14)	took	ทุก	thuk
15)	boot	บูด	but
16)	out	เอา	ao
17)	cut	คัด	khat

18)	term	เทอม	thoem
19)	about	อบาย	abai
20)	butter	เออ	oe

REMARKS

There are more vowel sounds in Thai, but they are omitted here because of their irrelevance.

8. Sound Conflicts

Even when the original words are chosen they are pronounced differently. One group pronounces them in the English or American way, another in the Thai way. One group pronounces 'fax' with the final sounds, another like /fæk/. Those who observe the one-symbol-for-one-sound rule of the Thai vowels pronounce 'label' /laa-beel/ , 'erase' /ʔii-ráat/ or /ʔii-ráas/.

For the general public the final sounds /f/, /l/, /s/, and /č/ in English are coming into the Thai sound system as well as the new initial clusters. Traditionally there are 12 clusters in Thai: /kr/, /kl/, /kw/, /khr/, /khl/, /khw/, /pr/, /pl/, /phr/, /phl/, /tr/, and /thr/. With the arrival of some high-tech terms some Thais are now able to pronounce the likes of 'block', 'break', 'drive', 'flip-flop', and 'free'.

Another conflict is in tone marks. Since Thai has tones and English does not, it is reasonable to omit tone marks when writing English words in Thai. However, since English words with Thai characters assume some tones, not necessarily like the original words, when used in Thai language, some Thais can't help putting a tone mark in some syllable, making them are Thai. For example, 'Pepsi' became เป๊ปซี่ /pépsî/ where a tone mark indicating high tone is placed above the first syllable , and a tone mark indicating falling tone is placed above the second syllable. 'Pepsi' without tone marks looks like this: เปปซี.

9. Conclusion

Despite the protest from the conservatives that Thai terms should be used instead of English, no one can stop the avalanche of high-tech terms which can be understood immediatedly . The world has been made so small by the communications systems that nothing is obscure anymore.

It was recently reported in *Asiaweek* that many Asian governments have tried to slow the infiltration of foreign words into their national languages. In Indonesia where some 200 indigenous tongues are spoken, authorities incorporated Bahasa Indonesia to unite the country linguistically. Jakarta has been fighting the encroachment of English words. Recently it banned the use of English in advertisements. And at one symposium, government officials and linguists called for improved efforts to promote the use of Bahasa as a language of science and technology. One minister called for experts to develop new words in order to keep up with scientific advances.

Asiaweek agreed that as an agent of national unity Bahasa Indonesia should be promoted. And the bastardized usages of "indoglish" can encourage both bad English and bad Indonesian. but not every language needs to have its own expressions for everything. Scientific words that are globally accepted could be adopted. Just like Latin is widely used by biologists and medical scientists to classify things, *Asiaweek* proposed the standardization of easy-to-pronounce, easy-to-spell scientific usage throughout the world. To do so would facilitate communication among scientists from different nations and make it easier for researchers and students alike to work from primary sources.

In Thailand the importance of English was realized long ago. As all nations of the present decade belong to a global community, English is the language of international commerce and information interdependence. English has lost its 'foreignness' in Thailand . Instead it is a powerful vehicle for carrying on international business, strengthening the economy and improving technical knowledge (Masavisut et al 1986).

Whether "standardization" of high-tech terms is a good idea or not, the Thais will continue to adapt and adopt them in a Thai way. More original words may be used and understood as most carry "international" concepts with them, despite different pronunciations. The Americans and the Thais have the same concepts when using the likes of 'remote control', 'xerox', 'fax', etc. Whatever conflicts there may be now, the original high-tech terms will be here to stay.

Footnotes

[1]Thaicom was launched on December 18, 1993 at French Guiana, South America. The Ariane rockets carried both the Thai and the US satellites.

[2]The Thai part is in transliterated form while the English part retains the original form for better understanding.

[3]Adapted from *the American Heritage Dictionary of the English Language*. 3 rd. edition, 1992.

[4]Thai words are chosen in order to illustrate consonant or vowel sounds only, not the translation.

[5]This paper uses the Royal Institute Romanization Rules in converting Thai scripts to Roman scripts except when underlining is used to indicate the difference between English and Thai sounds.

References

Anonymous. 1993. Modern Priorities: Pragmatism is as important as Purity of Language. *Asiaweek*, 19.49.26.

Changkhwanyuen, V. 1983. Development of Loanwords from English. In *Report of the Seminar on Thai Language and Thai Society*. 221-224. Bangkok, National Identity Bureau.

Masavisut, N., M. Sukwiwat and S. Wongmontha. 1983. The Power of the English Language in Thai Media. *World Englishes*, 5.2/3.197-207.

Prugsapramool, K. 1989. *Coined words before the Appointment of the Thai Terminology Committee of the Royal Institute.* Master of Arts' Thesis, Silpakorn University.

Royal Institute. 1992. *Computer Terms*. 2nd. edition . Bangkok, Royal Institute.

Wanwaithayakon, Prince . 1970. Coining Thai Words . *In Memoriam Phya Anuman Rajadhon*. 33-38. Bangkok, The Siam Society.

Common vocabulary of Sukhothai inscriptions and different Tai dialects

Prasert Na Nagara
The Royal Institute

A speaker of the Northern Thai dialect of Thailand (NT) can communicate easily with either a Tai Lue (TL) or a Tai Nuea (TN) speaker from China. This is also true for the Northeastern Thai (NET) and the Southern Thai dialects. Unfortunately, a person who knows only the Central Thai or Standard Thai dialect (ST) can hardly understand any Tai dialects of China, and vice versa. A friend of mine who speaks TN can clearly understand the inscription of King Ram Khamhaeng (1292 A.D.), but can read modern Bangkok newspapers only with much difficulty. Thus, it is expected that Tai dialects can help in the interpretation of old Thai inscriptions.

From the Inscription of King Ram Khamhaeng
(Inscription 1):

	Meaning in Standard Thai	in Some Tai dialects
tuu (ตู)	*we*	*all of us*
phĭa (เผือ)	*we*	*we two* (exclusive)
phûu ʔâai (ผู้อ้าย)	-	*the eldest (brother)*
tiam tàɛ̀ (เตียมแต่)	-	*from the time, since*

'khâu' (เข้า) which means *'rice or year'* comes from the clause, 'mîia kuu khîn yài dâi sìp kâau khâu' meaning *"when I was 19 years old."* 'khâu' means *'rice'* in ST, but *'year'* in many other dialects.

'ya yâai' (ญญ่าย) which means 'to scatter' in NT but no longer in use, comes from the sentence, 'phrâi fáa nâa sǎi phɔɔ kuu nǐi ya yâai' meaning "my father's men scatter in confusion."

phǽæ (แพ้) which means 'to be defeated or to win' comes from the clause, 'ton kuu ...phǽæ' meaning "because I won in fighting." 'phǽæ' means 'to be defeated' in ST, but 'to win' in many other dialects.

'phɪa' (เพื่อ) which means 'for (someone) or because' comes from the clause, 'phɪa kuu phûŋ cháaŋ khǔn sǎam chon phǽæ' meaning "because I won in elephants fighting with Khun Sam Chon." 'phɪa' means 'for (someone)' in ST, but 'because' in many other dialects.

'luu thâang (ลูท่าง) which means 'it is convenient.' in NT and NET, comes from the sentence 'câu miaŋ bɔɔ ʔau cakɔɔp nai phrâi luu thâaŋ phɪan cuuŋ wua pai kháa' meaning "the lord does not levy tolls to his subjects and so it is convenient for them to trade."

'phɪan' (เพื่อน) which means 'friend, neighbor, or they', comes from the sentence 'phɪan cuuŋ wau pai kháa' meaning "they herd their cattle to trade." 'phɪan' means 'friend' in ST, but 'they' in NT.

'yiia khâau' (เยียข้าว) is not used in ST, but means 'granary' in Shan, NT and NET.

'khǎa' (ขา) means 'both of them' in Phake and other dialects, but not in ST.

'chɔɔi' (ช่อย) is not used in ST, but it means 'to help' in many other dialects.

'nɪa fɪa' (เหนือเฟื้อ) is not used in ST, but it means 'to support' in many other dialects.

'mɪa' (เมื่อ) is not used in ST, but it means 'to go or to come' in many other dialects.

'màak laaŋ' (หมาก-ลาง) renders different meanings in different Tai dialects and tends to confuse readers when reading texts of different dialects. It means *'jack-fruit'* in Shan, *'areca nut'* in Chuang, the White Tai and the Southern Thai dialects, and *'coconut'* in many other dialects.

'ĺian' (เลื้อน) means *'glide'* in ST and *'to chant poetry or to recite in a singing manner'* in Phake and other dialects. The latter meaning seems to be more acceptable.

'khàp' (ขับ) means *'to sing'* in NT. It appears as 'khàp rɔ́ɔŋ' meaning *'to sing classical Thai songs'* in ST.

'lùak' (หลวก) is not used in ST, but it means *'to be wise'* in many other dialects.

'lúk...maa' (ลุก...มา) means *'to stand up and come'* in ST, but *'to come from'* in many other dialects which appears in a sentence in the Inscription as 'lúk tὲæ miaŋ sǐithammarâat maa' meaning *"(he) has come from the Province of Nakhon Si Thammarat."*

'mon' (มน) is not used in ST, but it means *'to be round'* in many other dialects.

'bîaŋ tiin nɔɔn' (เบื้องตีนนอน) means *'the direction of a man's feet when he is sleeping, which is the North.'* The NE Thais and the Southern Thais still sleep with their feet pointing north.

'dian bâaŋ pὲæt wan' (เดือนบ้างแปดวัน) means *'the eighth day of the waning moon.'* 'bâaŋ' in NT means *'to have a nick'* and so 'dian bâaŋ' means *'the waning moon.'* It is very unusual for the Inscription to use the eighth day instead of the eighth night which is used in nearly all Tai dialects, but nowadays TN still uses the eighth day.

'sùut' (สูด) means *'to chant, to preach'* in NT, but not in ST. The sentence appears in the Inscription as 'fǔuŋ pùu khruu thěen mahǎa thěen khîn nâŋ nǐa khadaan hǐn sùut tham kὲæ ʔùbaasòk' meaning *"a group of the monks sit on the stone slab to preach Dharma to the people."*

'laai sɨi' (ลายสือ), which means 'stripes' in ST and 'the alphabet' in TN which is equivalent to 'lik laai' in Phake, should be translated as 'the alphabet.'

'khrâi cai ' (ใคร่ใจ) is not found in ST, but it means 'to think' in Ahom, Phake, and TN. The sentence in the Inscription is 'phɔɔ khǔn raam khamhǎɛɛŋ hǎa khrâi cai nai cai lɛɛ sài laai sɨ thai nɨi' meaning "King Ram Khamhaeng thinks in his mind and devises the Thai alphabet."

'hǎa' (หา) in the phrase 'hǎa pen' (หาเป็น) is found in the Inscriptions 1 and 3 which means 'by oneself' in White Tai. The sentence in the Inscription is 'phɔɔ khǔn raam khamhǎɛɛŋ hǎa pen khruu ʔaacaan' meaning "King Ram Kamhaeng himself is a teacher."

'khɛɛ' (แคะ) is not yet found in other Tai dialects, but in one Kha: dialect meaning 'strong'. In the Inscription, the word is given together with its synonym, 'rɛɛŋ' (แรง). The sentence in the Inscription is 'dûai khɛɛ dûai rɛɛŋ hǎa khon càk samɔɔ mɨ dâi' meaning "there is no one to equal him in wisdom and strength."

samùt hǎa pen dɛɛn (สมุทรหาเป็นแดน) means 'the ocean itself is the boundary.' 'dɛɛn' means 'a certain region' in ST, but 'a boundary' in NT.

'rɔɔt' (รอด) which means 'to be safe' in ST, but 'to reach' in NT, comes from the sentence 'bɨaŋ tiin nɔɔn rɔɔt miaŋ phrɛɛ' meaning "In the north he conquered (or he reached) the Province of Phrae."

In Inscription 2 we have the following words:

'tɔɔŋ caarɨit wái' (ต้องจารีตไว้) which means 'in conformity with tradition' in ST but it means an inscription was carved' in NT. 'tɔɔŋ' means 'carve' in Chuang.

'sǔŋ' (สุง) means 'a kiln.' Vickery (1986) says that this word is derived from Mon. In fact TN uses 'sǔŋ' for 'a fireplace.'

In Inscription 3, we have the following words:

'hǎa raŋ bɔɔk' (หารังบอก) comes from the sentence 'kham phrá phútthácâu rau hǎa raŋ bɔɔk wâi ʔeeŋ sái' meaning "*Lord Buddha himself did say it*." 'hǎa' means 'to seek' in ST but it means 'by oneself' following the White Tai. 'raŋ' means '*to build*' in ST but it should be translated as '*to do*' in an emphatic sense. 'bɔɔk' means to '*say*' in ST.

'kɛ̂ɛ' (แก้) means '*to untie*' in ST., but '*to explain*' in Chuang. The given sentence is 'phì mii khon thǎam daŋ níi...hâi kɛ̂ɛ wâa daŋ níi' meaning "*If anyone asks this question, let the answer be explained to him.*"

'khǎan' (ขาน) is '*utter yes*' in ST, but '*to answer*' in TN and Phake. In Inscription 2 there is a sentence '...hâi khǎan wâa daŋ níi' meaning "*...let it be answered thus.*"

In Inscription 5, we have the following words:

'pii lón hǒn pii sân' (ปีล้นหนปีสิ้น) was translated by Griswold and Na Nagara (1973:78) as "the years that are too long and changed them back to short years," because 'pii' means 'year', 'lón' means 'to overflow', 'hǒn' means 'to retreat' and 'pii sân' means '*short years.*' This corresponds with the translation of Inscription 4 by Coedès. But according to '*A Handbook for an Interpreter*' from the Ming Dynasty period, 'dian lón' (เดือนล้น) means '*an intercalary month.*' Thus, 'pii lón' must mean '*a year with an intercalary month*' and 'pii sân' means '*a short (lunar) year* (with 354 days),'

'phûuk' or 'fûuk' (พูก, ฟูก) means '*mattress*' in ST., but '*mat*' in TL. 'Mat' corresponds with the translation of Inscription 4 (inscribed in Cambodian) by Coedès. It may be concluded that the Thais in the 13th century slept on mats.

The following words are collected from Chuang to be used in reading Thai classical literature.

'pɔɔp' (ปอบ) means '*suck.*' Thus, 'phǐi pɔɔp' means '*a vampire spirit.*'

'blɔ̀ɔk' (บลอก) means *a flower* in Ahom and 'byɔɔk' pronoucing 'pyɔɔk' in Chuang.

'fáa dὲæt' (ฟ้าแดด) means *a bright sky.*

'phlûŋ' (พลุ่ง) means *'to burn'*, but in ST it means *'to burst out as steam.'* The full sentence is 'klàau thĭŋ tàwan cὲt ʔan phlûŋ naám lέæŋ khâi khɔ̀ɔt hăai' is found in **Lilit Ongkan Chaeng Nam** (1986:6) meaning *"the seven suns burnt until the water was entirely dried up."*

'taa tɔ̀ɔk' (ตาตอก) means *'one eye.'* comes from a sentence 'phráyaa ciaŋ thùuk phráyaa mæǽn taa tɔ̀ɔk khɔ̀ɔk fáa taa yɨ̀n khâa taai' meaning *"Phya Chueng was killed by Phya Maen, a one-eyed king, who came from far away."*

'thûŋ' (ทุ่ง) means *'a bucket.'* I learned this word when I was a boy but did not understand the meaning of 'thùŋ' in 'náam thùŋ' which is *'a water bucket.'*

'wâai' (ว่าย) means *'to turn, to rotate.'* This explains the phrase 'wian wâai taai kɔ̀ɔt' (เวียนว่ายตายเกิด) which means *'to whirl in a cycle of birth and rebirth.'*

From **'A Handbook for an Interpreter'** of the Ming Dynasty period, we have the following words:

'pɨ̀n' (ปืน) means 'bow and arrow.'

'pɨ̀n fai' (ปืนไฟ) means *'a cannon'* but in NET it means *'a bow with flaming arrows.'* These two words can help scholars in finding out whether there was a cannon or just a bow with flaming arrows in King Borom Trai Lokkanat's reign (1448-1488 A.D.).

'théeŋ' (เท้ง) is *'to pound with a fist, to punch.'* It comes from the sentence 'phɔɔ tæ̀æ kam mɨi théeŋ thæ̀n khrǽæŋ' in **Yuan Phaai** (1969:21) meaning *"only in pounding with a fist, the platform was trembled."*

'ʔɔɔn' (ออน) which means *'before or first'* comes from the phrase 'maa yùu nai miaŋ ʔɔɔn ʔùat klâa' in **Yuan Phaai** (1969:21) meaning *"to come to the city first, and (thus)to boast that he is brave.'*

References

Anonymous. 1969. *Yaun Phaai*. (in Thai poetry). Bangkok, Khlang Witthaya.

Anonymous. 1986. Lilit Ongkan Chaeng Nam. (in Thai Poetry) *Wannakam Samai Ayutthaya*. Vol. 1, pp. 3-22.

Committee on Historical Researches and Publications. 1978. *Inscriptions 1-15*. Bangkok, Office of the Prime Minister.

Griswold, Alexander B. and Prasert Na Nagara. 1973. Epigraphic and historical studies. No. 11, Part 1. *Journal of the Siam Society* 61.1, pp. 71-182.

Vickery, Michael. 1986. Some new evidences for the cultural history of Central Thailand. *Siam Society Newsletter* 2.3, pp. 4-6.

Yongbunkoet, Chaloem. 1968. *A Handbook for an Interpreter*. (in Thai). Bangkok, Thai Baep Rian.

The change in meaning of Pali and Sanskrit words used in Thai

Pathana Pengpala
Ramkhamhaeng University

Pali(Pl.) and Sanskrit(Sk.) are classified as Indo-European languages.They were disseminated from the Near East where the Aryan people lived to the Northern part of India. These two languages have been developed into the Ancient Indo-Aryan, the Middle and the Modern Indo-Aryan languages.

Sanskrit is considered to have evolved into the Ancient Indo-Aryan language. This is exhibited in The Veda Scriptures in Brahmanism or Hinduism. Pali, on the other hand, is viewed as the Middle Indo-Aryan. This is evidenced by the Tripitaka Scriptures of The Hinayana School in Buddhism. Sanskrit has served as a tool to write Brahmanism Scriptures and the scriptures belonging to the Mahayana School in Buddhism. Pali is used to write The scriptures of The Hinayana School in Buddhism.

The dissemination of Sanskrit occurred in Thailand prior to that of Pali. Pali was spread to Suvannabhumi (the present Thailand), having Nakhon Pathom as the capital after the Third Buddhist Council in 308 B.C. (B.E. 235). When King Sri-Indraditya declared Sukhothai as an independent country in 1257 A.D. (B.E.1800), Sanskrit already had an influence on that country. When The Ramkhamhaeng Inscription was created by King Ramkhamhaeng the Great in 1283 A.D. (B.E.1826), Pali and Sanskrit were already used in that Inscription.

Pali and Sanskrit words are derived from their roots. Each root has its own meaning, but it is not ready to be used. Each root must have inflection of nouns and verbs before it can be used for communication. Unlike Pali and Sanskrit, Thai(Th.) is categorised as an isolating language. Each morpheme has its own self-contained meaning and it can be used in that form. This attribute makes Thai distinguishable from Pali and Sanskrit. The impact of Pali and Sanskrit words on Thai are the most significant, taking other foreign languages, namely, English, French, Chinese, etc. into account. You may ask why Thai is so significantly influenced by Pali and Sanskrit despite the fact that Pali and Sanskrit and Thai belong to different language families. This is because Brahmanism and Buddhism which utilized these languages are credited with having such a great impact on Thai people and Thai culture.

Pali and Sanskrit words are widely used in both spoken and written Thai. Thai people of all walks of life use Pali and Sanskrit in their own language. Pali and Sanskrit words used in Thai range from words used in daily life, words used on formal occasions, special terminology of certain disciplines, and royal language. Thais use Pali and Sanskrit words so much that there is a saying: " If one deletes Pali and Sanskrit words from Thai, a crisis will arise" The vocabulary of the Thai language may not be adequate on its own.

Pali and Sanskrit have been integrated into Thai in many ways. The two most obvious ways are the sound alteration and the change in meaning. This paper will mainly focus on the latter. Each morpheme of Pali and Sanskrit carries meaning. One morpheme may impart one or several meanings. When Pali and Sanskrit words are used in Thai, they are partially or fully adopted.

First, there is the restriction of meaning. That is, the meaning of words from Pali and Sanskrit have become more specific in Thai than in the original language. They impart either bad or good connotation. Second, there is the extension of meaning. This phenomenon has resulted in the fact that words with specific meanings have been extended to have general meanings. In some cases, new meanings have been attached.

Third, there is the complete change in meaning. That is, some Pali and Sanskrit words used in Thai carry meanings totally different from the ones they originally conveyed. Finally, there is the change of the original sound in Thai from that of Pali and Sanskrit words. This sound alteration thereby represents a change in meaning.

The following are the illustrations of these four categories and their sub-categories.

      1. **The restriction of meaning**: This is evidenced by the fact that Pali and Sanskrit words originally conveyed a general meaning, but in Thai the meaning becomes specific. This aspect of change in meaning can by sub-categorized as follows:

      1.1 Entailing good/bad connotation and specific meaning

      1.1.1 Entailing good connotation: This means that some of Pali an Sanskrit words with general meaning have been replaced by the ones with only positive connotation.

Pali/Sanskrit and Thai transcription	Meaning in Pali and Sanskrit	Meaning in Thai
Th. kìríyaa Pl. kiriyā Sk. kriyā	act, deed, performance	good manner, good behavior
Th. wâatsànǎa Pl. vāsanā Sk. vāsanā	former impression, recollection of the past	good fortune, fame and wealth
Th. lâap Pl. lābh Sk. lābh	gain, receiving, acquisition	godsend, windfall
Th. kháti Pl. gati Sk. gati	going, career, course, passing onto another existence, destiny, behavior	a proverb, a saying for practice
Th. sàkun Pl. kula cultivated Sk. kula	family; clan; caste	good, noble, or family

      1.1.2 Entailing bad connotation: As opposed to 1.1.1 the meanings of some Pali and Sanskrit words with general meaning have been restricted to convey negative connotation.

Pali/Sanskrit and Thai transcription	Meaning in Pali and Sanskrit	Meaning in Thai
Th. kam Pl. kamma Sk. karma	a volitional action, action, deed, good and bad volition	bad fortune, bad destiny
Th. wíbâak Pl. vipāka Sk. vipāka	result, fruition, consequence of one's actions	misery, misfortune, suffering
Th. khrɔ́ Pl. gaha Sk. graha	carrying, holding, catching, taking, seizing, a planet, a house	bad luck, misfortune
Th. càrìt Pl. carita pretentious Sk. carita	behavior, character, life	being affected and (showing disapproval)
Th. săndaan Pl. santāna Sk. santāna	1 continuity, succession, 2 offspring, 3 a cobweb	bad habits inherited from one's past continuity. (showing disapproval)

1.1.3 Entailing specific meaning: In this case, the general meanings of some Pali and Sanskrit words have been specific without showing good or bad connotation as in1.1.1 and 1.1.2 above. For example:

Th. nímon Pl. nimanta Sk. nimantra	invitation	invitation for a monk

Th. ʔaarâatthanaa invitation, accomplishment, invitation for

Pl. ārādhanā	winning of favor.	a monk, to
Pali/Sanskrit transcription	Meaning in Pali and Sanskrit	Meaning in Thai
Sk. ārādhanā		give sermon or precepts
Th. ʔàatsàná Pl. āsana Sk. āsana	a seat, sitting down,	monks' seat, dais or raised platform for monks
Th. ʔaaphâat Pl. ābādha Sk. ābādha	disease	being ill, illness (used with a Buddhist monk)
Th. líkhìt Pl. likhita Sk. likhita	writing, cutting, scratching	books, letter (monk's letter)

1.2 Singling out meanings from Pali and Sanskrit words: Some words in Pali and Sanskrit carry many meanings. However, when they are used in Thai one of their meanings has been singled out. That is, one meaning remains to be widely used in Thai. For example:

Th. săŋhăan Pl. saṅhāra Sk. samhāra	destruction, devastation, outline, summary, stopping	destruction
Th. khawróp Pl. gārva Sk. gaurava	heaviness, depth, greatness, prosperity, respect	respect
Th. phûut Pl. bhūta Sk. bhūta	become, born, produced, an element, a ghost, living being, truth what has happened	a kind of ghost

Th. phâatchâná division, classification,   vessels, containers

Pali/Sanskrit and Thai transcription	Meaning in Pali and Sanskrit	Meaning in Thai

Pl. bhājana   a bowl, dish, vessel, a
Sk. bhājana   container

2. The extension of meaning:

2.1 Some words in Pali and Sanskrit are used in a narrow sense. They, however, are extended to have general meanings. For example:

Th. khoŋkhaa   The Ganges River   rivers(in general),
Pl. gaṅga   water
Sk. gaṅga

Th. dontrii   string instruments   music (in general)
Pl. tanti
Sk. tanti, tantri

Th. booríween a separated residence of   a restricted area
Pl. pariveṇa   monks, a place for religious
Sk. pariveṇa   learning

2.2 Adding a new meaning to the original one: This means that a new meaning is added to the original meaning.

Th. phrommácaarii one who leads a holy or   a virgin
Pl. brahmacaři   chaste life
Sk. brahmacarin

Th. thêetsànǎa to preach   scold
Pl. desanā   to give a semon   to rebuke,
Sk. desanā   to castigate

Th. prànaam   paying respect   blame

Pl. paṇama

Sk. praṇama

Pali/Sanskrit and Thai transcription	Meaning in Pali and Sanskrit	Meaning in Thai
Th. săŋwâat Pl. sanvāsa Sk. sanvāsa	communion	sexual intercourse
Th. maalaa Pl. mālā Sk. mālā	discipline, flowers	a hat
Th. kàmon Pl. kamala Sk. kamala	a lotus	heart

3. **The total change of meaning**: This phenomenon indicates the complete change of meaning from the original one.

Th. ʔàpprii Pl. appiya Sk. apriya	not dear, not beloved, not pleasant	vulgar, malicious, spiteful, wanton
Th. ʔànàat Pl. anātha Sk. anātha	miseralbe, helpless	pitiable, pathetic agitation
Th. ʔìtchǎa Pl. iccā	wish, desire	envy
Th. ʔaacom Pl. ācama Sk. ācama	cleaning, something that should be cleaned	human excrement, the faeces, the stool
Th. sàwâat	taste, flavor, savor	love

Pl. sāda

Sk. svāda

Pali/Sanskrit and Thai transcription	Meaning in Pali and Sanskrit	Meaning in Thai
Th. ʔaakhom	1 coming, approach,	magic
Pl. āgama	2 religion, scripture	
Sk. āgama	3 an inserted consonant	

Th. ʔànètʔànàat	unstable, not lasting,	grief-stricken,
Pl. anicca anāth	helpless	wretched
Sk. anitya anāth		

4. **Sound alteration leading to a change in meaning**: For example Pali words may be pronounced differently from those of Sanskrit but they convey the same meanings. The opposite is true: if a Pali word and Sanskrit word are pronounced similarly, they impart different meanings. When it comes to their use in Thai, their sounds are slightly changed. Hence, their meanings are also altered. For example:

Th. ʔànàat	feel sorry, to pit, to be sympathetic with, to be
dismissed	
Th. ʔànaathăa	without someone to lean on, without parents, destitute
Pl. anātha	helpless
Sk. anātha	

Th. sămphaará	supplies, belongings, supporting, up-bringing
Th. sŏmphaan	an abbot, virtue, or merits accumulated
Pl. sambhāra	collection, compilation,
Sk. sambhāra	materials, commodities

Pali/Sanskrit and Thai transcription	Meaning in Pali and Sanskrit	Meaning in Thai
Th. pràweenii		having a sexual intercourse
Th. pràpheenii		a tradition,a custom
Pl. pavēṇi	a custom, a pattern,	
Sk. pravēṇi	a wig	sexual intercourse,
Th. wíthii		a proverb, a way, a means,a tradition, a custom
Th. phíthii		a rite,a ritual, a ceremony
Pl. vidhi	method, way, luck, destiny;	
Sk. vidhi	form	
Th. kháฺtĭ		role model, ways, principles,departure
Th. khádii		a lawsuit, a case
Pl. gati	going; career; course;	
Sk. gati	destiny; behaviour; passing onto another existence	
Th. phaawá		condition, state, circumstances
Th. phâap		a picture, drawing, a sketch,a painting, a photograph, a sight, scenery, an image
Pl. bhāva	condition, nature, becoming	
Sk. bhāva		

Pali/Sanskrit and Thai transcription	Meaning in Pali and Sanskrit	Meaning in Thai
Th. râatsàdɔɔn		people in a state or a country
Th. rát		a region, a domain, a state, a country
Pl. raṭṭha	a state, people in a state,	
Sk. raṣṭra	a region, a domain	
Th. thrítsàdii		a theory
Th. thiṭṭhì		opinion,
		conviction, pride, stubborness
Pl. diṭṭhi	idea, opinion, theory, view,	
Sk. drṣṭi	belief; speculation, dogma	

To sum up, the change in meaning of Pali and Sanskrit words used in Thai is four-dimensional: (1) the restriction of meaning, (2) the extension of meaning, (3) the total change of meaning from the original word, and (4) the change of meaning caused by sound alteration.

References

Anuman Rajadhon, Phraya. 1972. *Philology*. Bangkok, Aksonthai.

Banchob Bandhumedha. 1979. *Influences of Pali and Sanskrit in Thai*. Bangkok, Ramkhamhaeng University Press.

Banerji, S.C. 1964. *Introduction to Pali Literature*. Culcatta, Punthi Prestok.

Bapat, P.V.1959. *Buddhist Literature; General, 2500 Years of Buddhism*. New Delhi, Publication Division, Ministry of Information and Broadcasting.

Barau, Anomadarshi, (Bhikshu).1965. *Introduction to Pali*. Varanasi, Pracya Bharati Pakasan.

Buddhadatta Mahathera, A.P. 1957. *Concise of Pali-English Dictionary*. Columbo, Apothecaries' Co., Ltd.

Chanthaburinaruenat, Krommaphra, (His Royal Highness Prince Kitiyakara). 1972. *Pali-Thai-English-Sanskrit Dictionary*. Bangkok, Maha Makut Ratchawitthayalai.

Davids, Rhys T.W. and William Stede. 1966. *The Pali Text's Pali-English Dictionary*. London, The Pali Text Society.

Geiger, William.1968. *Pali Literature and Language*. Delhi, Oriental Books Reprint Corporation.

Gune, G.P.1962. *An Introduction to Comparative Philology*. Poona, Poona Oriental Book House.

Kamchai Thonglor. 1994. *Principles of the Thai Language*. Bangkok, Ruamsan.

Keith Berriedale, A.A.1973. *History of Sanskrit Literature*. Delhi, Oxford University Press.

Macdonell, Arthur A. 1971. *A History of Sanskrit Literature*. Delhi, Motilal Banarsidass.

Malalasikera, G.P. 1958. *The Pali Literature of Ceylon*. Columbo, M.D. Gunasena & Co. Ltd.

Plaek Sandhiraksa. 1963. *Dictionary of Pali-Thai.* Bangkok, Thai Wattana Panich.

Rajvaramuni, Phra (Prayudh Payutto) 1977. *A Dictionary of Buddhism*. Bangkok, The Religious Affairs Department.

Royal Institute of Thailand, The. 1987. *Thai Dictionary*. Bangkok, The Royal Institute.

So Sethaputra 1965. *New Model Thai-English Dictionary*. Bangkok, Thai Wattana Panich.

Sujib Punnanubhab 1961. *Dictionary of Buddhism*: Bangkok, Maha Makut Ratchawitthayalai.

Suthiwong Pongphaiboon. 1974. *Pali-Sanskrit-Related with the Thai Language*. Bangkok, Thai Wattana Panich.

Sathian Phothinan.1970. *A History of Buddhism*. Bangkok, Phosamton.

Uppakitsinlapasan, Phraya 1971. *Principles of the Thai Language*. Bangkok, Thai Wattana Panich.

Wooler, Alfred, C. 1975. *Introduction to Prakrit.* Delhi, Motilal Banarsidass.

Semantics in a holistic context -- with preliminary convictions and approaches

Kenneth L. Pike
Summer Institute of Linguistics

ABSTRACT: The study of semantics is related to the study of human behavior. Understanding meaning requires an appreciation of cultural needs and differences. In these, the person is involved in understanding, recognizing, and reacting to personal-social situations and their contents. In this sense, person gets priority above logic, and meaning involves multiple relations to multiple components or complex situations.

Some of the starting points for such a view are best stated as beliefs, or convictions, about human nature, rather than as the result of "proving" them by logical argument. From such starting points, the person wishing to understand human nature can begin some approaches to his/her study.

CONVICTION I: MEANING REQUIRES THAT SOME PERSON BE INVOLVED.

We start with the belief that meaning is not something abstractly "floating in the sky", with no people around. Rather it somehow joins person to thing, person to situation, person to understanding--or failing to understand--some part of the world. There is an "outside" objective world to be observed--but it is known only when it is known, in part, to a person. As the philosopher Kant pointed out ([1985] 1938), years before I had independently stumbled on to that fact, we do not know the thing in itself, but in relation to an observer (with us as observers).

Conviction Ia: The person has (and in part comprises) a "self". One can choose, e.g., to write an article, or to discuss linguistic theory, or to forgive (or condemn) someone who has damaged him. Kearney, an anthropologist, says (1954:68) that 'The first requirement for a world view is the presence of a *Self*--discernibly distinct from its environment, which I refer to as the *Other*.'

It is the presence of the self in relation to the world which allows us to have a holistic view of that world which includes us. Only a self can discuss such features as we are treating here. A shepherd dog can track a sheep much better than we can. But it does not write a book about it. And for a total holism (not a "fractionated" one), in my view, religion must enter in some way. A "secular" religion may assume that the self is somehow purely physical in its origin and outworking. A theistic view (which I hold) would treat the soul as distinct from body or mind, but integrating both in its decisions and actions. But, under any theory, it seems to me, the mind must somehow be given the power to influence body actions to some degree. Mind and body must both be included in a holistic approach to human behavior.

Conviction Ib: In order to understand an adult, the research scholar must in some sense first understand a child. It is the child, not the adult, who first learns through social interaction in a physical environment how to live in a culture. The Danish linguist Louis Hjelmslev told me that the reason for their considering Danish important for them was that a person "learns his moral structure at his mother's knee". It is the child who learns a deep-ingrained understanding of his culture. It is the child who learns his mother tongue as part of that culture.

Conviction Ic: Language is a crucial factor in establishing a cultural identity. The coherence of a community is more likely to involve a shared language than any other feature known to me. A positive contribution of language difference is specifically that it gives coherence to a community. In addition, it can be one of the greatest incentives to resist the tyranny of a single larger community. A negative feature, on the other hand, is that it divides the world community, where it would be nice if we could all understand one another, agree with one another and not fight with one another!

Conviction Id: The early naming of things, events, people, attitudes, situations, or other items is crucial to the ability of a child to be human (not just a "shepherd dog"). A holistic view of human nature must give this characteristic very high priority. Language, involving naming, is like a cultural "telephone exchange", without which a normal human society could not exist. (An animal society has a degree of communication, although it does not go to "graduate school" to study physics.)

The meaning of something, whether it be a name, or an event, or a situation, involves the reaction of a person (or persons, or society) involved, or observing, or thinking about it.

CONVICTION II: A PERSONAL PERSPECTIVE CAN FOCUS TEMPORARILY ON STATIC, OR DYNAMIC, OR RELATIONAL COMPONENTS OF A SITUATION.

We start with the belief that a person does not on every occasion look at a thing in the same way. A person can choose to look on a thing as if it were isolated, unchanging, and in a "permanent" form--even when that person knows very well that the item is in fact changing or changeable. The ability to choose to change perspective is part of human nature.

Conviction IIa: A person can choose to focus on an entity as if it were a particle. If the entity is viewed as a particle, it may be seen "as if" it were for the moment "static". In that case, it could be seen as a member of a list, or as a point (somewhat isolated), or in a sequence (in a line or in time). The particle is a structural thing, and comprises a part of the identification of a larger including item which is also seen as a particle, hierarchically. A chile viewed as a whole is seen as a particle. So, also, is a football game; of a "hunch"; or dream. This view (or any other view) of these items is part of their meaning-of-the-moment for the observer.

Conviction IIb: A person can choose to focus on an
entity as if it were a wave. The entity so viewed can be
thought of as changing, as part of a sequence, or as
developing to or from a nucleus, or as dynamic. The wave
can be growing, or decaying, as part of a larger process
involving the situation. When the child is looked at in
relation to its current visible changing characteristics
(getting more beautiful, for example), it is being looked at
from the wave perspective. So, also, is a baseball game
when one is watching its final inning when a player is in the
actual, momentary, process of making the winning run. The
process feature is part of the significance, and hence of the
semantic impact, on the observer.

Conviction IIc: A person can choose to focus on an
entity as if it were primarily a point in a larger pattern or
system, i.d., as a part of--or as comprising--a field. The
entity so viewed can be thought of as existing in relation to
the larger pattern, rather than being felt as somehow
"existing autonomously" in thought or "isolatable objective
reality". The field can be organized multi-dimensionally,
with its parts in intersecting relations one to another
simultaneously in the still-larger organized field context.
The shape of the baseball diamond is not only called the
"field" but is itself, semantically here, a field structure. So,
also, is the planned (by the coach) constituency of the team
as a whole. Holism, in linguistic semantics, requires whole
elements of systems of behavior, as well as of background,
and of the containing of larger systems.

Conviction IId: Units, as observed by a person,
include entities of various types, e.g., things, actions,
attributes. Each can be perceived as a particle, or a wave, or
a field (or a point in a field). Things are objectively (or
imaginatively) seen as physical chunks, which can in general
be touched or stared at (or thought about as if they could be
touched if one were close enough to do so). Actions are
movements of things, in which the process of change can be
observed. Attributes are characteristics of things such that
the observer can mentally abstract those components, and

talk about them as if they were in fact separable entities in themselves--"fatness" can be seen as a characteristic of a weighty person; "redness" can be perceived as a certain color of a thing via the light waves being physically reflected; and "unicorn" would be an animal mythically depicted, generally, "with the body and head of a horse, the hind legs of a stag, the tail of a lion, and a single horn in the middle of the forehead" (Webster's Collegiate, 10th ed., 1993:1291).

CONVICTION III: KNOWING ABOUT A CULTURE REQUIRES ASKING QUESTIONS OF PEOPLE, LISTENING TO THEM, AND OBSERVING HOW THEY REACT VERBALLY TO DIFFERENT SITUATIONS.

We start, also, with the belief that in order to understand a culture, we must hear what people say about situations and events, either by listening to them talk to each other, or by listening carefully as to what they say in response to our questions (which must be carefully formed, to be polite in relation to that culture).

Conviction IIIa: As people talk to each other about incidents which have occurred within their community, we can learn a lot about their interpretation of the motivation for such actions, or about their moral evaluation of such actions. In some contexts, people discuss things they approve of, or of things which they condemn. Human nature is sufficiently uniform that in every culture there is approval of some ways of helping others, but disapproval of other actions, which are treated as theft or as immoral behavior.

Such discussion, or presence of some gossip, is a human universal. The anthropologist Haviland (1977) gives us a book-length discussion of such situations. For example, he maintains (p. 170) that "one can gossip only in a culture one is competent in"; and (p. 163) "Gossip trades on rules and [on] 'should' statements,...and [on] throwing out other behavior by condemning it. [Whereas] the ethnographer makes do with only the brute facts of observed regularities."

In the Mixtec language of San Miguel el Grande, Oaxaca, Mexico (where I studied the language over a period of several years), various kinds of action, when talked about in the village, can lead to a person being ostracized: e.g., refusal to vote correctly, allowing surgery on a son, which may be interpreted as responsibility for later damage; discovered theft; or adultery. These lead to treatment that I have called (Pike 1986) loss of "credit rating" in the community.

Conviction IIIb: Granted that there are absolute general universals in all languages and cultures, nevertheless each culture has its own specific cultural forms and restraints, which may be said to be emic ones, as reacted to from inside that culture, versus the etic structures as noted by outsiders (which may or may not parallel the emic ones in part). Goodman (1978:x) says that "What emerges can perhaps be described as a radical relativism under rigorous restraints". And anthropologist Goodenough (1981:108-09) uses these concepts of the etic and the emic "as crucial for cultural theory".

The terms emic and etic were introduced by Pike (1954 Section 2) to parallel culturally the terms phonemic and phonetic (and to be created by abbreviating those words). In English, for example, the difference between /p/ and /b/ makes a difference between words such as "buy" and "pie"; but in Mixtec, no such difference occurs. To be emically different, nonlinguistic emic units must also be contrastive in that culture--as baseball differs from croquet. In order to behave properly in a culture, a person must know its emic structure. (See Alvarez-Pereyre & Arom 1993:7-33 for an extensive discussion, by four authors, of the relation of emics and etics to ethnomusicology.)

CONVICTION IV: FOLKTALES NEED TO BE UNDERSTOOD WITH HELP FROM INVOLVED MEMBERS OF A COMMUNITY, IN RELATION TO THE CONTENT OF THE TALES, THEIR TIME AND

PLACE OF USE, THE PURPOSE FOR WHICH THEY ARE TOLD, AND THE WORLD VIEW BEHIND THEM.

Anthropologist Dundes stated some years ago (1968:467) that "For most of the thousands of song and folktale texts recorded in the ethnographic literature, there is either no interpretation at all or else a passing speculative comment or two provided by the collector who tells what he thinks the song or tale means." Sparing, more recently (1984:47, 27), addresses "interpersonal relationships", and "the character, life, beliefs, and world view of the community".

In relation to Mixtec folktales, I have drawn on a number of them published by Dyk (1959). But I had extensive discussion about them, both in Mixtec and in Spanish, with a local speaker (whom I will call AM, since he prefers that his name not be mentioned). I could ask about the reaction to these tales from his grandfather, his father, and twenty-six grandchildren. Here, I am using only one of the tales (with the analytical data taken from Pike 1988:392-93).

(For further kinds of components needed for a fuller description, see Conviction VIII, below.)

Conviction IVa: Every emic unit needs, in its description, a mention of its class--i.e., its name or contents in relation to the larger set of other items (including phonology, grammar, and referential materials) that might be found appropriately in a comparable position in that language and culture.

The name of this folktale is "The Skunks Look for a Godfather". This is one of a member of the class of stories about animals. Its content: The skunk couple seek a godfather to go with them to have the child baptized. They recruit a lion--but the lion refuses at the feast to eat worms. So they search for food appropriate for the lion. For that purpose, the skunk tries to kill an ox, which is lying down, by spraying on it. But the skunk gets gored and dies. All the folk cry.

Conviction IVb: Every emic unit needs in its description a mention of its slot--i.e., a particular position (or set of alternate positions) in a larger social or linguistic context in which the unit is customarily used or mentioned.

The skunk tale is likely to be used by the Mixtecs at a feast, or at a lunch for workmen, where there is not enough food.

Conviction IVc: Every emic unit needs in its description a statement of its purpose, or role, or cause, explaining or constituting the function of the tale or the use of the tale.

The skunk tale may be used to shame people, or to put indirect pressure on them to take better care of their neighbors. It sometimes can also be used as a joke--but it will be poorly received if there is not enough food!

Conviction IVd: Every emic unit needs in its description a statement of the broader background structure, or belief, or experience, or cultural system--its cohesion--within which the tale takes place, and which in part controls the use or the form of the tale.

The skunk tale has as a background a belief system regarding baptism and the culturally appropriate relations to godfather and society. If the parents cannot provide food at the fiesta, it causes shame.

(For a much more complicated setting, with a tale told during a wake, combined with the acting out of the tale, with the audience taking a part in the action, see Howland 1981.)

CONVICTION V: PROCEDURES MAY SPROUT FROM TRUE PRINCIPLES--AND PRINCIPLES MAY GROW FROM USEFUL PROCEDURES.

Sometimes one hears of a theoretical hunch suggested by a scholar, and is able to try to apply it successfully. On the other hand, one sometimes, through trial and error, manages to get some work done without understanding just why the procedure worked; this can lead to philosophical reflection to try to arrive at principles which would explain the "result". There may be a "cycle" between principle and procedure and principle. We must be ready to move in whichever direction seems needed--or possible--or fun!--at the moment.

Conviction Va: The procedure of starting to learn a language without an interpreter, while using gestures and pointing at things, or acting, is very workable. I have done it many times, since my first attempt for my students in 1936. Usually, within half an hour, one can get a dozen words, a few noun phrases, a few clauses, a sentence or two, and know one is "under way". (For a video sample, see my Program No. 5: "Into the Unknown", in the University of Michigan Television Center series "Pike on Language", 1977.) A statement given by the language helper during the process, after one has pointed at something, may be called an "observation sentence". The philosophers Quine and Ullian ([1970] 1978:28) affirm that it is ultimately through observation sentences "that language gets its meaning, its bearing on reality. This is why it is that they convey the basic evidence for all belief, all scientific theory". This is an instance where a somewhat "accidental" approach has proved very useful--and has received philosophical acknowledgment as to its theoretical importance. (It was accidental, in that I began to learn Mixtec in a village where I was not using an interpreter, but was learning the language directly; later I applied this in the classroom, as mentioned.)

Conviction Vb: Procedures for the growth of knowledge must start with the child; knowledge must build on experience, but the growth from experience must increase via metaphor. Knowledge must be steadily "expansive"--adding to experience. but that addition comes when the child (or grown-up "adult child") compares its experience, or knowledge, including its knowledge of the past by "heard" history, with a bit of the current unknown, and hence makes the new partly intelligible. We cannot understand the "new" directly without this help.

This makes "basic" vocabulary, with its early experience, foundational to advanced knowledge, and in that sense as "basic" as that advanced knowledge itself. As Einstein said, in a discussion with a philosopher (1950), the word "table" is as basic as any word in physics.

This importance of childhood learning, or leaning as does a child, is as true in religion as it is in physics. For example, Jesus said (Mark 10:15, Living Bible) that "[Anyone] who refuses to come to God as a little child will never be allowed into his Kingdom".

Literature discussing the importance of metaphor is vast--I have barely begun to skim it. For example, note Brown and Witowski (1981:599, 600) who list metaphors in 25 different languages for the "human/pupil of the eye"; with eleven other languages using metaphors of seed, instead of humanness. Or note Büky (1984:784-85) with metaphors treated semiotically, with lists of different concept categories where a first concept is compared to a second.

Conviction Vc: Language uses metaphor as a tool to build abstract concepts and world view. Babies perceive, touch, hear, with innate capacities to learn to recognize things and movements. But to move from "a stumble" to a more abstract treatment of a failure as generalized to the broader situation in some business requires metaphorical capacity. Tyler said (1978:50) that "Our new visions of the world are metaphoric; we bring into contact concepts that were hitherto remote and unconnected; we predict new things of old concepts". An extensive discussion of metaphors and concepts we "live by" is seen in Lakoff and Johnson (1980).

Conviction Vd: Poetry utilizes metaphorical development to let the reader connect things or views which may be of potential interest to him, but which may not have been thought of as related in that way. Riming word pairs may force such a connection. Suppose I try it, here, using "pain/gain" to suggest an unexpected value from the hurt; and using "grow/sow" to force parallelism between the relation of trees to seed and of thoughts to their development out of pain:

> My foot is in pain
> But that is gain
> If thought may grow
> From seed which pain can sow.

And somewhere--I have lost the reference--the American poet Frost suggested that metaphors (or the like) are a ladder by which we climb to the sky. (For the detailed hierarchical tamemic phonological analysis of a poem, including its voice quality, see Pike and Pike 1983, Chapter 2.)

CONVICTION VI: THE THREE HIERARCHIES OF PHONOLOGY, GRAMMAR, AND REFERENCE INTERLOCK AND ALLOW FOR EXPERIMENTAL VARIATION WITHIN THE EMIC LOCAL STRUCTURE OF THEIR LEVELS.

One expects to find, in any language, three kinds of language structure in which parts make up wholes with differing levels of increasingly larger structures.

The phonological hierarchy has emic relevant sounds (phonemes) in its system, which are included in a larger unit, a kind of emic syllable (with consonants and vowels); which are included in some kind of rhythm unit containing one of more syllables that, in turn, enters still larger phonological units up to a special phonological kind of text (e.g., as a limerick, in English, may have a particular phonological pattern of rhythm and rime). (For the levels of rhythm in a phonological hierarchy treated as a "metrical constitutent structure" see linguist Everett 1988.)

The grammatical hierarchy is the structure from morpheme to word to phrase to clause to sentence to paragraph and to text or conversation. (And the limerick, in turn, may have typical grammatical characteristics, beginning, for example, with "There was an old [person] from [place])". The grammatical order is the order of "telling".

188

The <u>referential order</u>, on the contrary, is the order of "<u>happening</u>". And the referential material is structured in numerous simultaneous hierarchies of social or personal or language data--e.g., <u>kinship systems</u>, <u>social systems</u>, <u>personal appearance</u> and <u>personal form</u>, and <u>chronological history</u> of happenings. (For a sample analysis of the referential versus the grammatical structure of a text, in tagmemic structural holistic terms, see Evelyn G. Pike 1992.)

<u>Conviction VIa: Although the three hierarchies are structurally different in their function, they are simultaneously present in speech or action, and may share some of the forms in an overlapping manner</u>. That is, the physical material may simultaneously belong to more than one of the hierarchies--either with beginnings and endings in some instances the same, or with the divisions between their respective units coming at different points in the spoken or acted sequence.

<u>Humor</u> often exploits this fact with <u>puns</u> in which two words may share the same pronunciation but different lexical (referential) meanings. For example, a fisherman is said to have read a sign at the river as "Don't fish hear?", although, in fact, the sign was "Don't fish here!" So, the fisherman said to himself "I don't know", and he went on fishing. (See Pike 1981:32-37 for a more detailed discussion of this pun.)

<u>Conviction VIb: By experimental syntax one can artificially re-tell a story in a different order, changing the telling order (the grammatical form) but preserving unchanged the happening being discussed (the referential structure)</u>. This allows a change of <u>focus</u>, through grammatical change, without changing the (referential) event as such. For a simple instance, note the following story (taken from Pike 1983): "(a) John came home. (b) He ate supper. (c) He went to the movies." By shifting the order to (c)(b)(a) one gets: "(c) John went to the movies. (b) But before that he had eaten his supper, (a) after coming home." This shifts the focus to the movie event. In scores of

languages of Papua New Guinea, however, one cannot change the order in this way--and no word for "after" is available! Nonetheless, focus can be changed by using a different technique--by saying "Coming home, and eating supper, John went to the movie." (For a more extensive discussion of a different re-telling of a story with three participants involved see Pike 1981: 47-63. For some twenty further samples and discussions of experimental syntax in various languages and in a variety of circumstances, with material which might also be useful for language learning and teaching, see Pike 1993b.)

Conviction VIc: Paraphrase is a form of alternative grammatical (and phonological) expression of the same referential material. Paraphrase is intended to preserve or summarize the meaning as intended by the original speaker, and as acceptable to him/her, yet to put that meaning in a form which differs from, or changes, the focus or emphasis, in order to meet the summarizing needs of the listener. A student, for example, may be told by a teacher to "tell me in your own words what I have said"--and may do so by paraphrase acceptable to both. (An exact quotation would not suit an American teacher who would feel that the student had not understood the information if he/she could not rephrase it.)

Conviction VId: From this perspective, translation is one kind of paraphrase, in the sense that the grammatical form of the second language may require a different order. Some lexical referential material may also need to be added or substituted, because of the different knowledge and lexical structure of speakers of the second language. Metaphors, also, may be quite different from language to language, and affect translation acceptability. Since translation relates language to language via structure and meaning, translation is one kind of linguistics.

Conviction VIe: Whether in paraphrase, or in translation, or in general language learning, or in the ordinary social use of a language, both form and meaning are necessary for adequate results. An attempt to express meaning without using language (or some other symbolic means, such as gesture) is pointless. So, also, an assumption that one can use language socially with no attempt either to imply or to interpret meaning or purpose or intention must fail to lead to normal communication.

A holistic view of semantics in a linguistic context requires a holistic view of language structure, including relation of units to class, slot, role, and cohesion (see Section IVa-d), and relation to hierarchies of phonology, grammar, and reference. An approach to sign systems, which in semantic areas is somewhat holistic also, is semiotics, about which there is a large literature. As an interesting application of semiotics to the theatre and drama, see Elam 1980. For an excellent summary of semiotic development, see Sebeok 1991.

CONVICTION VII: PERSON HAS PRIORITY OVER LOGIC IN DETERMINING THE EMIC VALIDITY OF SOCIAL PATTERNS.

Conviction VIIa: Personal judgement must precede valid logical decision. The philosopher Angus Sinclair taught me years ago (1951), in personal discussion, that no truly basic premise can be proved. In the syllogism "All men are mortal; Socrates is a man; therefore Socrates is mortal", the conclusion is logically valid. For it to be known to be true, however, the premises such as "All men are mortal" must also be true. But to prove, logically, that these are true, further syllogisms are necessary--and they also may be valid but not "proved" in themselves. Eventually, Sinclair pointed out, one gets so far back in the discussion that one does not know how to get the premises any further back. Then one must resort to lower-level discussion utilizing a kind of metaphorical approach: "It is somewhat like this-- but not totally"; etc. If this is true, it follows that we, as persons, must first start with unproved beliefs before we can develop logically. (Note, in Sections Ib and Va, reference to the child as a starting point. Compare, also, philosopher Pepper--[1942] 1970:94--who shows that "a world theory" begins with a "root metaphor fresh from vital common sense". And, [p. 112], "If a man is to be creative in the construction of a new world theory he must dig among the crevices of common sense".)

Conviction VIIb: We need a belief system we can "live by", not merely argue by. For this, we need to start with a holistic view, growing from the unproved starting understanding of a child and building by metaphor to an adult abstract but applicable set of convictions. For this to be workable across cultures, however, there must be universals present that, in spite of variation within them, include moral components which can often be recognized across cultures. (See Pike 1972 for the relevance of this to debate with persons in disagreement.)

Conviction VIIc: Every culture grants that some things are "bad"; but the bad is always the deterioration of the good; it is never really original (Pike 1993a:63-76). Across cultures one expects to find objection to taking items felt to belong to someone else, or to sexual mis- conduct locally defined, or to the misrepresentation of truth, or to the mistreatment of persons in one's friendship circle. I have been surprised to find how quickly persons in a foreign culture may recognize kindness in a visitor, even if his habits are very different or even, temporarily, unintelli- gible to them.

Courts of law must rely on some such underlying feeling in the local culture. A jury is expected to react radically differently to an action which is obviously an intended murder (e.g., by using an automobile for that purpose) versus an action which is accidental and unintend- ed. The personal relation is at stake here (and, in tagmemic terms, note especially the role cell, cf. Section IVc, above).

CONVICTION VIII: MEANING IS NOT MADE UP OF SHARPLY SEPARATED BITS, BUT OF OVERLAPPING COMPONENTS, AS IN AN IRREGULAR "VENN DIAGRAM".

Conviction VIIIa: Variation is normal for the meaning of a word when it occurs in different contexts. The word "run" is different in meaning in the sentence "He ran home" versus "He ran the business". The wave component leaves room for this concept (cf. Conviction IIb).

Conviction VIIIb: Different contexts may contribute different meanings to (or force the selection among meanings of) a word or statement. The grammatical position of object, for the phrase "the business" in the preceding paragraph, plus the implicit referential context of a business structure, combine with the meaning of "activity in a direction" in that sentence to give the actual meaning, there, of "run". Compare the statement of the phenomenologist Ricoeur (1978:142) that we point "to the semantic event as to the point of intersection between several semantic lines; this construction is the means by which all the words taken together make sense". (The way a verb paradigm may have irregular overlapping phonological bits in rows and columns, and yet have the meaning unambiguous when the intersection of the rows and columns is looked at as a whole, can be seen in the Fore of Papua New Guinea [Pike 1963]. The technique has then been elaborated in Pike and Simons [1993] to show how these irregular formations can be used for reconstructing a language family when the smaller phonological bits may not be as readily visible.)

Conviction VIIIc: Complexity of structure is sometimes easier to understand than is apparent simplicity of form. It might be easier to understand the function of a head as a whole, than it is of a pimple on the face. The logician Langer said [1973:185, 2nd ed.], in an introduction to symbolic logic: "If we chance upon a fairly complex and even surprising proposition, from which very many simple ones would follow, we are perfectly justified in taking the former as a postulate and deriving the others from it". It is precisely this position that I have been taking here in affirming the value of dealing with holistic semantics in holistic contexts.

SUMMARY: Meaning in its more complex forms, involves the <u>interaction</u> of academic modules of phonology with referent lexicon in purpose or rimes. It also involves interaction of sound and grammars--or grammar and referential cognitive material.

REFERENCES

Alvarez-Pereyre, Frank, and Simha Arom. 1993. Ethonomusicology and the emic/etic issue. The World of Music 35(1).7-33.

Brown, Cecil H., and Stanley R. Witkowski. 1981. Figurative language in universalist perspective. American Ethnologist 8.3.596-615.

Büky, Béla. 1984. The system of metaphors semiotically considered. Semiotics Unfolding, ed. by Tasso Borbé, 783-90. Berlin: Mouton.

Dundes, Alan. 1968. Every man his way: Readings in cultural anthropology. Englewood Cliffs, N.J.: Prentice-Hall.

Dyk, Anne. 1959. Mixeco texts. Norman, Okla.: Summer Institute of Linguistics.

Elam, Keir. 1980. The semiotics of theatre and drama. London: Methuen.

Einstein, Albert. 1950. A letter from Dr. Albert Einstein, in Essays in Physics, 1952, by Hebert L. Samuel, 157-62. New York: Harcourt, Brace and Co.

Everett, Daniel L. 1988. On metrical constitutent structure in Parahã phonology. Natural Language and Linguistic Theory 6.207-46.

Goodenough, Ward H. 1981. Culture, language, and society. Menlo Park, Calif.: Benjamin-Cummings.

Goodman, Nelson. 1978. Ways of worldmaking. Indianappolis: Hackett Publishing Co.

Haviland, John Beard. 1977. Gossip, reputation, and knowledge in Zinacantan. Chicago: University of Chicago Press.

Howland, Lilian G. 1981. Communicational integration of reality and fiction. Language and Communication 1.89-148.

Kant, Immanuel. [1785] [1938] 1966. The fundamental principles of the metaphysic of ethics. Otto Manthey-Zorn, translator. New York: Appleton-Century-Crofts.

Kearney, Michael. 1984. World view. Novato, Calif.: Chandler and Sharp.

Lakoff, George, and Mark Johnson. 1980. Metaphors we live by. Chicago: University of Chicago Press.

Langer, Susanne K. [1937] 1953, 2nd ed. An introduction to symbolic logic. New York: Dover Publications.

The Living Bible, paraphrased. 1971. Translated by Ken Taylor. Wheaton, Ill.: Tyndale House Publishers.

Merriam Webster's Collegiate Dictionary. 1993, tenth edition, Mish, editor-in-chief. Springfield, Mass.: Merriam-Webster.

Pepper, Stephen C. [1942] 1970. World hypotheses--a study in evidence. Berkeley: University of California Press.

Pike, Evelyn G. 1992. How I understand a text--via the structure of the happenings and the telling of them. Discourse Description, William C. Mann and Sandra A. Tompson eds., 227-61. Amsterdam/Philadelphia: John Benjamins.

Pike, Kenneth L. 1954, 1955, 1960, Vols. I-III; first edition, Language in relation to a unified theory of the structure of human behavior. Glendale Calif.: Summer Institute of Linguistics; 1967, second edition, The Hague: Mouton.

----. 1963. Theoretical implications of matrix permutation in Fore (New Guinea). Anthropological Linguistics 5.8.1-23.

----. 1972. Morals and metaphor. Interchange 12.228-31.

----. 1977. Program No. 5: Into the unknown [Learning an unknown language by gesture--a monolingual

demonstration]. Ann Arbor: University of
Michigan Television Center.

----. 1981. Tagmemics, discourse, and verbal art.
Michigan Studies in the Humanities, ed. Richard
W. Bailey. Ann Arbor: University of Michigan.

----. 1983. Experimental syntax: A basis for some new
language-learning exercises. Arab Journal of
Language Studies 1.2.245-55.

----. 1986. Mixtec social "credit rating"--the particular
versus the universal in one emic world view.
Proceedings of the National Academy of Sciences
83.3047-49.

----. 1987. The relation of language to the world.
International Journal of Dravidian Linguistics.
14.1.77-98.

----. 1988. Cultural relativism in relation to constraints on
world view--an emic perspective. Bulletin of the
Institute of History and Philosophy 59.2.385-99.
Taipei, Taiwan: Academia Sinica.

----. 1993a. Talk, thought, and thing--the emic road
toward conscious knowledge. Dallas: Summer
Institute of Linguistics.

----. 1993b. Experimental linguistics and language
learning. Word 44.2.302-08.

----, and Gary F. Simons. 1993. [in Russian]: Toward the
historical reconstruction of matrix patterns in
morphology. Moscow: Voprosy jazykoznania
[Problems of Linguistics] 1.21-44. (To appear, in
English, with the Georgetown University Press).

----, and Evelyn G. Pike. 1993. Text and tagmeme.
Norwood, N.J.: Ablex.

Quine, W. F., and J. S. Ullian. [1970] 1978. The web of
belief. New York: Random House.

Ricoeur, Paul. [1974-75] 1978. The philosophy of Paul
Ricoeur: An anthology of his work. Charles E.
Reagan and David Stewart, eds. Boston: Beacon
Press.

Sebeok, Thomas A. 1991. Semiotics in the United States. Bloomington: Indiana University Press.

Sparing, Margarethe W., 1984. The perception of reality in the Volksmarchen of Schleswig-Holstein: A study in interpersonal relationships and world view. Lanham: University Press of America.

Tyler, Stephen A. 1978. The said and the unsaid--Mind, meaning, and culture. New York: Academic Press.

KEN PIKE'S THANKS

Thanks to Udom and Hopple
The mouse and the cat.

All's well that ends well.
   [=tone glides?] (well well!)

Edmondson: "I'm able to cut off
   the heads of the speakers."
      [=ends the conference?]

Tones leave bones from heads
   in history's graves,
But no groans are heard
   since tongues got lost
      when heads got tossed--
         although "tongues" remain
            in social domain.

In this report finalizing, finally.
   I must try, not lie, re-Thai-
      although I'm not the Rector
   to "rectify" (Rector's task).
      (or rector-ify) the data.

From Bauer: "We can believe it or not"
   when showered with words.
So just relax--
   there is no tax to pay today--

So fax the facts to friends
   from brain on left
      to brain on right--

We say "Bye bye"
   in tune and tone.

The socio-semantic influence of religious beliefs and concepts on Thai language

Taweesak Yanprateep
Ramkhamhaeng University

INTRODUCTION

Since Thailand is a democratic country with the king as Head of State, Thai people have freedom to worship any religions or beliefs, such as Buddhism, Christianity, Islam, Hinduism and Confucianism. As a result, the Thai language is liberally sprinkled with words from various religions, for example Parajika (ปาราชิก), Karma (กรรม), Tripitaka (ไตรปิฎก), Trilakkhana (ไตรลักขณ์), Ariyasacca (อริยสัจ), from Buddhism; Bible, Catholic, Protestant, Jesus, Valentine's day, Christmas day and Pope from Christianity; and mosque, masjid, Mohammed, hadji from Islam. Brahmaa(พระพรหม), Vishnu (วิษณุ), Shiva (ศิวะ), Indra (พระอินทร์), Ramayana (รามายณะ), Mahaapharata (มหาภารตะ) Brahmacari (พรหมจารี) from Hinduism; Cheng Meng (เช็งเม้ง- Chinese Family Day to pay respect to the ancestors) Si-kow (ซิโกว-การทิ้งกระจาด-a custom of throwing baskets to poor people) from Confucianism. These loan-words have been well-accepted and incorporated into the Thai language.

The vocabulary concerning religious beliefs and concepts enters the Thai language in many ways.

1. **Moral preaching.** Though every religion aims at the same thing-to do good and avoid evil, the means to the goal is different. In Buddhism, people wish to go to heaven not to hell. However, the ultimate goal is Nibbana (นิพพาน), which is the Ultimate Truth. As for Christianity, the ultimate goal is to be with God in heaven. Muslims also

want to be reunited to Allah (พระอัลเลาะห์เจ้า). In Hinduism, Brahma (อาตมัน) will be united with Mahabrahma (ปรมาตมัน). In brief all these things are concerned with the relationship between good and evil.

2. **Allusion.** It is the reference to religious stories from the Bible, the Koran (คัมภีร์อัลกุรอ่าน) the Veda Scripture (พระเวท) and the Tripitaka (พระไตรปิฎก). Those of Buddhism and Hinduism which have been deeply rooted in Thailand for a long time are most often quoted. For example, the separation of lovers because of past karma (past deed) is usually referred to Rama-Sita (พระราม-นางสีดา), and Unnarudda-Usa (พระอุณรุท-นางอุษา) from Hinduism; and Sudhana-Manoraha (พระสุธน-นางมโนราห์) from Buddhism. Moreover, some references derive from traditional beliefs such as Lohasimbali Naraka (งิ้วนรก-a red cotton tree planted in hell), Khuen Ton Ngiw (the punishment for those committing adultery), Sriarya (พระศรีอาริย์), Malaya (พระมาลัย)

3. **Religious Festivals.** Buddhists celebrate Songkran Day (the former Thai New Year Day), Wan Khao Phansa (Buddhist's lent or the Rainy Retreat), Wan Asalha Puja (The day of Buddha's first sermon to his first five disciples), Thot Kathin (the ceremony of presenting the yellow robe to the monks at the end of the Rainy Retreat). Christians also celebrate Easter and Christmas.

4. **Idioms.** It is the connotative or the secondary meaning of the language. Many are seen both in everyday spoken and written language.

5. **Sayings and proverbs.** Sayings are intepretations of a story, while proverbs are written in concise and precise styles.

Examples for 4 and 5
A. The concepts of 'karma' in Thai

กงกำกงเกวียน /koŋ kam koŋ kwian/

      circle spoke circle cart

"Come home to roost"

"Sow the wind and reap the whirl wind."

"One reaps what he has sown."

(In Buddhism's law of causality, good deeds beget good results whereas bad deeds beget bad results.)

ก่อกรรมทำเข็ญ /kɔ̀ɔ kam tham khěn/

      create deed do adversity

"Always give troubles or problems to others(those who do bad things repeatedly)."

บุญทำกรรมแต่ง /bun tham kam tæ̀æŋ/

      merit make past deed arrange

"What will become of a person depends upon the good and the bad that he did in the past."

(This idea is based upon Buddhist beliefs about the law of causality or karma.)

บุญมาวาสนาส่ง /bun maa wâatsànǎa sòŋ/

      merit come fate send

"Fate was favorable and personal merits helped."

กินบุญเก่า /kin bun kàw/

      eat merit past

"To live a happy life because of the merit of deeds in the past."

B. Rituals in Buddhism

กรวดน้ำคว่ำขัน

/krùat náam khwâm khǎn/

pour water put upside down bowl

"To break the relationship after doing something together for some time."

(Buddhist usually pours water into the ground so that the dead might benefit from this merit-making.)

คว่ำบาตร /khwâm bâat/

      put upside down alms-bowl

"To excommunicate"

(During Lord Buddha's period, some heretics annoyed the priests when going out to receive alms, so the priest stayed away from them.)

ตักบาตรอย่าถามพระ /tàk   bâat   yàa thăam phrá/

put in alms-bowl don't ask monk

"When you want to give something don't bother to ask whether it is a favorite or not."

(In Buddhist doctrines, the monks must accept whatever be offered and bless that person since everyone usually offers the best he can find.)

เถรส่องบาตร   /thĕen   sɔ̀ɔŋ   bâat/

senior monk look at alms-bowl

"To do like the others but not knowing the reason."

(In Buddhist rules, the bowl of a senior monk must be taken care of by the young ones. So after every wash the latter must examine the bowl carefully to see if there is any crack. The new monk does the same but he does not know what for.)

วุ่นเป็นจุลกฐิน

/wùn pen   cunlá kàthǐn/

busy be (as) small a ceremony of presenting a
                yellow robe to the monk at the end of
                Buddhist Rainy Retreat.

"To work busily." (It's a kind of Kathin when the process of making the yellow robe must be done within one day starting from collecting the cotton from the field.)

เดาสวด   /dau sùat/

guess chant prayer

"guesswork."

(This refers to some new monks who cannot remember all the prayers. Then, they have to listen to the senior ones and guess. This may be correct, or incorrect.)

ตื่นแต่ดึก สึกแต่หนุ่ม

/tɯ̀ɯn tɛ̀ɛ dɯ̀k sɯ̀k   tɛ̀ɛ nùm/

get up while late   leave the monkhood while young
          at night

"an early bird" (Those who get up early will have a better chance.)

(As a Buddhist, a man should be ordained once in his lifetime. If he becomes a monk and leaves the monkhood while still young he still has strength and energy to be successful in his careers.)

ชายสามโบสถ์ /chai sǎam bòot/

man three temple

"A man who has entered the monkhood three times is believed to be a weak-minded person."

"Those who always change their mind."

ปิดทองหลังพระ /pìt thɔɔŋ lǎŋ phrá/

stick gold leave back Buddha statue

"To do good by stealth"

"To do decent thing without expecting any reward or gain."

(In Buddhist beliefs, if you stick the gold leaves in the front part of Buddha statue, it will be noticeable. If you stick them at the back, it will remain unseen.)

ไปวัดไปวาได้ /pai wát pai waa dâai/

go temple go - can

"To be good looking enough to appear in public."

(This refers to the merit-making at the temple. Beautiful women will dress in their best clothing and go to the temple late. However the less beautiful will go to the temple very early when it is still dark in order not to be seen by many people.)

ทำคุณบูชาโทษ โปรดสัตว์ได้บาป

/tham khun buuchaa thôot pròot sàt dâai bàap/

do good pay homage guilt show mercy animal get sin

"To cherish (nourish) a viper (snake, serpent) in one's bosom"

"To do a good deed in homage of a bad return."

ทำบุญเอาหน้า /tham bun ʔau nâa/

make merit get face

"To show off when making merit."

(Some who wants his name be publicized when making merit so that everyone will know and give a compliment.)

วันพระไม่มีหนเดียว /wan phrá mâi mii hǒn diau/

day monk no have time one only

"Buddhist days of worship do not occur once."

"Every dog has his day."

"Every man has his moment."

(Buddhist sabbaths usually come on the 8th and 15th day of the new moon and the waning moon on the lunar calendar. On that day Buddhists go to the temple to chant prayers and listen to the sermon.)

C. Special vocabulary from Buddhism used in Thai.

พระมาลัยมาโปรด /phrá maalai maa   pròot

Phra Malaya   come bless

"One who is helpful to person in need."

(Phra Malaya was a Buddhist monk who was believed to have gone to hell to temporarily stop the torturing)

สอนหนังสือสังฆราช /sɔ̌ɔn nǎŋsǐi sǎŋkhárâat/

teach book Supreme Patriach

"To teach someone who already knows best."

(In former times, the priests educated the children in both general knowledge and morality)

เจ้าไม่มีศาล สมภารไม่มีวัด

/câa mâi mii sǎan sǒmphaan mâi mii wát/

Spirit no   have shrine abbot   no   have temple

"Those who do not have a place to settle down."

(Thai people have a belief that a god or the spirit of the dead should reside in a shrine whereas an abbot should stay in a temple.)

ลูกสมภาร หลานเจ้าวัด

/lûuk sǒmphaan lǎan   câo   wát/

son abbot   offspring noble temple

"Children of the nobility or important people are of some importance in the eyes of society."

เสือเฒ่าจำศีล /sǐa thâu cam sǐin/

tiger old   dormant
"Those who are not what they seem to be."
มือถือสาก ปากถือศีล

/mii thǐi sàak pàak thǐi sǐin/

hand hold pestle mouth hold precepts
"A wolf in sheep's clothings.
"The hand holds a pestle while the mouth utters
Buddhist precepts."
(If you tell people how they should behave, you
yourself must be the model.)
พลั้งปากเสียศีล พลั้งตีนตกต้นไม้

/phláŋ pàak sǐa sǐin   phláŋ tiin tòk   tônmáay/
slip   mouth lose precepts slip foot fall down tree
"To speak carelessly may be to cause of trouble."
สวรรค์อยู่ในอกนรกอยู่ในใจ

/sàwǎn yùu nai ʔòk nárók yùu nai cai/

heaven is in   chest hell   is in mind
"The good and the bad will both affect our mind."
ตกนรกทั้งเป็น /tòk nárók tháŋ pen/

fall hell   still alive
"Almost be dead because of sufferings."
(In Buddhist beliefs, the hell is where a person with
bad deeds will be tortured.)
พระอิฐพระปูน /phrá   ʔit   phrá   puun/

Buddha statue brick Buddha statue plaster
"To sit still or to be indifferent ."
(This refers to the statues of Lord Buddha that only
sit still because they are made of brick or plaster.)
เถรตรง   /thěen   troŋ/

senior monk straight
"To call spade a spade"
"To be straight as a senior monk."
(Someone who is too frank, and has no wit to
conceal his feelings or to be flexible.)

ชักแม่น้ำทั้งห้า /chák mɛ̂ɛnáam tháŋ hâa/

                  pull   river   all   five

"Beat around (about) the bush."

   "To give a long explanation to get what one wants."

(A reference to Vessantara story.)

ไม่เชื่อน้ำมนต์ /mâi chɯ̂a   náam mon/

                  not believe water consecrated

"Not believe in the words or promise of that person."

(In Hinduism or Buddhist beliefs 'náam mon' is thought of as the holy water.)

ชั่วช่างชี ดีช่างสงฆ์ /chûa châaŋ chii dii   châaŋ sŏŋ/

                    evil   let   nun good let monk

"To be indifferent to the nun and the monk no matter how good or bad they behave."

(Thai Buddhist have high respect for the monks. They dare not criticize them, being afraid that they may go to hell.)

ตัดหางปล่อยวัด /tàt hǎaŋ plɔ̀ɔi wát/

                  cut tail   leave temple

"To cut off a shilling."

(Buddhist temple is usually a shelter for all kinds of unwanted animals. Especially, those that are naughty, will have their tail cut off and are left at the temple.)

แพ้เป็นพระ ชนะเป็นมาร

/phɛ́ɛ   pen phrá cháná pen maan/

be defeated is   monk win   is   demon

"It is sometimes better to be patient and lose the game."

(Buddhist monks must tolerate all kinds of passions.)

เห็นกงจักรเป็นดอกบัว /hĕn koŋcàk pen dɔ̀ɔk   bua/

                     see   disk   is   flower lotus

"Do not mistake evil for good."

กิ้งก่าได้ทอง /kîŋkàa   dâay thɔɔŋ/

                  chameleon get   gold

"to have vanity."

D. Influences from Hinduism, Christianity and other religions.

วัดรอยเท้า   /wát   rɔɔi tháau/

measure print foot

"To prove himself better or be more powerful."

(In the Ramayana, when Thoraphi, a son of Thorapha, grew up having the same size of footprint as his father, he then went to fight with his father.)

ทรพี   /thɔɔráphii/

Thoraphi (a water buffalo.)

"Those who are ungrateful. They do not appreciate the favors done to them."

(This refers to the story of Thorapha and Thoraphi in Ramayana.)

งอมพระราม /ŋɔɔm   phrá raam/

overripe   Rama

"to be over-tired because of sufferings."

(In Ramayana, Vishnu, reincarnated as Rama, had to wander in the jungle for 14 years.)

บนบานศาลกล่าว /bon   baan sǎan klàau/

pledge vow shrine say

"Make a vow to offer something to a god if your problem can be solved."

พระศุกร์เข้าพระเสาร์แทรก

/phrá sùk khâu phrá sǎu sɛ̂æk/

Venus   enter Saturn   come in between

"It never rains, it pours."

"Misfortunes never come singly."

(Sufferings usually occur in our life repeatedly.)

แพะรับบาป   /phǽ ráp   bàap/

goat   receive sin

"a scapegoat."

"The innocent who suffers in the place of the others."

(In Hindusim, an animal may be killed as an offering to God in return for blessing.)

พาลีหลายหน้า /phaalii lǎai nâa/

Phali many face

"To be unreliable, untrustworthy."

(from the Ramayana)

6. Buddhist sayings.

1) ตนแลเป็นที่พึ่งของตน

One is his own refuge.

2) บุคคลไม่ควรลืมตน

Don't over estimate yourself.

3) ความประมาทเป็นทางแห่งความตาย

Imprudence leads to disaster.

4) สิ่งที่ทำแล้ว ทำคืนไม่ได้

What has been done cannot be undone.

5) พึงประกอบธุระให้เหมาะแก่กาลเทียว

Manage your affairs at proper times.

6) พึงรักษาความดีของตนไว้ ดังเกลือรักษาความ

เค็ม

Safeguard your virtue againt decline, just as salt never loses its saltiness.

7) บุคคลหว่านพืชเช่นใด ย่อมได้ผลเช่นนั้น ผู้ทำ

กรรมดีย่อมได้ผลดี ผู้ทำกรรมชั่วย่อมได้ผลชั่ว

One reaps whatever one has sown. Those who do good receive good and those who do evil receive evil.

8) ความอยากมีอารมณ์หาที่สุดมิได้เลย

Desires are unlimited.

9) จิตที่ฝึกแล้ว นำสุขมาให้

A well-disciplined mind can bring happiness.

10) ภูเขาศิลาแท่งทึบ ไม่สะเทือนเพราะลมฉันใด บัณฑิตย่อมไม่หวั่นไหวเพราะนินทาและสรรเสริญ ฉันนั้น

As a mountain of solid rock remains unshaken by the storm, so the wise man remains unmoved by praises.

11) ผู้ให้ย่อมผูกไมตรีไว้ได้

Giving brings friendship.

12) ความจนเป็นทุกข์ในโลก

Poverty is a cause of suffering.

13) ธรรมแล ย่อมรักษาผู้ประพฤติธรรม

The virtuous are protected by their own virtues.

14) ปัญญาพึงรู้ได้ด้วยการสนทนา

Wisdom can be known in discussion.

15) คนไม่ถูกนินทา ไม่มีในโลก

Never is there a person who is not gossipped about.

16) คบคนใดก็เป็นเช่นคนนั้นแล

You will become what your associates are.

17) เปล่งวาจางาม ยังประโยชน์ให้สำเร็จ

Good words get things done.

18) ความพร้อมเพรียงของหมู่ให้เกิดสุข

Unity within a group creates happines.

19) ความไม่มีโรค เป็นลาภอย่างยิ่ง

Health is wealth.

20) เมตตาเป็นเครื่องค้ำจุนโลก

Loving-kindness enhances the world.

21) ความกตัญญูกตเวที เป็นเครื่องหมายแห่งคน ดี

Gratitude is an earmark of the virtuous.

22) ร่างกายของสัตว์ย่อยยับได้ แต่ชื่อและสกุลไม่ย่อยยับ

Bodies perish, but not honour and fame.

23) ได้ยศแล้ว ไม่ควรเมา

Don't be infatuated by honor.

24) ต่อหน้าประพฤติเช่นใด ถึงลับหลังก็ให้ประพฤติเช่นนั้น

Behave the same way both before and behind others.

25) เวรย่อมระงับด้วยไม่มีเวร

Enmity is ended by forgiving.

26) ความบริสุทธิ์และไม่บริสุทธิ์มีเฉพาะตัว

A person's stain or purity belongs to its owner.

27) ความรู้จักประมาณ ยังประโยชน์ให้สำเร็จทุกเมื่อ

Moderation is always advisable.

28) กำลังใจพึงรู้ได้ในคราวมีอันตราย

Danger is the measure of courage.

29) พึงชนะคนไม่ดีด้วยความดี

Overcome an evil person with virtue.

30) คำสัตย์แลเป็นวาจาไม่ตาย

Truth is immortal.

CONCLUSION

Even though the Thai lauguage is influenced by many religions, Buddhism plays the most important role since it is the religion of the country. Buddhist idioms, sayings and proverbs in Pali (the language of Theravada Buddhism) are most often seen. Stories from Hinduism in Sanskrit (the language of the Brahmin's Hinduism) are also widely-spread since Hinduism was well founded in Thailand long before Buddhism. Some children of the

Royal family are named after Hindu Gods such as Rama and Narayana. These can also be traced in the name of some important places such as Bueng Phra Ram (Rama's Lake), Thale Chup Son (Dip Arrowhead Lake).

Religion is the stronghold of the mind and sets guidelines in life for a human-being. The language is affected greatly by every religion.

References

Duangtip Somnapan Surintatip.1985. *On Thai Proverb and Sayings.* Bangkok, National Identity Board, Prime Minster's Office.

Maha Makut Ratchawitthayalai. 1985. *Dhammapadattha-katha.* Vol.1-8. Bangkok, Maha Makut Ratcha witthayalai.

Nikom Kaolad. 1993. *Having Fun with Proverbs and Sayings.* Bangkok, International Book.

Rachanee Sawsottikun. 1983. *English and Thai Idioms.* Bangkok, ChulalongkornUniversity Printing House.

Rajavaramuni, Phra. 1975. *A Dictionary of Buddhism.* Bangkok, Maha Chulalongkorn Buddhist University.

Religious Affairs Department, Ministry of Education. 1978. *The Tripitaka.* Vol. 1-45. Bangkok, The Religious Affairs Department Press.

Royal Institute of Thailand, The. 1987. *Thai Dictionary.* Bangkok, The Royal Institute.

So Sethaputra. 1965. *New Model Thai-English Diction-ary.* Vol. 1-2. Bangkok, Thai Wattana Panich.

Taweesak Yanprateep. 1977. *Religious Literature.* Bangkok, Ramkhamhaeng University Press,

Vajirañanavarorasa, Somdet Phra Mahasamana Chao Krommaphraya. 1978. *Buddhasasanasubhasit.* Vol. 1-3. Bangkok, Maha Makut Ratchawitthayalai.

Deixis and implicit argument of Japanese verbs of giving

Yukiko Sasaki Alam
San Francisco State University

INTRODUCTION

1. Japanese has five verbs of giving which are used as both independent and supporting verbs. It has been known that these verbs can be divided into two groups, i.e. the *kureru* and *yaru* groups[1], but what the essential element is that distinguishes the two groups has been the subject of considerable debate. The present paper examines the previous analyses of these distinguishing features of giving verbs as presented by Ooe 1975, Kuno & Kaburaki 1977, Wetzel 1985, 1988, Tokunaga 1986 and Kuno 1987, and presents a new analysis. Although it is in line with Wetzel's analysis, the current analysis sheds light on several points previous analyses fail to capture.

The existing analyses fail to notice the fact that the syntactic case, dative, of independent verbs of giving ceases to be a syntactic case but becomes an implicit semantic role, beneficiary, when the verbs of giving are used as supporting verbs. And although the use of the dative with the supporting verb would give rise to an ungrammatical sentence, it is vital to recognize the referent of the implicit argument for a complete comprehension of the sentence. Furthermore, this paper demonstrates that independent verbs of giving as well as their supporting counterparts have this implied beneficiary role as an integral element in their lexical entries in addition to the direct beneficiary referred to by the syntactic dative case. That is, this paper argues that the Japanese verbs of giving, whether used as independent or as supporting verbs, includes the implicit semantic case of beneficiary as an integral semantic element.

In addition, this paper focuses on the point that the use of two types of giving verbs, the *kureru* group and the *yaru* group depends upon where the speaker stands in the benefactive event world. This is analogous to the use of the English deictic verbs *come* and *go* in which one can be used to describe motion from one place to another but the other cannot, depending upon where the speaker (or the addressee) is. Therefore, this paper claims that these verbs of giving are deictic and terms the deixis `benefactive deixis'. While the English verbs *come* and *go* describe the motion relative to the speaker or the addressee,

Japanese verbs of giving express the benefactive relation between the speaker and the event. And the implicit argument in question is the very element signaling the speaker's position as a beneficiary or as not a beneficiary, thus presenting the deictic egocentric property of these verbs.

PREVIOUS ANALYSES

2. Although the two verbs of giving, *kureru* and *yaru*, can be used on appropriate occasions to describe the very same event of giving, it is often the case that one can be used to describe the event but the other cannot, depending upon who is the speaker. This is similar in its context dependent property to the use of *come* and *go*: one can be used to describe motion from one place to another but the other cannot, depending upon where the speaker (or the addressee) is. While much research has been conducted on Japanese verbs of giving from various points of view, special attention was paid to the difference of the lexico-semantics of the *kureru* and *yaru* groups of verbs by Ooe 1975, Kuno & Kaburaki 1977, Wetzel 1985, 1988, Tokunaga 1986 and Kuno 1987.

Ooe 1975 treats verbs of giving as verbs that indicate the speaker's subjective description of a giving event. He explains the difference between *kureru* and *yaru* by using the terms *point of view* and *intention* (1975: 61).

(1)

		giver	------>	receiver
kureru		X		(X)
		ø		@
yaru		X		(X)
		@		ø

The symbol @ denotes the locus where the speaker's point of view lies, and the letter X indicates that the referent performs the designated act intentionally. The parentheses indicate optionality. According to Ooe's analysis the speaker uses *kureru* to describe an event of giving from the point of view of the receiver while he uses *yaru* when he views the giving event in the giver's perspective. Ooe calls *kureru* a `receiver-oriented' verb and *yaru* a `giver-oriented' verb. The intention of the givers of both verbs is lexically specified while that of the receivers is ambiguous but can be evoked in an appropriate context. Therefore, although the following sentences in 2 and 3 all describe giving events, an appropriate verb of giving must be chosen in each event according to the perspective of the speaker relative to the event.

(2) a. *Hanako-wa watashi-ni   ningyoo-o kureru.*
        -Topic I   -IO   doll -DO give
        `Hanako will give me a doll.'
     b. **Watashi-wa   Hanako-ni ningyoo-o kureru.*
        I   -Topic   -IO doll -DO give
        `I will give Hanako a doll.'

(3) a. **Hanako-wa watashi-ni   ningyoo-o yaru.*
        -Topic I   -DO   doll -DO   give
        `Hanako will give me a doll.'
     b. *Watashi-wa Hanako-ni   ningyoo-o yaru.*
        I -Topic   -IO   doll -DO give
        `I will give Hanako a doll.'

Both 2a and 2b use *kureru*, but 2a is an acceptable sentence while 2b is not. Because *kureru* is a `receiver-oriented' verb, in 2a and 2b the speaker should describe the giving event in the receiver's perspective. Given only two event participants, the speaker and Hanako, 2a, having the speaker as the receiver indicates that the speaker describes the event in his perspective rather than in the other person's perspective, and therefore it is semantically an acceptable sentence. On the other hand, 2b, with Hanako as the receiver, denotes that the speaker places the other person's perspective over his, which is unnatural, and therefore it is a semantically incongruous sentence. Likewise, a similar argument applies for the explanation of the difference in acceptability of 3a and 3b. Because *yaru* is a `giver-oriented' verb, the speaker should view the events from the point of view of the giver and therefore he must be the referent of the giver, as in 3b, and he must not be the referent of the receiver of *yaru* as in 3a.

Kuno & Kaburaki 1977 and Kuno 1987 discuss verbs of giving in the framework of the theory of Empathy. According to them, Empathy is a term which refers to the `speaker's identification, with varying degrees (ranging from degree 0 to 1, with a person who participates in the event that he describes in a sentence.' It is a technical linguistic term, distinguished from the concept of sympathy, to capture linguistic phenomena found universally. Kuno & Kaburaki formulate the Empathy relationships between the participants in the lexico-semantics of *kureru* and *yaru* as in 4.

(4) Empathy conditions on independent verbs of giving
    (a) *kureru* `give': $E(\text{subject}) < E(\text{dative})$
    (b) *yaru*   `give': $E(\text{subject}) \geq E(\text{dative})$

Kureru is called a `dative-centered' verb while *yaru* is called a `subject-centered' verb. According to Kuno & Kaburaki, acceptability and unacceptability of the sentences in 2 and 3 are due to conformity and violation of the Empathy conditions listed in 4: 2b above is unacceptable since the Empathy condition on the `dative-centered' verb *kureru* is $E(\text{subject}) < E(\text{dative})$, and the speaker, who should empathize most with himself, is instead in the subject position, whereas 3a is anomalous for the opposite reason that the Empathy condition on the `subject-centered' verb *yaru* is $E(\text{subject}) \geq E(\text{dative})$, and the speaker is instead in the dative position.

The equity sign for the Empathy condition of *yaru* (but not for that of *kureru*) is necessary because *yaru* is used to describe a giving event when the speaker places himself at a distance from the referents of both giver and receiver (cf. 5a below). Giving verbs are used not only as independent verbs, but also as supporting verbs. Kuno 1987 assumes that the Empathy conditions on the supporting verbs *yaru* and *kureru* are the same in nature as those on the independent counterparts except that the supporting verb *yaru* cannot be used for a neutral description, based on the observation of such examples as in 5 and 6.

(5) Independent verbs of giving
    a. *Toorigakari-no-hito-ga Taroo-ni   okane-o   yatta.*
       passerby   -Subj   -IO   money-DO gave
       `A passerby gave Taro money.'
    b. *Taroo-ga toorigakari-no-hito-ni   okane-o   yatta.*
       -Subj passerby   -IO   money-DO gave
       `Taro gave a passerby money.'

(6) Supporting verbs of giving
    a. *Toorigakari-no-hito-ga Taroo-ni   okane-o   kasita.*
       passerby -Subj   -IO   money-DO   lent
       `A passerby lent taro some money.'
    b. *?Toorigakari-no-hito-ga Taroo-ni okane-o kasite-yatta.*
                                          lending-gave

According to Kuno 1987 the awkwardness of 6b can be accounted for if we assume that the supporting verb *yaru* requires that $E(\text{subject}) > E(\text{dative})$, but does not permit the relation that E(subject) = E(dative).   That is, the use in 6b of the supporting verb *yatta*, the past form of *yaru* assumes that E(Subject) > E(Dative), and thus indicates an unnatural Empathy relation, E(a passer-by) > E(Taro). Because the speaker should be closer to Taro than to an unfamiliar passer-by, 6b is a semantically awkward sentence.   This absolute subjectivity of the supporting verb *yaru* differs from the possibility of objective description by the independent verb *yaru*, as indicated in 5a and 5b by the feasibility of interchanging *Taro* and *a passer-by*. Thus Kuno 1987 proposes two sets of Empathy conditions for *yaru*, but one set for *kureru*, which denotes a subjective description whether in its use as independent or as dependent verb.

(7) Empathy conditions on giving verbs
   a. *kureru* `give': independently and for supporting verb
                    E(subject) < E(dative)
   b. *yaru* `give':   independently
                    E(subject) ≥ E(dative)
                  supporting verb
                    E(subject) > E(dative)

Wetzel 1985 `broadly' defines *kureru* and *yaru* as in 8.

(8)   *kureru* :   give to in-group
       yaru :   give to out-group

This definition seems to be intended for both independent and supporting verbs of giving, because the previous examples include both. Wetzel claims that the following Empathy relation holds.

(9)   E(in-group) > E(out-group)

She lists as in-group a group of friends, playmates, a family, and the speaker himself, who is the ultimate in-group, noting the observation by Lebra 1976 that `the in-group/out-group distinction is drawn by constantly varying situations.' This means that an individual regarded as in-group in a situation can be regarded as out-group in another situation. Take the following situations in 10 for example: the speaker's father is regarded as in-group in 10a, but as out-group in 10b.

(10) a. *Tomodachi-ga chichi-ni sore-o oshiete-kureta.*
     friend   -Subj. my father-IO that-DO informing-gave
     `My friend informed my father about it (and I am
                                  grateful.)
    b. *Chichi-ga tomodachi-ni sore-o oshiete-kureta.*
     my father   friend
     `My father informed my friend about it (and I am
                                  grateful.)

10a shows that the speaker has placed himself closer to his father than to his friend, which is justified by the fact that his father is a family member. 10b indicates that the speaker has placed himself closer to his friend than to his father and that he and his friend share a common interest. Although the situations in 10 illustrate the flexibility of the in-group/out-group distinction, it is highly predictable in most cases who the speaker considers closer to himself, because the judgment on intimacy is in essence based on (a) a general concept of the socially recognized in-group hierarchy or (b) shared interests in a specific context.

Tokunaga 1986 studies the independent verb *kureru* and treats it as `affective deixis'. According to her, affective deixis indicates `the speaker's personal or emotional relation with a particular participant in the speech-act.' In 11, for example, the use of *kureru* suggests the speaker's `personal and emotional relation' with Mary. (This is somewhat similar to Kuno & Kaburaki's Empathy interpretation that 11 indicates that the speaker feels closer to Mary than to Tom.)

(11) *Tom-wa   Mary-ni   hon-o   kureta.*
      -Top   -IO   book-DO   gave
     `Tom gave a book to Mary.'

In Tokunaga's analysis, *kureru* and *yaru* belong to different classes: respectively as a `speaker-oriented inward directional' verb (which indicates that the inherent directionality of giving is toward the speaker) and as a `subject-oriented outward directional' verb (which denotes that the inherent directionality is toward someone other than the speaker).

The table below gives a general picture of the differences among the analyses reviewed above.

(12)

		GIVER	**RECEIVER**
Ooe	*kureru*	+intention	±intention
		-point of view	+point of view

(called the receiver-oriented verb)

		GIVER	**RECEIVER**
	yaru	+intention	±intention
		+point of view	-point of view

(called the giver-oriented verb)

Kuno &
  Kaburaki

		SUBJECT		**DATIVE**
	kureru	E(mpathy)	<	E

(called the dative-centered verb)

		SUBJECT		**DATIVE**
	yaru	E	≥*	E

(called the subject-centered verb; *the equity sign
is required only for the independent verb.)

Wetzel

		RECEIVER
	kureru	in-group
	yaru	out-group

Tokunaga

		SUBJECT	**IO**
	kureru	giver≠speaker	receiver=speaker
			or speaker-in-law
			(personally &
			emotionally related
			with the speaker)

(called the speaker-oriented verb)

		SUBJECT	**IO**
	yaru	giver=anyone	receiver≠speaker

(called the subject-oriented verb)

THE PROBLEM

3. In all the above analyses except for Kuno's, which makes a slight distinction between the independent and supporting verbs of giving by adding the equity sign to the independent verb *yaru*, the implications are that the lexico-semantic descriptions for the independent verbs of giving are generally applicable for the supporting verbs as well, because example sentences used for their analyses include supporting verbs of giving.[2] However, there are several syntactic and semantic differences between them.

3.1. SYNTACTIC DIFFERENCES. An important syntactic difference between the independent verbs and supporting verbs of giving is that while the independent verbs of giving subcategorize for the dative NP, the supporting counterparts do not, as shown below.

(13) a. *(Anata-ga)*   *soko-e*   *itte-kureru?*
       you-Subj   there-TO   going-give
       `Can (you) go there (for me)?'
    b. **(Anata-ga) watashi-ni*   *soko-e itte-kureru?*
                I-IO
       `Can (you) go there (for me)?'

(14) a. *(Boku-ga)*   *soko-e*   *itte-yaru.*
        I-Subj   there-TO going-give
       `(I'll) go there (for you).'
    b. **(Boku-ga) kimi-ni*   *soko-e itte-yaru.*
               you-IO
       `(I'll) go there (for you).'

Because the supporting verb *kureru* does not subcategorize for the dative NP, an addition of the dative NP *watashi-ni* `to me' to 13a gives rise to an unacceptable sentence 13b, even though the identification of the referent of the beneficiary of the event is an integral part of the understanding of the sentence. The same is true of the supporting verb *yaru*, as shown in 14a and 14b. The insertion of the dative in 14a results in an unacceptable sentence 14b, but nonetheless the identification of the referent of the beneficiary of the event is of vital importance.

When a dative NP appears in a sentence with the supporting verb *kureru* or *yaru*, it is the one that is subcategorized for by the main verb, as is the case with the following example.

(15) *Chichi*   *-ga*   *(boku-o)*   *kaisha-no-shachoo-ni*
     my father-Subj.   I-Obj.   company-OF-president-IO
                      shookaishite-kureru.
                      introducing-give
       `My father will introduce (me) to a company president (and I am happy about it).'

The overt dative NP *kaisha-no-shachoo-ni* `to a company president' is subcategorized for by the verb *shookaisuru* `introduce', but not by *kureru*. As a result, because the Empathy conditions refer to the syntactic category dative, they often predict wrong Empathy relationships. Take 15 for example. The Empathy condition on the supporting verb *kureru*, E(subject) < E(dative) suggests the Empathy relationship of 15 that E(subject=my father) < E(dative=a company president), which is a wrong interpretation of 15.[3] Thus, as shown above, reference to the syntactic category dative is misleading, but yet for a complete comprehension of the sentence it is vital to identify the referent of the beneficiary of the event even though it is not syntactically present. That is, the dative of the independent verb of giving ceases to be a syntactic case but becomes an implicit semantic argument, beneficiary, when it is used as supporting verb.

3.2. SEMANTIC DIFFERENCES. The difference in subcategorization of the dative NP between the supporting and independent verbs of giving seems to be due to a significant semantic difference between them. Although the semantics of the dative NP of an independent verb of giving denotes a recipient of a given object, that of the implicit argument of a supporting verb no longer indicates such a recipient, but instead denotes a beneficiary. This point is demonstrated by the default interpretation of the speaker as the beneficiary in 16a in the absence of prior context or an overt beneficial phrase, and by the default interpretation of the addressee as the beneficiary in 16b in the same situation.

(16) a. *(Anata-ga)*   *soko-e*   *itte-kureru?*
         you-Subj   there-TO   going-give
         `Can (you) go there (for me)?'
     b. *(Boku-ga)*   *soko-e*   *itte-yaru.*
         I-Subj   there-TO   going-give
         `(I'll) go there (for you).'

Likewise, as indicated by the expression in parentheses in the gloss of 17 below, the independent verb of giving also implies that the speaker thinks that the giving in question is beneficial not only to his child but also to him by membership in the same group.

(17) *Mary-san-ga*   *uchi-no-ko-ni okane-o*   *kureta.*
         -Subj.   my child-IO   money-Obj.   gave
         `Mary gave my child money (and I am grateful to her).'

The verb *kureru* not only enables the speaker to express the speaker's position as a beneficiary, but also to imply his gratitude. Even in the case in which the direct beneficiary is someone other than the speaker, the use of *kureru* entails the speaker's expression of gratitude, as is shown in the gloss of 18 below, unless otherwise specified.

(18) *Kodomo-no-tame-ni   soko-e   itte-kureta .*
child -OF-SAKE-FOR   there-TO going-gave
`(He) went there for my child (and I am grateful to him).'

Thus it can be said that while the meaning of an independent verb of giving includes both the recipient of a given object and the implied beneficiary, a supporting verb of giving implies only the beneficiary. In other words, the role of beneficiary is implicitly present in both independent and supporting verbs of giving, but the role of recipient is lexically specified only in independent verbs of giving. Therefore, not only is the reference to the dative of the supporting verb of giving misleading, but the reference to the beneficiary as the recipient, as in Ooe and Wetzel, is as well.

BENEFACTIVE DEIXIS

4. Observations made above suggest that in Japanese, giving events are viewed from the perspective of benefactive effects on the speaker and that other events are also screened for benefactive effects on the speaker. In particular, the semantics of the implicit argument of the supporting verb *kureru* denotes that the speaker views himself as a beneficiary, whereas that of the supporting verb *yaru* indicates that the speaker thinks that he is not a beneficiary but someone he does not share interest with. And this implicit expression of his position as a beneficiary or as not a beneficiary is the very reason why Japanese has two sets of verbs of giving. An event is filtered through the speaker's perception for benefactive effects of the event, and when he perceives himself as a beneficiary, whether directly or indirectly through shared interests with the direct beneficiary, he uses *kureru*, but when he does not consider himself a beneficiary, he uses *yaru*. That is, both verbs denote benefactive events, but differ in implication of the speaker's role as a beneficiary. This usage is analogous to that of *come* and *go* , which both denote motion from one place to another, but differ in implication of the speaker's location: that is, *come* denotes motion toward where the speaker (or the addressee) is and *go* , motion toward where the speaker (or the addressee) is not (Fillmore 1966; Batari 1982). If deixis refers to that egocentric aspect of language with which `a human being establishes a relation between what may be generally called his "ego" and the "non-ego"' (Rauh 1983:

230), *kureru* and *yaru* are deictic verbs as *come* and *go* are. In the use of *kureru* or *yaru*, the speaker establishes a benefactive relation between himself and the event, whereas in the use of *come* or *go* the speaker establishes the direction of motion relative to his own location (or the location of the addressee). Because benefactive effects on the speaker is the central issue in the deictic property of *kureru* and *yaru*, I call this deixis benefactive deixis.

Based on the deictic property of these verbs discussed above, I call *kureru* the beneficial-to-self verb and *yaru*, the beneficial-to-other verb. The term *self* here refers to several non-mutually exclusive dimensions of self. One dimension of self is represented by the `empathetic self' defined in Lebra 1992 as `the intimacy-seeking, empathetic self, the second orientation of the interactional self.' Lebra states that `(i)nvolved here is the awareness of self as an insider of a group or network, or as a partner to a relationship.' Another dimension of self is the `subjective, experiencing, internal self', and yet another is the `objective, observing, external self' (Lyons 1982). The speaker who expresses his own feelings of gratitude is the experiencing self. The speaker who expresses acknowledgment of a favor granted to his in-group as a customary convention expected by a social norm is represented by the external as well as the empathetic self. In this regard the use of *kureru* denotes the speaker's acknowledgment of the `collectively shared *on*' incurred from the event he perceives to be beneficial for his in-group and himself. According to Lebra 1976 *on* is a culture-bound notion of reciprocity for the Japanese. It is `a relational concept combining a benefit or benevolence given with a debt or obligation thus incurred: it refers to a social debt from the viewpoint of the beneficiary, and a social credit from the perspective of the benefactor.

The term *other* employed here denotes someone with whom the speaker does not have shared interests. As self is a variable, so is other. In a given context a speaker may view his own family member as other, and his friend, as an insider out of shared interests, and in another context the relationship may be reversed, as discussed in 10 above. The following examples give a clear picture of the deictic property of these verbs.

(19) Supporting verbs of giving
    a. *Soko-e*   *itte-kureru*?
      there-TO   going-give
      `(Can you) go there (for me)?'

b. *Soko-e   itte-yaru.*
   there-TO   going-give
       `(I'll) go there (for you).'

(20) Independent verbs of giving
   a. *Kureru* ?
      give
         `(Can) (you) give (it) (to me)?
   b. *Yaru* .
      give
         `(I'll) give (it) (to you).'

Given only two discourse participants, the speaker and addressee, in 19a and 20a, the beneficial-to-self verb *kureru* implies the speaker as the beneficiary and the addressee as the benefactor, even though the referents are not explicitly mentioned. Similarly, in 19b and 20b, the beneficial-to-other verb *yaru* implies the addressee as the beneficiary and the speaker as the benefactor.

CONCLUSION

5. The current analysis focuses on the benefactive aspect of the verbs of giving since the role of beneficiary is implied in the lexico-semantics of both independent and supporting verbs of giving while the role of recipient, a primary focus of previous analyses, is lacking in the lexico-semantics of the supporting verbs of giving. Kuno & Kaburaki's analysis centers on the interaction between the syntax and the Empathy principles. However, as discussed above, because of absence of subcategorization of the dative NP of the supporting verbs of giving, reference to the syntactic category in the Empathy conditions often results in wrong interpretations of sentences with a supporting verb of giving. For general explication of the lexico-semantics of both independent and supporting verbs of giving, reference to a semantic role is called for. The terms *receiver* or *recipient* would be correct if we specify that independent verbs of giving have an (implicit) recipient semantically equivalent to a beneficiary in addition to the recipient denoted by the dative argument. But to avoid ambiguity and confusion I call the role of the implicit argument *beneficiary*. The synopsis of the present analysis can be shown as follows.

(21)
	BENEFICIARY
kureru	self
(called the beneficial-to-self verb)	
yaru	other
(called the beneficial-to-other verb)	

The research of giving verbs mentioned above refers to a special relationship the speaker holds with the referent of the dative NP or the receiver argument of *kureru*: the speaker takes his point of view rather than that of the giver (Ooe); the speaker identifies himself more with him than with the referent of the subject NP (Kuno & Kaburaki); the speaker has a personal and emotional relation with him (Tokunaga). Wetzel's analysis in terms of the in-group/out-group division offers an explanation for a special relationship between the speaker and the referent of the receiver in question. In this respect the present analysis is in line with Wetzel's analysis. According to the current analysis, the use of *kureru* indicates that the speaker considers himself a beneficiary directly or indirectly through his in-group or those with whom he shares interest.

A supporting verb of giving denotes the speaker's viewpoint of an event (i.e. modality) while the main verb indicates the propositional content of the event. The following diagram shows the relationship of the two functions.

(22) Sentence contents consisting of
EVENT	+	SPEAKER'S VIEWPOINT
(expressed		(expressed by a supporting
by the main verb)		verb of giving)

EX. *Soko-e*   *itte-*   *kureru?*
there-TO   going   give
`going there' (= Event)  `is beneficial to me'
(= Viewpoint)

When events denote giving, independent verbs of giving alone are used to indicate both events and the speaker's viewpoints, as exhibited below.

(23)   GIVING EVENT
SPEAKER'S VIEWPOINT
(expressed only by independent verbs of giving)

The current analysis is able to account for the fact that the lexico-semantics of *kureru* often expands to imply the speaker's gratitude in an appropriate context, because the present analysis in essence claims that a supporting verb of giving denotes the `effect' part of the chain `cause and effect' while the main verb is the `cause' part. For the feeling of gratitude is a natural effect resultant from the recognition of one's position as beneficiary. The use of the Japanese verb of giving enables the speaker to express implicitly and economically gratitude resultant from the perception of self as beneficiary, as structures by social and cultural norms of Japanese society.

NOTES

[1] The *kureru* group consists of *kureru* and *kudasaru*, and the *yaru* group constitutes *yaru*, *ageru* and *sashiageru*. In addition to this division, these five verbs can be categorized according to their honorific levels. This paper will not touch on this dimension, but focuses on features distinguishing between the *kureru* and *yaru* groups. Another point of note is that in present Japanese, among *yaru*, *ageru* and *sashiageru*, *ageru* is replacing many uses of *yaru*. *Ageru* rather than *yaru* might be more appropriate to represent this group, but this paper follows the predominant practice of use of *yaru* in previous literature under discussion of this paper.

[2] In reality the use of giving verbs as supporting verbs is much more pervasive than the use of giving verbs as independent verbs. Weztel reports that there were found 29 of giving and receiving verbs in a spoken discourse text of approximately 1950 words and that all 29 were used as supporting verbs (1985:146).

[3] Kuno (1978:152-154) uses the terms *nonsubject* instead of *dative*. As understood from (15) above, this term is ambiguous and difficult to identify the referent in question without considering the semantic role of beneficiary.

REFERENCES

Clark, Eve V. and Olga K. Garnica. 1974. Is he coming or going?: on the acquisition of deictic verbs. Jr. of Verbal Learning and Verbal Behavior 13, 559-572.

Fillmore, Charles J. 1966. Deictic categories in the semantics of *come*. Foundations of Language 2, 219-227.

_____. 1971. Santa Cruz lectures on deixis. Bloomington: Indiana University Linguistics Club.

_____. 1972. How to know whether you're coming or going. Linguistik, ed. by Karl Hyldgard-Jensen, 369-359. Frankfurt: Athenaum Verlag. [Reprinted in Essays on deixis, ed. by Gisa Rauh. Tubingen: Narr, 1983.]

_____. 1973. May we come in? Semiotica 9, 97-116.

Horiguchi, Sumiko. 1984. Jujuhyoogen-ni-kakawaru ayamari-no bunseki. Nihongo-Kyooiku 52, 91-103.

_____. 1987. *Te-kureru te-morau*-no gokansee-to muudoteki imi. Nihongogaku 6, 59-72.

Ishiguro, Hiroaki. 1985. Nihongoji-ni-okeru jujudooshi koobun rikai-no hattatsuteki kenkyuu. The Japanese Jr. of Psychology 56, 192-199.

Kuno, Susumu. 1973. The structure of the Japanese language. Cambridge, Mass.: MIT Press.

_____, and Etsuko Kaburaki. 1977. Empathy and Syntax. LI 8, 627-672.

_____. 1978. Danwa-no bunpoo. Tokyo: Taishukan.

_____. 1987. Functional syntax anaphora, discourse and empathy. Chicago: University of Chicago Press.

Lebra, Takie Sugiyama. 1976. Japanese patterns of behavior. Honolulu: University Press of Hawaii.

_____. 1992. Self in Japanese culture. Japanese sense of self, ed. by Nancy R. Rosenberger, 105-120. New York: Cambridge University Press.

Lyons, John. 1982. Deixis and subjectivity: *loquor, ergo sum*? Speech, place and action studies in deixis and related topics, ed. by Robert J. Jarvella and Wolfgang Klein, 101-124. New York: John Wiley & Sons Ltd.

Okutsu, Keiichiroo. 1983. Jujuhyoogen-no taishooteki kenkyuu. Nihongogaku 2, 22-30.

Ooe, Saburoo. 1975. Nichieigo-no hikaku kenkyuu - shukansei-o megutte. Tokyo: Nan'undo.

Perkins, Revere D. 1992. Deixis, grammar, and culture. Philadelphia: John Benjamins Publishing Company.

Rauh, Giza (ed.) 1983. Essays on Deixis. Tubingen. Narr.

Taylor, Kenneth A. 1988. We've got you coming and going. Linguistics and Philosophy 11, 493-513.

Tokunaga, Misato. 1986. Affective deixis in Japanese: a case study of directional verbs. Ann Arbor: University of Michigan dissertation.

Ueno, Tazuko. 1978. Jujudooshi-to keigo. Nihongo-kyooiku 35, 40-48.

Wetzel, Patricia J. 1985. In-group/out-group deixis: situational variation in the verbs of giving and receiving in Japanese. Language and social situations, ed. by Joseph P. Forgas, 141-157. New York: s-Verlag.

_____. 1988. Japanese social deixis and discourse phenomena. Jr. of the Assoc. of Teachers of Japanese 22, 7-27.

Features and types of insulting, teasing, and sarcastic utterances in spoken Khmer

Kenneth D. Day
Department of Communication
University of the Pacific

This study examines lexical, paralinguistic, kinesic, and situational features of insulting, teasing, and sarcastic utterances by Cambodians in the Khmer language in terms of Khmer-language terminology for classifying these utterances. While, as with spoken English, there is considerable overlap between the categories used to classify such utterances, this study seeks to identify key features which place utterances in particular categories.

Examples of insulting, teasing, and sarcastic utterances were collected from over 100 Cambodian videocassettes produced in Cambodia since 1990.[1] While most of the videos were low-budget theatrical movies, videocassettes of on-stage comedy performances were also included. Five Cambodian-American informants aided in validating the interpretations made of the content and intent of the utterances as well as in corroborating that particular features were relevant in how an utterance should be classified.[2] Khmer-language categories for classifying utterances were obtained not only from English-Khmer dictionaries but also the Institut Bouddhique's Vacananukram Khmer (1968).[3]

Informants frequently related utterances more to perceived intent than lexical, paralinguistic, or kinesic features in the performance of an utterance. Although there was agreement among informants on the classification of many of the utterances, some utterances were not consistently classified. This seems to reflect not only the difficulty in classifying utterances with subtle cues but also some disagreement among the informants in terms of the semantic boundaries of some of the categories. In the following discussion regularities across utterances are described and examples of utterances in a number of specific Khmer-language categories are presented.

Common Features

Ladd (1980) has suggested that some features tone of voice may be relatively universal across languages. Tone of voice, as a paralinguistic feature, and kinesics for the utterances examined in this study were generally found to resemble those in English. Intonational and lexical features were, as Ladd (1980) would also predict, specific to Khmer.

Utterances aimed at hurting another individual often included one of more of the following features: sentence intonation associated with anger, facial expression associated with anger, confrontive eye contact, and lexical choices showing disrespect.

Based on the examples observed it seems that anger is evidenced in Khmer speech by a general rise in pitch and volume. Angry statements thus seem to be spoken in a higher tone of voice and a louder manner than non-angry statements. In some angry statements pitch rises across the sentence with the highest pitch occurring on the last syllable which may be given particularly strong stress. Depending on whether the utterance is a statement or question, the voice falls or rises on the last syllable.

Hurtful utterances were also usually spoken with eye contact with the person to whom the remark was addressed. Sometimes this occurred only as a glance while at other times a stare was maintained.

Speakers of hurtful utterances also tended to display facial expressions associated with anger. These included frowns and the tightening of the muscles around the eyes in the manner of the scowl.

Hurtful utterances also tended to display certain lexical features that indicated disrespect. The most common feature was the choice of familiar pronouns, ឯង (ʔaeŋ) for you and

អញ (ʔaɲ) for I, and the use of the address particle អា (ʔaː).

អា precedes a name, pronoun, or other word of address in speaking to another or may be used as a term of address by itself (Jacob 1968; Huffman 1970). Placing this particle before a word decreases the amount of respect that would otherwise be associated with the term of address. For example, អា សំឡាញ់ (familiar address particle followed by friend) takes a term of address which is not particularly respectful and converts it to a term of contempt unless the interaction is between intimates. Although these pronouns and vocative particles also occurred in non-hurtful statements in which close friends talked, these words clearly marked disrespect and hurtful intent when interactants were not well-acquainted. Less commonly, hurtful statements also displayed the choice of disrespectful terms when choices were possible, for example, the use of the most disrespectful term for eat (ស៊ី) rather than more respectful forms.

Utterances that were intended as non-hurtful teasing contrasted with the above features. Such utterances were often marked by smiles, non-derisive laughter, and softer and more relaxed vocal qualities. They were often accompanied by terms of address followed by the addition of a syllable produced by lengthening the last consonant of the term of address to become the first letter of an unstressed syllable with the remainder of the syllable consisting of (əh). Ehrman (1972) described such added unstressed syllables as deriving from particles. Huffman (1970) described this particular modification of the final particle as resulting from ហ៎, a particle soliciting agreement or a yes answer from the hearer. Huffman (1970) noted that some speakers generalize this particle to use at the end of nearly any sentence. The application of this particle to terms of address seems to have produced another address particle.

Sarcastic utterances often displayed some of the same features as hurtful utterances in general, but such features were often less marked. Some types of sarcastic utterances relied primarily on subtle lexical features.

Types of Utterances

Informants tended to classify utterances more on the basis of intent and situation rather than other features. The most common term used for an insult was ជេរ (ce:+r)) but informants often added that the best examples were those in which cursing occurred (something rarely seen in Cambodian movies). ជេរ statements are well-described by the general features described above for hurtful statements.

ចំអក (cɔmʔɔ:k) conforms rather closely with the English verb to mock. A hurtful intent accompanies these statements. In the samples from Cambodian videos ចំអក was often accompanied by a haughty facial expression. Some statements were accompanied by unusual intonation or derisive laughter. The use of ឯង and អា were also common. A good example of this type of statement is the following:

Source: ហ៊ានស្តុគិនៅឯណា?   (Angkor Wat Video)

ធ្វើ	ប្រក	ដូច	គេ	ទើប	ចុះ	មក	ពី	ហ៊ានស្តុគិ
Acts	behavior	like	he		just	descend	come	from	heaven.

This statement, which was spoken by a young woman who was fed up with her boyfriend, ends with an unusual intonation of the word for heaven with a slow fall on the last syllable that starts from an unusually high pitch.

ចំអាន់ (cɔmʔan) contrasts with ចំអក់ in not having a hurtful intent. It aligns closely with the English verb to tease. Speakers using these statements often smiled or laughed during the utterance.   Such statements were always spoken between people (characters) who knew each other well.   Although ឯង and អា occur in such statements, the use of the particle ហ្គើ as an address particle seems to further distinguish such statements from those intended to be hurtful. A terse example of this type of statement is:

Source: អាយៃយ៉ស្យ៉ើនម៉ាញ្ចាប្រាជ្ញជ្ឈុន   (CMI Video)

អញ្ចឹង	បានតែ ធាត់
then	reason why fat

This statement from an ayae performance is spoken by a woman who has just endured teasing about how skinny she is. After her male ayae partner declares he is a doctor and can help her gain weight, she expresses surprise that he is a doctor then teases him with the above statement that means "Oh, that's why you are fat!" Informants explained that not being thin was seen as a sign of being healthy and that doctors are expected to be healthier than other people, because they know how to stay well. Her intonation and accompanying smile as well as the fact that she is turning the tables on his previous teasing, identify this statement as merely teasing. Nonetheless, her male partner does not greatly appreciate the comment.

A common type of hurtful statement in Cambodian videos is the មើលឃាយ (mvːlɲiːəy). This term comes from the two words "see easily". Jacob (1974:152) notes that this phrase means "do you see?". These statements have the same features as ចៃៃ statements but are limited to situations in which someone puts someone in their place. In Cambodian films this occurs when someone of a higher social class criticizes someone of lower social standing for engaging in behavior which is not acceptable for someone of their social status. The following example illustrates the above features:

Source: អ្ននជាតែរវៃក្នកបង (K. K. Productions)

ហ៊ាន:	នាង	ងង	មិន	សុំ	ពន្លត់	ភ្លើង	ទាន
status	miss	you	not	ask for	blow out	flame	candle

នេះ	ទេ
these	at all

This statement, taken from a movie, reminds a young woman from the country that she should not be helping a temporarily blind, middle class man, whom she is caring for as a nurse, with successfully blowing out the candles on his cake. The angry intonation pattern and use of ងង to a non-intimate are important features.

Some types of teasing statements were neutral enough that informants suggested that they were best called ប៏ឃាប៏ (bɔŋʔap), embarrassment. Such statements were delivered in a rather dead-pan manner. Consider the following statement:

Source: ចុះខ្ញុំខុសអ្វី!   (Preah Vihear Video)

ញ៉ាំ	ដូច	ជ្រូក	អញ្ចឹង	បាន	ទំនិញ	ឡើង
eat	like	pig	then	result	merchandise	climb

ថ្លៃ	រាល់	ថ្ងៃ
expensive	everyday	

The statement means something like "It's because you eat like a pig that the prices have been going up so much at the market. (e.g. you eat so much that there is a scarcity of food thus driving up prices"). This statement is spoken by a man to a household visitor whom he perceives as an inconvenience. It is spoken as a matter of fact without features associated with other forms of teasing or mocking.

Another type of insulting statement is the ចំអាស

(cɔmʔaːh). Dictionary definitions (Vacananukram Khmer 1968; Jacob 1974) give two entries for this word. The first means to wash a corpse, while the second is to speak very coarsely or obscenely to a woman. In non-theatrical usage, these statements are normally insults that involve sexual references. Such statements occur almost exclusively in Cambodian videos in ayae and live comedy performances where they are intended to be crude but funny. Curiously, in these performances women often insult men with sexual reference as well. A good example of this statement as it occurs in ayae is:

Source: ក្រមុំស្រស់កម្លោះចោម   (S. M. Productions)

ចិត្ត	មិន	បាន	ដូច	ឆ្កែ	ខែ	ក្ដឹក
heart	not	have	like	dog	month	in-heat

This statement which means "You aren't capable of love and act like a female dog in heat" is spoken by a character who has just found his wife flirting with another man. The statement is spoken with intonation associated with hurtful statements. Such statements often rely on double entendres with sexual meanings.

A number of additional categories were important in how informants interpreted insulting, teasing, and sarcastic

235

statements. For some of these categories, insulting, teasing, or sarcastic statements may occur as variations of the type of statement. These categories are ផ្លែផ្កា , ពែ្យបខាយ , ការមិនឃ្យើ, and ពេ្ញ.

ផ្លែផ្កា (phlae-phka:) literally means "fruit-flower". The term is used to identify statements relying on subtle word play. These statements at one level appear to be about something else other than their actual intent. Two examples are helpful in illustrating this concept.

Source:　　　ចុះខ្ញុំឧសអ្វី!　　　　(Preah Vihear Video)

ទ្រលន់	ដល់	ហើយ	អា	ស្យារ	ជើង	ជ្រូក
fatty	arrive	already	address particle	soup	foot	pig

ជាមួយ	ត្រឡាច	ហ្នឹង
with	wintermelon	right there

In this first example taken from a Cambodian movie, a young woman who has just been embarrassed about her behavior responds with what appears to be a comment about the soup. The statement appears to say "The meat is really fatty in this pigsfeet with wintermelon soup". But the key here is the use of

the address particle អា which is not likely to be used to get the

attention of the soup. Informants understood this statement as directed to the man who embarrassed her at the table telling him that he is not a nice person. Pig is a common word in Khmer insults. This interpretation is also brought about by the use of the word meaning "right there" and by the fact that at the end of the statement the young woman points not at the soup but at the young man across the table. In this way ផ្ទេផ្ទា is a means for expressing subtle insults.

ផ្ទេផ្ទា can also be used as a means of flirting or criticizing another. In the following example a lower-status male comments on the fact that his middle-class friend is having an affair. He does this with a parody on a Cambodian primary school tune used to learn arithmetic operations.

Source: អណ្ដាតដុះឆ្អឹង   (Angkor Wat Video)

បើ	ចង់	ស្រណុក	ឲ្យ	យក	មួយ
បើ	ចង់	ព្រួយ	ឲ្យ	យក	ពី
បើ	ចង់	ឃ្លាន ស្ងី	ឲ្យ	យក	បី
បើ	ចង់	ដេក ដី	ឲ្យ	យក	បួន
បើ	ចង់	ងាប់ ខ្លួន	ឲ្យ	យក	ប្រាំ

Each line of this song is of the form "If you want to" _____ "take " some particular number from one to five. The first line means "If you want to have life easy take one". The second means "If you want to worry, take two". The third means "if you want to be hungry, take three". The fourth line means "If you want to sleep on the ground, take four. The final line means "If you want to die, take five". This rhyme is intended as a statement that the younger man knows about his friend's affair and does not approve.

For ផ្ទេផ្ទា examples, kinesic and paralinguistic features were less obvious and consistent. Lexical and semantic features appear to be the primary means of conveying statement intent.

លេបខាយ (lɛːpkhaːy) as a term has two meanings.

Jacob (1974:174) defines the term as to flirt while Huffman and Proum (1977:114) define this term as "to extemporize appealingly and provocatively." Informants were also split on this. However, it seems that the first definition is simply a narrower demarcation of the concept since men who engage in flirting often use such statements. An example of an utterance in the more general meaning of the term is:

Source: នេះគឺរឿងខ្ញុំ   (Angkor Wat Video)

គេ	ថា	ប្រុស	ញញឹម	ស្រី	ញញែម
they	say	man	smile	women	smile

ដូច	ស្ករ	ផ្អែម	ស្រមោច	អញ្ចឹង
like	sugar	sweet	ant	like that

This statement is uttered by an older woman who teases/scolds two young people. ពែបខ្មាយ statements have the potential to be insulting, teasing, or sarcastic.

ការមិនជឿ (ka:+r` mɯn cɯə) simply means disbelief.

Informants had no consistent term for classifying statements delivered with this intonation but indicated that such remarks indicated disbelief. Such statements are a form of sarcasm. In these statements the speaker contradicts what is said through special intonation. The following example displays this.

Source: ប្រធុំក្រុមកំម្មែង៩៣   (Preah Vihear Video)

Wife: មក   ពី   ណា?
come from   where?

Husband: ធ្វើការ
working

Wife: ធ្វើការ រហូត!
work   throughout

This last statement normally is a statement that someone has been working all day. While most of the utterance is spoken with normal statement intonation, the last syllable is spoken with a high rapidly falling and highly stressed intonation on the last syllable of the final word which has the effect of contradicting the overall statement. This intonation has the effect of changing the statement into "I don't believe you've been working all day". More examples will be needed to better understand sarcastic remarks of this type.

The last category to be discussed is ញែ (ɲae) . The Vacananukram Khmer (1968:321) defines this as a way of speaking in a thin and hoarse voice. Informants explained that this represented a tone of voice and behavior that men adopt when they flirt with a woman. It is often characterized by hesitancies and almost cough-like sounds in speech as well as nonverbal behavior associated with flirtation or shyness.

Most utterances of this type in Cambodian movies are also examples of ចំអាន. However, these statements are understood to express interest in the woman being teased. The woman's role in such encounters seems to be to respond with anger or even insults. Consider the following example:

Source:	នាងធីដា	(CMI Video)

Guy:	ភ្លៀង	ខ្លាំង	យ៉ាង	នេះ
	rain	hard	how	this

អ្នកនាង	ខ្លាច	ទទឹក	ភ្លៀង	ទេ,
miss (polite)	afraid	get wet	rain	? particle

អ្នកនាង	ហ៎
miss	particle

Girl:	ខ្លាច	ឆ្កួត	អី?
	afraid	crazy	what

Guy:	ព្រោះ	ថា	នៅ	លើ	ខ្លួន
	because	say	located	on	body

អ្នកនាង

miss (polite)

សុទ្ធតែ   របស់   ក្លែងក្លាយ ទាំងអស់
only   things   fake   all

The young man says, "Aren't you afraid to get wet?"   The
woman answers, "Why should I be afraid, you lunatic?"   The
young man responds, "Because everything about you is fake
(and will wash off in the rain).   Although there are features here
of ចំអាន់, there are other vocal and behavioral features that
distinguish such instances as a special case.

Implications

This study is only an initial exploration of insulting,
teasing, and sarcastic remarks in the Khmer language. While
some paralinguistic and kinesic features associated with the
utterance types examined in this study appear to be universal,
some lexical and intonational features of types of utterances
were identified which are specific to Khmer.   Results suggest
that additional work on the Khmer language on the use of
unusual intonational features as markers of contradiction and
lexical choices as markers of insulting and teasing remarks may
be fruitful.

The results also underscore the pragmatic, contextual
nature of utterances.   Categories used by respondents remind us
that the interpretation of language depends on the pragmatic
considerations of context.   Use of categories obtained from
informants has the potential to aid foreign students of the Khmer
language in better understanding the intent and relevant features
of messages.

However, there are some limitations in generalizing
these results to day-to-day interaction.   Several informants
periodically reminded me that we were watching theatrical
presentations and that people did not talk this way in real life.
Certainly, some types of statements such as the ចំអាស់ were
only observed in a stage comedy form.   On the other hand,
theatrical performances may offer fruitful examples of utterance
types even though these utterances may be somewhat

exaggerated in comparison to everyday speech.   Entertainment videos do seem to have potential as a source of utterances to be analyzed in the study of the pragmatics of Cambodian speech.

Notes

1. For the examples used to illustrate types of utterances, the name of the video from which the statement was taken and American video company distributing the video are given.

2. The author wishes to thank Polly Miech, Sophy Lim, Heang Taing, and particularly, Morokoth Ouk and Suos Sarin for their assistance in interpreting and transcribing the utterances.

3. Romanization of Khmer terms follows the system used by Jacob (1974) with the exception that the accent mark used to distinguish registers was omitted.

References

Ehrman, Madeleine. 1972. Contemporary Cambodian: grammatical sketch. Wasington, D.C.: Foreign Service Institute.

Jacob, Judith. 1968. An introduction to Cambodian. Oxford: Oxford University Press.

Jacob, Judith. 1974. A concise Cambodian-English dictionary. Oxford: Oxford University.

Huffman, Franklin. 1970. Modern spoken Cambodian. New Haven: Yale University Press.

Huffman, Franklin, and Proum, Im. 1977. Cambodian-English glossary. New Haven: Yale University Press.

Ladd, D. Robert, Jr. 1980. The structure of intonational meaning: Evidence from English. Bloomington: Indiana University Press.

Vacananukram Khmer. 1968. Revised edition. Phnom Penh: Institut Bouddhique.

A pragmatic look at sarcasm in Thai

Archara Pengpanich
Ramkhamhaeng University

This paper is the investigation into the use of sarcasm in Thai. The term SARCASM employed will cover related phenomena (its synonyms) which are included in the definition of SARCASM in Webster's New Twentieth Century Dictionary of the English Language (unabridged, second edition, 1983).
Sarcasm is defined as:

" a bitter laugh
1) a taunting, sneering, cutting, or caustic remark;
   a gibe, jeer, general ironical remarks
2) the making of such remarks
   Synonym: irony, banter, jeer, derision, satire."

This study will mainly focus on the making of a cutting and caustic remark. The investigation is based on the speech acts theory and Grice's Cooperative Principle. As Levinson (1983:226) says:

"speech acts remain, along with presupposition and implicature in particular,one of the central phenomena that any general pragmatic theory must account for."

Thus, this study is intended to address two questions: (1) To what extent can speech acts and Cooperative Principle theories help explain sarcasm in Thai? (2) What are other factors (if any) involved?

On the basis of speech acts, a speaker expresses his/her intention by means of illocutionary acts or sometimes fails to do so. In other words, the speaker's intention or meaning is conveyed by his/her utterance (locution) and at the meantime the speaker aims it to be effective i.e. to urge the hearer's response (perlocutionary act). Speech acts only, however, cannot fully explain how conversation works, let alone sarcasm. As Grice (1975) points out, in order for conversation to be effective and perhaps even to be conversation, it must involve cooperation between the speaker and the hearer. Hence, Grice (1975:45-46) formulates maxims of conversation which jointly express a general cooperative principle. By this Grice means that when speaking, one has to, or may be expected to make one's contribution such as is required. The four maxims constituting the Cooperative Principle (CP) are described as follows:

I. Quantity: Provide the right amount of information, i.e.
　　　1. Make your contribution as informative as is required.
　　　2. Do not make your contribution more informative than is required.
II. Quality: Try to make your contribution one that is true:
　　　1. Do not say what you believe to be false.
　　　2. Do not say that for what you lack adequate evidence.
III. Relation: Be relevant
IV. Manner: Be perspicious
　　　1. Avoid obscurity of expression
　　　2. Avoid ambiguity
　　　3. Be brief
　　　4. Be orderly

Grice (1975:49) also coins the term " implicature" to designate inferences deriving from observing and flouting the maxims. For example, the speaker may deliberately flout a maxim. The latter Grice calls exploitation of the maxim. This is achieved by means of figures of speech, namely, irony, metaphor, hyperbole etc.. Clark and Haviland (1977:32) claim that this deliberate violation is perceived by the hearer interpreting what the speaker intends to say. As for the unostentatious infringement of a maxim, it will result in a breakdown in communication. But more likely it will be misattributed, leading to implicatures which may be utimately recognised to be false (Coupland,1981) . This is due to the speaker's negligence. As far as my analysis and interpretation of sarcasm in Thai is concerned, I will focus on only the speaker's deliberate violation of the maxims of quality and manner. The flouting of the maxim of quantity is not included because of the lack of evidence involving this phenomenon. As for the flouting of the maxim of relation, Grice (1975:54) says that it is perhaps rare. My data also lend support to this claim. This means that almost all of the utterances are relevant. To help the hearer to draw an appropriate implicature, Grice (1975:50) suggests that he/she should rely on the following data:

"(1) The conventional meaning of the words used, together with the identity of any references that may be involved.
(2) The CP and its maxims; (3) the context, linguistic or otherwise, of the utterance; (4) other items of background knowledge; and (5) the fact (or supposed fact) that all relevant items falling under the previous headings are available to both participants and both participants know or assume this to be the case."

To put it more simply, the hearer should seek the help from the context both linguistic and extra-linguistic together with their background knowledge when deriving an implicature of what the speaker intends to say. Similarly, Hymes regards the role of context as the backbone of utterance interpretation. As he remarks:
The use of a linguistic form identifies a range of meanings. A context can support a range of meanings. When a form is used in a context it eliminates the meanings possible to that context other than those the form can signal: the context eliminates from consideration the meanings possible to the form other than those the context can support.
(Hymes, 1962, quoted in Wooten, 1975:44)

As people speak different languages, they have mastered different concepts and convey their thinking differently. For example, Thai greetings are distinct from those of English. In English when people meet for the first time on a day, they say "Hello, how are you?" whereas Thais mainly say "Where have you been?" or in Thai English "Where you go?" These locutionary acts are predictable and yield the same illocutionary and perlocutionary acts. The opposite is true of the uses of sarcasm. This is because sarcasm can be expressed in many ways, namely, in figurative speech (simile, metaphor, irony, hyperbole etc..) and intonation (in English) and tones (in Thai). Besides, sarcasm varies according to the speaker's style as Sperber and Wilson (1986:218) write:

"Choice of style is something that no speaker or writer can avoid. In aiming at relevance, the speaker must make some assumption about the hearer's cognitive abilities and contextual resources, which will necessarily in what she chooses to make explicit and what she chooses to leave implicit."

The data were collected from a famous Thai novel called "khâa khɔ̌ɔŋ khon" or "The value of humans" and also from Thai informants.   I have classified Thai sarcasm into two main categories in terms of their forms and the ways the speaker violates Grice's maxims.

Classification according to forms:

A. the speaker's violation of the maxim of quality : the
   use of figurative speech.
B. the speaker's violation of the maxim of manner.
   1. the use of puns
   2. the change of vowels, consonants and tones to
      convey the contrast of meanings

The following examples are intended to illustrate the classification. I have added context for every sarcastic utterance in order to clarify what the speaker purports to convey. After the description of the context, Thai version followed by the representation of Thai transcription together with Englsih literal translation and English broad translation will be provided.

A. The speaker's violation of the maxim of quality: In this category, the speaker flouts the maxim of quality by means of figures of speech, namely, irony, simile, metaphor and hyperbole etc..

1. IRONY:

(1) Context: Mali had an appointment with Chuchai and
    he was two hours late so Mali said to Chuchai:

ทำไมไม่มาเสียพรุ่งนี้ล่ะ

thammay mây maa sĭa phrûŋ nîi lâ
why not come tomorrow this PARTICLE
Why don't you come tomorrow?

(2) Context: The husband saw his overweight wife
eating greasy pork stew wholeheartedly said
sarcastically to her:

กินเข้าไปเถอะ ยังผอมอยู่

kin khâw pay thə̀ yaŋ phɔ̌ɔm yùu
eat in go yet thin still
Darling, you should eat a lot more of it, you are still
thin.

2. SIMILE:

(3) Context: Chuchai asked Nirut for a comment on his
pretty girl friend's look, who he thought was
shapely. Nirut said:

เอวบางเหมือนยางรถยนต์

ʔew baaŋ mĭan yaaŋ rótyon
waist thin like tyre car
Her waist is as thick as a car tyre.

(4) Context: By being sarcastic, a wife is criticising her
husband for being too generous to others.

ใจดีเป็นพระเวสสันดรเชียวนะ

cay dii pen phrá wêtsăndɔɔn chiaw ná
heart good be Phra Vessantara PARTICLE
You are as generous as Phra Vessantara. (Phra
Vessantara is an earlier incarnation of the Lord
Buddha. He gives away even his wife and children.)

3. METAPHOR:

(5) Context: Chuchai is extremely indifferent to what has
been happening around him so his colleagues
sarcastically say to him.

เขาทำตัวเป็นพระอิฐพระปูน

khăw	tham	tua	pen	phrá	ʔit	phrá	puun
he	make	self	be	Buddha	brick	Buddha	stucco

He is a plaster statue.

(6) Context: A was very cross with B who always pushed
him around and made him do many things at a time.
A said sarcastically to B.

ฉันไม่ใช่พระนารายณ์สี่กรนะ

chăn	mây	chây	phrá	naaraay	sìi	kɔɔn	ná
I	not	be		Narayana	four	hand	PARTICLE

I've got only two hands.

(Narayana is a God with four hands).

4. HYPERBOLE:

(7) Context: Sak, who is very fond of having his meal hot
from the oven has been complaining about the lunch
in front of him i.e. it is not hot enough. His wife says
sarcastically to him:

กินไฟเสียเลยดีไหม

kin	fay	sĭa	lɔɔy	dii	măy
eat	fire	all		good	QUESTION PARTICLE

Why don't you eat fire?

(8) Context: Mother thought her son's room is as untidy
as a pigsty. Then she asked him when he last tidied
it up. Her son replied:

เมื่อปีมะโว้มาแล้ว

mîa	pii	máwóo	maa	lɛ́ɛw
when	year	long time	come	then

I tidied it up million years ago.

B. The speaker's violation of the maxim of manner: In this
classification, the speaker flouts the maxim of manner by being

deliberately ambiguous through (1) the use of puns, (2) the change of vowels, tones, and consonants.

1. The use of puns
   (9) Context : A looks down upon B who is going to do a difficult job.

A: เธอทำไม่ได้หรอก

    thəə   tham   mây   dây   rɔ̀ɔk

    you   do   not   can   PARTICLE

    You can't do it.

B: ไม่ต้องมาดูถูกฉันหรอก

    mây   tɔ̂ŋ   maa   duu thùuk   chǎn   rɔ̀ɔk

    not   must come look down upon   I   PARTICLE

    Don't look down upon me.

A: ใช่สิ ฉันดูไม่ผิดหรอก

    (says sarcastically)

    chây   sî   chǎn   duu   mây   phìt   rɔ̀ɔk

    yes   I   look   not   wrong   PARTICLE

    I don't think I'm wrong saying that.

    ดูถูกแล้ว

    duu   thùuk   lɛ́ɛw

    look   right   then

    I think I'm right .

    (In the example, the word *thùuk* is a pun. *thùuk* can be a part of *duuthùuk* meaning *to look down upon* . Also, *thùuk* can mean right.)

(10) Context: A and B are looking out of the window and they happen to see an old lady who is dressed up as a teenager. Both of them take turns to make comments on the look.

A: แหม ทำตัวเป็นวัยแรกแย้ม

mǎæ   tham tua pen way rɛ̀æk yǽæm

EXCLAMATION make self be   age   first   bloom

She's dressed up as a teenager.

B. แย้มฝาโลงน่ะซิ

(says sarcastically)

yǽæm   fǎa   looŋ   nâ sî

pry...open lid   coffin   PARTICLE

She is mutton dressed as lamb.

(The word yǽæm has two meanings: (1) to bloom
and (2) to pry open

2. The Change of Vowels, Consonants and Tones:
   (11) Context: By being sarcastic, A says to B ,who wants
       to be rich and famous:

ไม่ดังก็ดับนะ

mây daŋ   kô   dàp   ná

not famous then dead PARTICLE

Published or perished.

   (12) Context: A. says sarcastically to B, who always
       applies too much cosmetics to her face and looks
       over-ripe.

ไม่ใช่นางงามแต่เป็นนางงอม

mây châa naaŋ ŋaam   tɛ̀æ pen naaŋ   ŋɔɔm

not be   Miss beautiful but be woman over-
                                           ripe

If you don't become a beauty, you will be as
beautiful as a mud fence.

   (13) Context: By being sarcastic, A says to B, who wants
       to become rich and famous.

ก่อนเป็นมวยจะม้วยเสียก่อน

kɔ̀ɔn pen muay cà   múay   sǐa kɔ̀ɔn

before be   boxer will dead   all   before

Before you got there you'll be dead.

(14) Context: Having to get to his office on time, A came
to his office by driving on an expressway. So he was
held up for nearly an hour. His colleagues who
came with him said sarcastically:

นี่น่ะหรือทางด่วน ทางด้วนน่ะไม่ว่า

nîi	nâ	r̆i	thaaŋ	dùan	thaaŋ	dûan
this	PARTICLE	Q	way	express	way	amputated

nâ   mây wâa

PARTICLE not   say

This should not be called an expressway. It should
get another name i.e. a crippled way because there
are a lot of traffic jams on it

Discussion and Conclusion:

When it comes to the notion of perlocutionary acts or the
effectiveness of sarcastic utterances, it is difficult to measure it.
This is because perlocutionary acts resulting from sarcastic
remarks are not as noticeable as those of requests or greetings
etc.. To be precise, they are exhibited in the form of the hearer's
being angry, looking sulky, being flushed etc.. In addition , the
degree of effectiveness of sarcasm is a continuum   i.e. it ranges
from being 'slightly hurtful' to 'very hurtful'. This depends on
many factors involved: the speaker's style, the speaker's and the
hearer's relationship (i.e. it is a good or bad relationship), body
language (i.e.contemptuous attitude etc.) Consider the example
(14) as an illustration.

If it is said by a frustrated driver to the Director of the
Department of Expressway or the chief engineer who has been
proudly involved in the construction of the expressway, the
perlocutionary act yielded will be more hurtful than when it is
said by a friend to complain about traffic jams.

The findings can partly answer the questions addressed.
As agreed earlier, speech acts alone cannot account for sarcasm.
To interpret meaning as the speaker intends to convey, one has
to resort to the notion of implicature based on Grice's
Cooperative Principle.

References

อุดม วโรตม์สิกขดิตถ์. 2535. *ความรู้เบื้องต้นเกี่ยวกับภาษา (An Introduction to Language)*. Bangkok, Ramkhamhaeng University Press.

Austin, J.L.1962. *How to Do Things with Words*. Oxford, Clarendon Press.

Brown, G. and G.Yule. 1983. *Discourse Analysis*. Cambridge, Cambridge University Press

Clark, H. and S.Haviland.1977. Comprehension and the given-new contract. *Discourse Production and Comprehension*. ed. by R. Freedle,1-40. Norwood, NJ, Ablex Publishers.

Coupland, N.J.R.1981. *The Social Differentiation of Functional Language Use: A Sociolinguistic Investigation of Travel Agency Talk*. Ph.D. dissertation, UWIST.

Grice, H.P.1975. Logic and Conversation. *Syntax and Semantics 3: Speech Acts*. ed. by P.Cole & J. Morgan, 41-58. New York, Academic Press.

Hymes, D.1962. The Ethnography of Speaking. *Anthropology and Human Behavior*. ed. by T. Gladwin & W.C. Sturtevant, 13-53. Washington, DC, The Anthropological Society of Washington.

Levinson, S.C.1983. *Pragmatics*. Cambridge, Cambridge University Press.

Searle, J.R 1975. Indirect Speech Acts. *Syntax and Semantics 3: Speech Acts*. ed. by P. Cole & J.L. Morgan, 59-82. New York, Academic Press.

Sperber, D. and D. Wilson.1986. *Relevance: Communication and Cognition*. Oxford, Basil Blackwell.

Wooton, A.1975. *Dilemmas of Discourse*. London, Allen & Unwin.